Minutes to Doomsday invites you into the muddied waters of
espionage—where often the rules are: befriend your enemy,
ur friends, and watch extra carefully so that your own head-
doesn't stab you in the back. The price paid by our men in the
s, whose job is to keep us safe, is rarely seen; nor is it visible
se our nation is to disaster at any moment. Joe Navarro's book
d chills into readers as they consider the grave dangers we
t, and it will make them ache at the losses suffered by those
equently risk all."

—Glenn L. Carle, former CIA officer
and author of *The Interrogator*

is mystery, intrigue, high drama, and humor. However, it
ental ballet between author and superhero FBI agent Joe
o and Ramsay that borders on breathtaking. The reader is
ging on every word, every movement, and wanting more.
ook truly is a page-turner and one that doesn't come along
. . . A must-read."

—Sandra Grimes, former CIA operative
and coauthor of *Circle of Treason*

sterful work of suspense rivaling the work of any popular
se novelist . . . For all those who want to know how these
gations get done, this book should be required reading. More
hat, we should all feel lucky that at a perilous time in our na-
history we had Joe Navarro covering our backs."

—Gary Noesner, former chief of the
FBI Crisis Negotiation Unit and
author of *Stalling for Time: My Life
as an FBI Hostage Negotiator*

scinating behind-the-scenes look at one FBI agent's fight
pture a Cold War spy. Despite endless setbacks and chaos,

Navarro never gave up. For our nation's sake, you will come away hoping there are more Joe Navarros in the trenches, trying to do their job."

"[This] is one of the most unusual espionage stories of the modern era. The pace of Navarro's gripping first-person narrative never slackens."

THREE MINUTES TO DOOMSDAY

AN AGENT, A TRAITOR, *AND* THE WORST ESPIONAGE BREACH IN US HISTORY

JOE NAVARRO

BANTAM PRESS

LONDON • TORONTO • SYDNEY • AUCKLAND • JOHANNESBURG

TRANSWORLD PUBLISHERS
61–63 Uxbridge Road, London W5 5SA
www.penguin.co.uk

Transworld is part of the Penguin Random House group of companies
whose addresses can be found at global.penguinrandomhouse.com

Penguin
Random House
UK

First published in the United States of America in 2017 by Scribner
an imprint of Simon & Schuster, Inc.
First published in Great Britain in 2017 by Bantam Press
an imprint of Transworld Publishers

A CIP catalogue record for this book
is available from the British Library.

ISBNs 9780593079003 (hb)
9780593078167 (tpb)

Typeset in 12.5/15.5 pt Arno Pro
Printed and bound by Clays Ltd, Bungay, Suffolk

Penguin Random House is committed to a sustainable
future for our business, our readers and our planet. This book
is made from Forest Stewardship Council® certified paper.

MIX
Paper from
responsible sources
FSC   FSC® C018179
www.fsc.org

1 3 5 7 9 10 8 6 4 2

To my daughter Stephanie—so you might finally understand why I was so often gone.

It's not what happens to you, but how you react to it that matters.

—Epictetus

CONTENTS

PROLOGUE

April 17, 1961

The place is Cienfuegos, at the crest of a large, sheltered bay on the south coast of Cuba. The time: early morning. I'm seven years old, on my way to the corner bodega to pick up fresh bread for our family breakfast, when the sky suddenly roars with the sounds of planes, flying low with guns blazing. I can hear my mother yelling at me, but I'm frozen, transfixed by what is happening above, when suddenly I'm tackled to the ground. My father is on top of me, his breathing heavy as he gathers his knees around me, enfolding me so nothing will be left exposed. My face is inches from a utility pole. I smell the black tar around its base as I study the cleat marks left behind by countless utility workers.

My father is whispering urgently in my ear to stay still, to keep down, but I stretch to see above me all the same. I can't help myself. Something metal and shiny falls from the planes as they fire—not bullets (I later learn) but their shell casings. Afterward, we neighborhood kids will search for them for hours, but not now. Unknown to us, less than an hour's drive away, at *Bahia de Cochinos*, the American-led Bay of Pigs invasion has begun.

The next day, Castro's thugs come for my father.

He has been detained for nineteen days—roughed up, threatened, barely fed, one of thousands being held without charges at a local sports facility—when a fellow prisoner loans him an identification card. The man knows my father hates Castro and eventually will be fingered as a counterrevolutionary. The ruse is thin but, in the confusion, just enough to set him free. He comes home to us— my mother, me, and my two sisters: one older than me and one younger—but only for a precious hour or two. Father gathers a few things, no luggage, and tells my mother he must leave before the guards realize their folly and he ends up like so many other coun- terrevolutionaries—on the *paredon* (the wall), awaiting execution. And indeed within weeks, thousands are shot, or simply disappear.

Where will he go? My father won't say. He doesn't want us bur- dened with that knowledge when the soldiers return. Instead, he hugs us all and kisses me last. True to the patriarchal society that Cuba is, his final words to me are: "You're now in charge of the family. You must be a man." Tears are falling down my face, my skinny legs shaking: This is the moment my childhood ends.

A week after my father's departure, Cuban soldiers—who've been secretly surveilling our house—arrive one night and thunder from room to room, searching. Eventually they go, but only after herding all of us into the living room and flashing their gun barrels at us. The message is clear: We have to leave, and America is our only hope.

JUMP AHEAD TO 1971, ten years to the day since the Bay of Pigs invasion. The place is South Florida. I'm seventeen years old, finishing my final year at Hialeah High, where I've played defensive end well enough to attract more than thirty scholarship offers. Evenings, I work at the Richards Department Store on 103rd Street in Hialeah, minding the cash register in the sports department. That's where I am when the manager calls my extension and says in an urgent voice, "Stop the two men walking side by side down the middle of the store. They've just robbed us!"

As I race toward them, they disappear into a rack of clothes. I run ahead and am blocking the store exit when one of the men reappears from the rack and runs straight toward me. At the last moment as he lunges, I see the knife. My body twists, my left arm tries to move away and up to avoid the blade, but it's not enough.

By the time the doctors are through with what the knife has done to me, I have 180 stitches, internal and external, in my arm. The doctors have sewn my bicep and tricep together. They've repaired my slashed arteries. The severed muscles in my arm have retracted into my chest, and the surgeons have pulled those back into my arm, too. For twenty-one days I linger in the hospital. I've lost immense amounts of blood. My arm is badly infected, and I can barely feel my fingers or move them.

I do recover, but my athletic career is over. I won't be able to lift my arm above the shoulder for another two years. But once I finally come out from all the medications, electrical stimulation, plastic surgery, and rounds of vocational therapy and rehabilitation, there's a letter waiting for me from President Richard Nixon, thanking me for my "heroism." Nixon's worst days—Watergate most dramatically—still lie ahead. For now I'm honored that an American president would take the time to thank this immigrant for doing nothing more than his civic duty.

FROM AN EARLY AGE, three powerful forces have combined to set my True North: a love of America for taking in my family, an abiding sense (still with me) that I can never pay this country back in full for the opportunities handed us, and a deep belief that, in Emerson's words, "When Duty whispers low, 'Thou must,' / The youth whispers, 'I can.'"

In the years ahead, Rod Ramsay will test that call to duty in ways I can't yet imagine. At times I'll fear he might even beat us. His intellect and interests will prove jaw-dropping, and yet it will be clear that he cares deeply about few things—least of all what matters most to me: country, honor, patriotism. That's what will make him so dangerous, not just to this nation but to the entire world.

1

"SUBJECT RAMSAY WAS NAKED . . ."

August 23, 1988

I'm thirty-five now, and I've been working for the FBI most of my adult life, since I was twenty-three years old. My recruiter told me back when I joined up that I was the second youngest person ever offered a position with the Bureau. I don't know about that, but strangely enough—since I can never play football competitively again—the sport is what landed me on the FBI radar screen, at least in a roundabout way.

While I lay in that hospital in Miami, watching my senior high-school year drift away, thirty-one of my thirty-two athletic scholarship offers disappeared. A single one survived, from Brigham Young University. LaVell Edwards, BYU's coach, called one afternoon to say that he still liked me, that I was big and fast. Why not give it a try? I did just that, for three days, by which time the arm I'd nearly lost a few months earlier was swollen to three times normal size and the docs were talking blood clots and possible nerve damage.

That was the official dead end of my dreams of gridiron glory, but I stayed on at BYU, supporting myself with a mix of scholarship money, loans, and odd jobs, including one as a campus policeman, at the suggestion of my criminology professor. And thus when the

NSA, the CIA, and the FBI came recruiting at BYU, as they always do in abundance at Mormon-dominated schools, my background seemed particularly apt: campus cop, graduate of the Utah Police Academy, a devout anti-Communist in general and a Cuban émigré stridently opposed to Fidel Castro in particular, and ardently in love with America. Maybe I really *was* the second-youngest recruit. What better combination of traits could the Bureau have been looking for?

As for me, I was so desperate for paying work that I said yes on the spot, really without giving it another thought.

ONE THING I SOON learned: There are no normal hours in the FBI. Contractually, I work ten and a half hours per day, but I'm constantly being asked to do more and more with less and less. It's not just my own cases that eat away time. There's always some new shortage, always "the needs of the Bureau"—a term that pecks at me every time I think I'm going to have a weekend off and instead have to cancel family time once again.

While I'm stationed in Puerto Rico, they need SWAT operators to work on terrorism cases, so I get volunteered by my supervisor—"volunteered" as in one day I see my name on a list to attend Basic-SWAT for four weeks and that's that. Not that I mind all that much. The training is fun, and really, who *doesn't* want to have an MP-5 Heckler & Koch suppressed submachine gun in the trunk of his car? But suddenly, every few weeks, on top of my regular work, there are the SWAT operations, and some of those last days. They can involve anything from an airplane hijacking to a takedown of the Machetero terrorist group (*macheteros* means "machete wielders," but these guys were good with guns, rifles, and bombs, too).

But what really eats up my spare time is the flying. In researching my background, the Bureau learns that I received my pilot's license in high school. Once I come on board, it isn't long before I start getting calls to help with aerial surveillance. Do I complain? Not really. Going from the bare-bones Cessna 150 I'd trained in to a Cessna 182 with retractable gears and air-conditioning is a huge step up, and this time I'm being paid to fly, not the other way around. But the hours are killers. Often, I work a regular shift, then pilot 6 p.m. till midnight—a great time to fly because the air is generally calm at night—but add it all together and I'm putting in way too many sixteen-hour days. When my family does see me, I'm so tired I sometimes doze off standing on my feet in line at the supermarket.

Ultimately, the flying and the SWAT operations take a mental backseat to what I really enjoy—counterintelligence work or "CI." The thing about CI work is that it connects you to the world. It makes you pay attention to what's happening in faraway places. Any country can tolerate bank robberies, carjackings, rapes, even riots, but espionage is the only crime a nation can potentially *not* survive. With the right kind of intelligence, you can render another nation inert or change the course of history. That's why I love CI—because it really matters.

I start just about every work morning with the daily intelligence brief that comes clacking in over our teletype machine a little after sunrise. Today's no different. Last night I was up almost to midnight, flying lazy circles over Tampa Bay, helping out another squad short on surveillance agents. This morning, I'm touring the world's hot spots, searching for anything in the overnight synopsis that might find its way back to Central Florida.

Example: Police in Lima, Peru, yesterday raided the plant that prints the newspaper *El Diario*, thought to be the voice of the Maoist guerilla group Sendero Luminoso, aka Shining Path. Sounds like a stretch, I admit, but when Maoist guerillas in South America get upset, I take notice because Cuba's Americas Department funds extremism in the region, and the Marxist ex-guerilla in Havana can sometimes get a little itchy himself.

Some things I can pretty much take a pass on. I'm sorry that hundreds died and thousands were injured in an earthquake that rocked northern India and Nepal, but there's not much I can do about plate tectonics that far away. The state of national emergency just declared in Pakistan is another matter. A few days ago President Zia and ten of his top generals disappeared in a midair explosion. Now Zia's successor, Ishaq Khan, is telling reporters that "the enemy has penetrated the inner defense of the country." Does "enemy" mean India? Probably, but unrest on or near the Subcontinent can easily spill over borders, and Tampa has been home since 1983 to the United States Central Command, whose responsibilities include Central Asia. Part of my job is to watch CentCom's back. The Pakistan-India conflict is also a proxy tug-of-war between China and the USSR— this could get ugly overnight.

As always, the Middle East is thick with violence and intrigue. In Haifa, a hand grenade tossed into a crowded sidewalk café has wounded twenty-five, including seven members of a single family that had been admiring the window display at a toy store.

Another dog-bites-man story: The IRA has struck again in Northern Ireland—eight dead and twenty-eight wounded this time when a bomb explodes aboard a civilian bus carrying British soldiers. The bomb, which the IRA said was fashioned from two hundred pounds of Czech-made Semtex, left a crater six feet deep. This story is also less distant than you might think. We have IRA financial supporters in Tampa who probably woke up cheering this very morning.

Counterintelligence is inevitably biased toward the biggest gorilla in the room, and that's the Soviet Union. They have the most spies, the most money, and they get most of my attention, but the Warsaw Pact countries are nothing to snicker at. East Germany is far smaller than the USSR, but its intelligence service, run by the legendary Markus Wolf, is even tougher to crack than the KGB. Not just tougher. *Better*—in a very scary way.

In Poland, I read, seventy-five thousand coal miners are out on strike, demanding that Solidarity, the outlawed trade union, be legalized. Moscow can't be happy with this. The KGB would love nothing better than to get rid of Pope John Paul II and his influence over his fellow Poles. In fact, the Soviets via the Bulgarians have already made one assassination attempt. Now Moscow is witnessing what it sought to erase: influence over power. The Pope is making the KGB quake. Yet another hot spot: In Czechoslovakia, source of the Semtex that blew the British police to smithereens in Northern Ireland, a small group gathered two days ago in Prague's Wenceslas Square to sing the Czech national anthem on the twentieth anniversary of the day two hundred thousand Warsaw Pact troops and five thousand tanks rolled into the country to crush the so-called Prague Spring.

By itself, none of this Soviet stuff is particularly alarming: Even seventy-five thousand angry miners pose no serious threat to the world's Other Superpower—the USSR has crushed the yearning of people to be free before and they'll do it again. But put it all together, and something is happening. Courage is breaking out behind the Iron Curtain, or maybe just the multiple failures of the Soviet system at all levels—economic, political, moral—are finally becoming impossible to ignore and cover up.

Either way, it might be a little early to start celebrating the Soviets' decline. The KGB has both the power to quash and suppress, and the incentive. I remember talking to a Soviet KGB defector once. "We can never afford to let go," he told me. "We've all seen how the crowds hung Mussolini's body when his government fell. That's what will happen to us, especially in Eastern Europe—they hate us there."

I'm thinking there's nothing more dangerous than a wounded Russian bear when Jay Koerner, my supervisor, approaches my desk. The time is 7:57 a.m. The date: Tuesday, August 23, 1988, and while I have no way of knowing, the next decade of my life has just been spoken for.

"Yours," he says, handing me a teletype from FBIHQ. "Now."

"Mine?" I've got a full day ahead of me and am scheduled to help out with surveillance tonight.

"Lynn's out of town. The army intel guy will be here in half an hour."

Jay is halfway back to his office by the time I look down at the teletype. I like Jay. He never gets in the way, but he's not a conversationalist. The message is from the National Security Division, and in typical Bureau style it reads:

> Anytime after 0400 hrs Zulu 8/23/88, you are to locate and interview Roderick James RAMSAY, last known to be living in Tampa, Florida, regarding his knowledge of or association with Clyde Lee CONRAD while stationed at 8th ID, Bad Kreuznach, West Germany: service years 1983–85. INSCOM [Army Intelligence] will liaise and assist: locate, interview, report.

In criminal investigations, information is power, which means that the document I'm holding is the equivalent of a five-watt bulb, barely enough to light a glove compartment. Still, I'm intrigued. The very fact that INSCOM—the US Army Intelligence Security Command—is involved means there's probably more at stake here than selling PX cigarette coupons on the black market. By the time my army CI counterpart walks in the door, I'm actually anxious to talk with him.

Al Eways, the INSCOM liaison, turns out to be a nice guy, but time is short, and his obligations are many. Roderick James Ramsay, our interviewee, is but one of multiple interviews on his overstuffed calendar.

"Let's get going" are not quite his first words to me, but close enough. To emphasize the point, Al hands me an address and adds, "We think this is where he is." A minute and a half later, I'm behind the wheel of my Bu-Steed—agent-speak for our drab government-issue sedans. Al, at the other end of the front seat, has his nose buried in notes, presumably a backgrounder on Ramsay, but I'm only guessing. I drive, he reads. It's not my place to pry.

CI operates on a strict need-to-know basis. Al is free to fill me in on the details, but the protocol is very straightforward: Unless he tenders the information to me, I'm going to be in the dark until he starts interviewing the subject. Sounds a little counterintuitive, I know, but observing carefully and learning on the go is sometimes the best way.

The first challenge is to find the address I've been handed. I know the general area—a sprawling enclave of single-wide trailers northwest of the Tampa airport, in an area once known for its oranges. A month or two back I flew surveillance over this same patch of ground, following a low-level drug dealer. We'll find the place, I know that, so I start thinking safety.

Where am I? Where's the closest hospital? Who's in the area? Young people or old? Mothers pushing strollers or out-of-work males standing on street corners? Are there teenagers roaming the streets?

As I look for the address, I'm also thinking of where to park. I want the driver's side away from the residence so if I need to, I can use the engine block for cover and have the advantage of distance. We're near now, but I circle a few more times to get the lay of the land in case I need to get away in a hurry or have to call for help.

And then there's the real purpose of all this: the interview itself. What are we going to talk about? How will we get this Ramsay guy to relax? People tell you a lot more when they feel in their comfort zone than when you have them sweating on the rack. One more thing: At the end of the day, I'm responsible for more than our safety. I'm on the hook for this interview, too. Ramsay is a civilian, and INSCOM technically has no jurisdiction over a civilian. Still, I have to give Al leeway because he's holding the cards; he knows more than I do. If anything goes wrong, though, it's going to be my ass on the line.

Al and I are silent as we drive past a well-kept single-wide trailer with a dark-green latticework skirt. "That's the place," Al says a little quizzically as I glide past and circle the neighborhood one more time.

"Got it," I reply. "Just making sure I know the territory."

Al is paying attention now, too, and I appreciate that. A lot of counterintelligence involves running down blind alleys, but we've got a saying in the FBI: There's no such thing as a routine interview or stop. Take it too casually, and it might be the last one you ever do.

One time, I was helping the local sheriff's office in Yuma, Arizona, with an arrest when the guy we were looking for stuck a gun out his front door and blasted away. One round grazed the head of the deputy I was standing inches away from. A year later, still in Yuma, I was on the phone arranging a basketball game with a couple of FBI agents in the El Centro, California, office, sixty miles west, while they waited for an interviewee who'd promised to stop by to see them. He did, also with gun blazing, while I was still on the line. One of the agents was alive, writhing in his own blood, when I got there. He died moments later. The shooter was lying there, too, dead by his own hand. These things stay with you forever, like the smell of a dead body—something you never forget.

THIS TIME, AT LEAST, the drama is minimal. Turns out, no one is home when we knock on the trailer door. All this driving around has accomplished nothing except to alert local residents that strangers are on their turf. One of the locals steps forward and asks if we need help. We tell him we're looking for Rod Ramsay.

"This is his mother's place," he says. "Rod's house-sitting a little ways over."

Al and I look so much like law enforcement that the guy doesn't even bother asking why we're here, but he does helpfully provide us with an address and points with his chin in the general direction we're to follow, and the new neighborhood, in fact, is no more than two minutes away—small tract homes built back in the early sixties. Now it's twenty-five years later, and their best days are long behind them. After I find the right house, park, and lock the Bu-Steed's door, I see a shadow crossing in front of the front picture window. Unless I'm mistaken, it's the shadow of a man not wearing a stitch of clothing.

"Was that person *naked*?" I ask, but Al is already at the door—directly in front of the door, in fact, pretty much exactly where you don't want to be. In the Bureau, we call doors "lethal funnels." Stand dead center in front of one, and you're so well framed that even a piss-poor, myopic, astigmatism-ridden shooter would have trouble missing you.

We can hear movement inside the house through the open windows—maybe cabinets opening and closing, someone tramping around—but no one is coming to the door, and I hate standing there for so long.

"Wonder what's going on," Al says.

By this point, I wonder so much what's going on that I slip back the right side of my suit coat just enough to easily get to the Sig Sauer P-226 I'm carrying in a holster right by my kidney. Ninety percent of gunfights take place from less than seven yards—narrower than most living rooms. The quicker you can get your handgun in play, the sooner it all ends—so my hand loiters just behind my hipbone.

Al is starting to look a little nervous himself when the chain slips off its bracket, the door opens, and there stands Rod Ramsay in all his gawkiness: six-foot-one and maybe 150 pounds. Thank goodness, he's fully clothed, in jeans and a sleeveless checkered shirt.

"Can I help you?" Rod asks with a slight Boston accent.

Instead of answering, we show him our credentials—INSCOM and FBI. If he's fazed, he does a good job of hiding it. Rod looks over both credentials carefully, but his eyes stay on my FBI creds just a tad longer. I suspect I'd do the same. In any event, I take it as an invitation to break the ice.

"Are you Rod Ramsay?" Seems an obvious question to ask, but I've known agents who've spent a half hour interviewing someone before figuring out they're talking to the wrong person.

Rod nods.

"Would it be okay if we come inside to talk?"

Now I see the first little bit of concern. His hand comes up and just grazes his neck. This is the legacy of sixty million years or more of human evolution. In the old days, when big cats were the greatest threat to our hominid ancestors, they learned to protect their throat first when threatened.

"What's this about?" Rod asks. Another sign of nervousness: His Adam's apple rises.

"Well," I say, with a smile, "you can relax, we're not here to talk about you—we just need to pick your brain about the Eighth ID." This is crucial because if he says, "Take a hike," we have nothing. You can prepare for days, and screw everything up in minutes if you put the subject immediately on the defensive.

Happily, Rod is buying what I have to sell. Relieved, he says, "Sure, come on in." As we enter, my eyes have a hard time adjusting to the darkness.

Just to make certain Rod understands I am not a Bureau suit like you see on TV, I stare at him with a grin on my face as Al gathers his paperwork. "Was that you walking across the room when we arrived?" I ask.

"Yeah," he answers with a little giggle. "I'd just gotten up. I was still naked."

"I just wanted to make sure I wasn't seeing things or someone else," I said, probing to see if there's another person here we need to worry about.

"No, that was me. Sorry, I forgot the windows were open."

ARMY INTELLIGENCE GUYS ALL go to the same interview school and use the same interview manual. Their techniques are spelled out for them—by the book, detailed, rigid—and that just isn't my style. These guys are true pros, no question about it, but their interviews are like forced marches, from A to Z. They rarely look up from their legal pads and notebooks long enough to study the nonverbal reactions of the people they're talking with—or more often, talking *to*.

Al is no different, but for now, I'm perfectly happy to let him plow on ahead with his agenda because it gives me time to assess Rod Ramsay, not for guilt or innocence—he's committed no crime so far as I know—but for how I'm going to accumulate face time with him, today and maybe in the future if needed. When I talk to people, I want to know how they communicate, and everyone is different. I want to get a sense for how they think about questions, how quickly they answer, their speech cadence, what words they use, how they hide their sins, minor and major. Interviews are always about people. The more I know about their idiosyncrasies, the easier it is to assess what they're really saying.

Example: Al is asking Ramsay a string of rote questions about his service record—"Ever confined to barracks or busted a rank?" . . . "Ever get written up?" . . . that sort of thing—when all of a sudden Ramsay jumps in with almost reptilian coldness.

"Are you interested in my peccadilloes, Mr. Eways? Is that it? Digging for a little dirt, are we?" Ramsay says.

"Not at all," Al answers affably, slowing down his note-taking just long enough to look up with a smile and hold up his pen in mock surrender. "Just filling in the blanks. You know how it is in the army."

But Rod isn't ready to let it drop.

"A chimpanzee can fill in blanks. Probably a rat could if you arranged the Skinner Box to sufficiently reward it for trying." There's an edge to his voice now, a kind of intentional pummeling.

"What I would suggest, Al, is that you try for some higher-order questions—you know, shoot for the stars. We'll have a much more enlightening conversation that way."

Ramsay favors both of us with a knowing smile at this point and nods at Al to continue with his dull recitation. Meanwhile, I'm left to wonder why a guy who lives in a single-wide trailer with his mother would be so ready to lord it over a decent, solid person like Al Eways.

Is Ramsay a narcissist? Quite possibly. He clearly has a higher opinion of himself than circumstances would justify. And maybe a predator, too. Al has given him almost no opening, but Ramsay has leapt all the same. One more thing: Despite his seemingly snotty attitude, Ramsay is damn smart. We've already learned his education stopped with high school, but dropouts don't toss around "peccadilloes" and Skinner Boxes. Maybe Rod is a big reader, maybe he's self-taught—all I know is that he's playing mind games with Al Eways even as he answers his questions.

WE'VE BEEN AT THIS for almost thirty minutes now, and one thing has held absolutely constant. Rod's movements are still as jittery now as when we first walked in. Is that always the way with him? Jacked up on speed, maybe? Or has the sudden appearance at his front door of two federal agents thrown him off kilter—and if so, why? Maybe he's naturally hyperkinetic. Some people are, but he remains jittery and that's something I just can't ignore.

Neither can I ignore his smoking. He's already on his third cigarette. Nerves? Nicotine addiction? There's not much to do at this point but note it.

Rod has led us into the kitchen, where there's no choice but to stand as his cigarette smoke swirls around us—the eight-foot ceiling and lack of ventilation don't help. Maybe he simply lacks social skills and that's why he hasn't invited us to sit down in the living room, or maybe by keeping us standing in the kitchen, he's assuring that this interview will be brief.

I take advantage of a pause in Al's questioning to ask a question of my own.

"Did you hear that?" I ask. "Was that someone . . . ?"

"No, no," Rod says. "I'm the only one here. The owner won't be back for another day."

I haven't stopped wondering if we're alone in the house. We don't have any legal standing to search to find out, but I'm satisfied with Rod's reply. No hand to the neck this time, or to the mouth as he talks. I listen distractedly for another couple minutes as Al and Rod talk about the average soldier's life in Germany, then I jump in with another question:

"Are there any guns in this house?"

Rod (speaking slower, chin pulled down): "Yeah, there's a gun in this room."

Crap, Navarro, I tell myself, *this is how you end up with a hole in your chest.* Now Al is looking at me to deal with the situation.

I stare at Rod, keeping my eyes on his hands because only his hands can hurt us. Fortunately, at least one of them is occupied with his cigarette, so I say, "Look, do me a favor, just stand where you are and tell me who owns the weapon and where exactly it is."

"Sure," he says, "it belongs to the guy who owns the house. He keeps it in the cabinet."

"Which cabinet?" And Rod points with his chin to the one just above the refrigerator, about a half-second lunge away from where he's standing. Far too close for comfort. Now I'm really uneasy. We've still got a lot of questions to ask. There's no air-conditioning, I can feel my weapon resting against a wet shirt, and we're standing near what might be a loaded gun—not exactly a conducive interview setting.

"Look, Rod," I say, "I know this isn't your doing, but that gun makes me nervous. What's more, it's blazing hot in here—this is going to ruin my sperm count. How about if the three of us just continue this interview outside? What do you say?"

"Sure," Rod says again. "Why not?" And in fact, he seems to relax almost immediately once we relocate to the great outdoors. Who knows, maybe he's thinking there'll be more witnesses if we decide to rough him up.

Al, for his part, barely misses a beat. He marks the last question with his thumb and starts up right where he left off as soon as we're settled in the shade of a small, raggedy grove of palms out the back door. Just to check Rod's veracity, I ask to use the bathroom. Once inside, I head straight for the cabinet above the refrigerator. Sure enough there it is: a dusty .38 revolver, from a manufacturer I've never heard of, but it can still put a lethal hole in you.

When I get back outside, Al is ever closer to the issue at hand. I know about criminal work and I know CI, but I never served in the military. Ranks, acronyms, army shorthand—they're all whizzing far over my head. I decide to join in only where I can.

Al: "So, you worked where?"

Rod: "In G-3 Plans [whatever that was]."

Al: "And you got out in 1985?"

Rod: "Yeah, I failed the piss test."

Me: "What the hell's the piss test?"

Rod, displaying a Cheshire cat grin: "Well, they did an impromptu test on us, and I guess they found cannabis in my urine."

Me: "Gee, I wonder how it got there."

Rod: [Laughter].

So now I'm thinking I know a little more of the puzzle. Not only is Rod a drug user; since he must have known about random piss testing, he's also either a risk taker or someone who doesn't think all that clearly or often about the consequences of his actions. The smart-ass way he enunciates "cannabis" tells me something about his intellect, but I also sense from how he answered that he didn't expect to get caught and wasn't happy to get bounced from the army.

While I'm processing all this, Al gets to the heart of the matter: "Didn't Clyde Conrad work in G-3 Plans for the Eighth ID back then?" And that's when all the baselines I've been laying down since we arrived start crashing into play. Quick with an answer otherwise, Rod stretches this one out, as if he has to access the deepest reservoirs of his memory. Mostly precise, too, in his responses, he stumbles through a reply before finally bringing this one to a close: "Oh, sure, Clyde Conrad—of course." He says this with little emphasis, but what really catches my eye is in his hand.

His cigarette shakes—not the familiar jitters I've been seeing but a good, hard tremor—like a seismograph announcing Mount St. Helens.

Before the question, a velvety, smooth contrail of smoke. Thirty seconds afterward, smooth again. But in between, at the precise moment Al Eways mentions Clyde Conrad's name, the contrail breaks up into a sharp zigzag that Rod has no more control over than his circulation.

Is it meaningful? You bet. Anything we do that potentially threatens us—burning a finger on the stove, say, or committing a criminal act—gets stored deep in the brain, in the hippocampus, and anything that awakens that threat—a glowing heating unit, mention of our partner in crime—puts us instantly on guard. That's what happened to Rod: For just a moment he trembled and froze, the same way any of us would temporarily freeze if we rounded a bend and saw a snarling dog in front of us.

Why would the words "Clyde Conrad" threaten Rod Ramsay?

"Rod," I say when Al takes a pause, "your recall is exceptional. I thought this would be a short interview, but I can see where you can fill in a lot of the holes. Here's the deal, though. It's hot as hell, and we could use more of your help. What if we move to a hotel nearby? We'll get a room, sit in comfort, enjoy the AC, and order a nice lunch if you want to join us."

Rod is holding still as he listens to what I'm saying. I sense this, so I shift my weight back and angle my feet so that I'm standing just a very precious few inches farther away from him, with a more oblique angle that presents less of a threat. As Al is giving me a stiff glance, Rod responds to my slight backing away, so I raise my shoulders and smile, nonverbally saying: "What do you think?" With that, he relaxes his arms once more, and the deal is done. If he was thinking we'd put him in the trunk of my Bu-Steed and feed him to the alligators, he's no longer worried.

"Tell you what," I say. "You think your mom is home yet?"

"Most likely," he says.

"Then call her. Tell her we're headed to the Pickett Hotel, over on US 60, where we can do our business in comfort, and see if she has any concerns. Fair enough?"

In part, I'm just being practical here. In that close-knit trailer park, the neighbors are sure to tell Mrs. Ramsay that the feds came looking for her son. The last thing I need is a panicked mother calling an attorney at the start of a simple inquiry. But something about Rod tells me he's not loaded with friends. Maybe his mother is all he's got to hold on to.

"Yeah, fair enough," he answers back, with just enough relief to make me think I'm right.

YOU NEVER KNOW WHAT seduces. Sometimes it's a combination of things: tone of voice, a smile, standing at a slight angle so you don't appear threatening, or maybe just the prospect of a free lunch in an air-conditioned hotel. Whatever it is, Rod agrees to come with us and that's all that matters—more face time. Ten minutes later, Al is checking us in at the Pickett Hotel, obtaining a suite with ample room for everyone to sit and spread out. I don't want either of us too close to Rod—this isn't the movies, comfort is key here—and of course we have to make allowances for Rod's smoking. While Al signs us in, Rod and I bond off to the side.

"So, what were the girls like in Germany?" I ask. Rod immediately perks up.

Honestly, I'm pulling a cheap trick, but the worst thing you can do in interviewing is set the bar at confession. What you want is what I was just talking about: face time. Get enough of it, and eventually you'll learn everything you want to know. Rod, as I said earlier, is a bit gawky. His face seems weathered, even at his early age, by acne scars and heavy smoking. I doubt that the city's most sought-after females lie in bed at night dreaming of Rod Ramsay's thin lips pressed against theirs. But I'm also betting Rod likes to think of himself as a ladies' man, and if I treat him like one—feed his narcissism—he'll want to be near me so I can feed it some more. The reemergence of that Cheshire cat grin tells me I'm right.

"Did you know prostitution is legal in Germany?" he asks.

"No! Were they really good-looking?"

"Oh," he says with a little moan, "there was this one I frequented a lot. She was unbelievably good-looking, built like a supermodel. I'd call in to the service just for her. I spent a fortune on that woman." Rod has his eyebrows arched again as he says this.

"How much?"

"Sometimes a couple hundred a week. Once I dropped twelve hundred dollars on her in one week alone, but God was she worth it. What a body!"

"How about the marijuana?" I say, bending the subject. "Just between us girls, what would a bag go for in Germany back then?"

"Well," he answers, all businesslike, "a three-finger bag might be the equivalent of twenty-two bucks. I'd go through one of those a week."

By the time Al gets back to our corner of the lobby with the room key, I've not only learned about Rod's lifestyle during his tour in Germany—dope and whores—I've also developed a pretty good feel for his personal economics, and they're troubling. I might never have served in the military, but I worked beside army sergeants in my Yuma posting, and I happen to know that they earn less than $100 a week. Rod's marijuana tab alone would have eaten up a quarter of that. Unless he's got a trust fund not readily evident from his current circumstances, his prostitute bill even in a slow week would have put him seriously in debt, and this (like cannabis) is a service *not* discounted at the base PX. Either Rod was living far beyond his means in Germany, or he had means far beyond his rank. And if so, where did they come from?

Every new thing I learn about Rod makes him more of a mystery, but in America, you're allowed to be an enigma . . . so long as you stay on the right side of the law.

*   *   *

UPSTAIRS, THE HOTEL HAS just the effect I'd hoped for. The AC soothes us, after an hour-plus on our feet in and around that little oven of a house; the ample sofa and two easy chairs are just what the doctor ordered. Even Al eases off long enough to let me jump in with some questions.

"Tell me about this G-3," I say to Rod. "I don't know the Eighth Infantry Division from the 'Twelfth of Never.'" Rod wasn't even born when Johnny Mathis recorded that song, but a little nod of his head says that he appreciates the cultural allusion and the tacit assumption that he'll pick up on it.

"G-3 is where the plans are made and stored for going to war."

"War?"

"With the Soviets. In case you haven't noticed, Joe, the Warsaw Pact is just across West Germany's eastern border."

The "Joe" part intrigues me. It's been "Al-this" and "Al-that" almost since we showed him our credentials, but he hasn't called *me* anything previous to this, not even "Agent Navarro." I'm starting to realize that in almost everything Rod says there is calculation. So where's he going with the "Joe" bit?

"Indulge me," I say. "Dispel my ignorance." And he does.

"When it comes to us against them, it's all how a given side reacts, how it deals with contingencies. Everything is constantly changing, so the plans have to be updated almost weekly. What's the troop force count? What's the air force going to do? Or NATO forces? What happens if the space shuttle goes down in Siberia instead of the Mojave Desert? Remember when we lost the three H-bombs over Spain?" (I do. January 1966. A midair collision between a US B-52 and a US KCK-135 jet tanker, and I know Rod is testing me with the question.) "What if something similar happens tomorrow over, say, Bulgaria? We need contingency plans for any number of scenarios."

This is good. Rod likes educating me, likes showing off his knowledge. And when it comes to G-3 and related subjects, he's got a ton of it—I'm impressed. He talks as I'd expect a senior army officer to brief. He understands tactical and strategic matters at a level that is startling. Plus, he also understands history and how it factors in—I'm fascinated by what he knows . . . and deeply aware that if this interaction between us continues beyond today's meeting, Rod will be a challenge.

A lot of times when I interview people with highly specialized knowledge—doctors and lawyers, for example—they quickly become very arrogant, so disdainful that they forget we agents are the ones who'll throw the full weight of government at them if they don't turn it down a notch. Rod isn't like that, not that obvious—he doesn't have the educational credentials. But I *can* feel him edging toward a red line as I ask questions and he answers.

Though Al likely doesn't realize it yet, Rod seems to have dismissed him as a threat. He's smart enough to know that because he's a civilian the army and INSCOM have no hold on him. Poof! In Rod's head Al is already gone—a zero threat. Now he's trying to figure out how to get the upper hand with me.

"Joe," he asks, patronizingly, "how high is your clearance?"

"Pretty high," I answer.

"No, Joe, exactly *how* high? Do you have a top-secret clearance?"

"I do."

"How about SCI?" he asks, referring to sensitive compartmented information.

"That too."

It's obvious he's going to keep walking up this ladder, and I'm getting tired of his increasingly snotty tone, so I decide to end it right there.

"Roderick," I say, lowering my voice, leaning forward while making sure our eyes don't break contact, "I am cleared for weird, do you understand? I have a higher clearance than anyone in this room, including Mr. Eways, and that's why I'm here." At this point even Al is sitting still—you can feel the chill in the room—but I'm not through. I take our uncomfortable silence and hold on to it as the muscles in my jaw intentionally throb. After a few moments Rod gathers himself up on the couch, breaks eye contact, and looks at me contritely. Message received.

It's by far the sharpest tone I've taken with Rod since we met, but I've done it without raising my voice and for a very specific reason: I don't want him to feel threatened, but I don't want him to feel superior to me either. If Rod is going to have to be interviewed again on this matter—whatever the *matter* might be—I'll most probably be the one doing it, and I don't interview people who feel superior. That's a losing proposition. No one confesses to a fifteen-year-old, which is exactly the situation when an interview subject feels superior.

Surprisingly, Rod seems to like me enough to tolerate being put back in his place. His look softens, and he nods amiably. I said what I had to say and I move on—no harangue. Rod, I'm noticing, gets it quickly. For both of us it's game on.

THERE'S STILL THE MATTER of that shaking cigarette to puzzle over. It's happened twice now. Maybe twenty minutes ago, back when we first got onto the G-3 stuff, Al happened to blurt out something like "Didn't Clyde Conrad have something to do with those plans also?" Al didn't look up from his notes long enough to see Rod's response, but I did. Rod's cigarette trembled again and sent another zigzag of smoke curling to the ceiling.

That's two in a row. Three's the charm, I figure, but this time I want to do the test myself, in the most controlled circumstances possible in a hotel room. To set that up, I have to calm Rod down.

Fortuitously, about this time lunch shows up: a pile of sandwiches with pickles and chips on the side, rolled in by a bellboy in a purple uniform with gold piping. Rod settles in immediately. For him and his current lifestyle, this is a nice treat, but I always like to introduce food into an interview, even when the subject has been living high on the hog. Food changes the dynamic; it's much harder to resist someone who has just fed you. To keep the spirit going, and to give Al a chance to swallow, I revert to my conspiratorial kidding mode.

Me: "Rod, I get a sense from what you're telling us that officers really were not minding the store and that lower enlisted men were doing as they pleased: bending rules, smoking dope . . ."

Rod, his smile sneaking back: "It was loose. Everyone was doing dope, even many of the officers, and of course there was the black market of PX items you could sell at a discount on the street."

"You, of course, lived at the foot of the cross?" I say with a big grin. Rod grins back—more confirmation that laws and rules for Rod are just something to get around.

"How about wine? Was it cheap on base?"

"Really cheap."

"You like it?"

"Oh, yeah, especially the Riesling. Everyone was drunk all the time over there. There's nothing else to do on base."

This is now the fourth or fifth time Rod has said "everyone," a verbal tell signaling guilt. In his mind "everyone" else is doing something bad, so why shouldn't he? I wonder if he even pays his taxes (assuming he even makes enough these days to owe Uncle Sam) or if that isn't necessary because "everyone" cheats.

Al goes back to asking questions about the kind of travel soldiers were allowed. Rod answers that he often walked in the countryside as many Germans do on the weekends, but he says nothing about visiting other countries. More important than the answer, though, he's obviously relaxing. He's talking at a normal speed. His hands aren't flying all over the place when he answers. It must be fifteen minutes since he last lit a cigarette when he finally shakes a new one out of his thinning pack. I wait until he has it lit and has pulled that first heavy puff into his lungs before I ask the question that all this has been leading up to.

"The people you worked for, this Clyde Conrad—was he a good guy? What was he like?"

Rod is listening intently. The tissue just under his left eye and just above the cheekbone quivers slightly; usually you see that only in poker players who are bluffing. But it's his cigarette I need to track.

"Conrad's really smart," he finally answers. "He used to read a lot—knew more about plans than most of the officers." That's when I see his cigarette shake for a third time, and I have the confirmation I've been looking for.

These autonomic reactions, as they're known, are very word-specific. Kill someone with a machete, for example, and "ice pick" and "knife" aren't going to have any effect on you. Only the word or phrase directly and specifically associated with the act triggers the threat reflex. For Rod, that phrase, I've now confirmed, is "Clyde Conrad," but why? Even when they carry all that extra weight, proper nouns are hard to pin down. Maybe Conrad and Rod hung out with whores together, or as he has already hinted, they sold PX cigarettes on the black market. But to see these reactions over and over, there has got to be *something* serious that happened between these two.

Obviously, this has to be pursued further, but there's a practical issue to be gotten around. Al has run out of time. Rod can take care of himself—he followed us over to the Pickett in his own down-at-the-heels Dodge Aries, which I held tight in the rearview mirror all the way to the hotel, but if I don't get Al to the airport in the next half hour, he's going to miss his flight.

"Why don't you call your mom before you leave," I suggest to Rod, "just so she doesn't have to worry."

"Oh, she'll be fine," Rod says. "I'll call her when I get back." He's smiling again—a *real* smile this time, not a smirk. He seems glad about the answers he gave us, and really, we didn't press him at all. If you were a fly on the wall, you might well wonder, "What the hell was achieved here?" This all sounded like storytelling and bragging, with a little Cold War historical garnish and the occasional BS. But that fly on the wall would be very, very wrong.

As Rod heads for the hotel-room door buoyed by our gratitude and no doubt glad this is over—or so he thinks—I wait until he has his hand on the doorknob to lob one last question at him.

"By the way," I say, "did Conrad ever give you anything?"

In the interrogation business, this is known as the doorjamb confrontation. The interview is over; the subject is feeling psychologically safe—freedom is only steps away, literally a turn of the doorknob. You never know what you might get when you try it.

"No, nothing much," Rod says, "but he did give me a telephone number."

Without missing a beat, he pulls a wallet out of his rear pocket, picks out a worn piece of paper, and holds it up for us.

"Can I have it?" I ask.

"Sure," he says. "Take it."

I pinch it by the corner, turn it over carefully, and read the number that has been written there: 266-933. I quickly notice that the number nine is written in the German style so it looks like a "g" with a curled tail, so I'm guessing Rod didn't write it.

"What's it for?" I ask.

"A telephone, I guess. He said to use it in the future if I had to get hold of him." And with that Rod walks out and closes the door.

Before Rod gets to the elevators, I've placed the paper carefully into a hotel stationery envelope. Forget about the numbers. Something about the paper—its density, the fibers and the texture—feels very odd.

2

LIFESTYLE ISSUES

Turns out, Al Eways isn't quite the sphinx I'd pegged him for. The drive from the Pickett Hotel to Tampa International is no more than ten minutes, but on the way, Al goes off script (on my prompt) and gives a good fill on the Conrad case.

Someone recruited by US intelligence—Al can't or won't say more—tipped INSCOM to a spy burrowed deep among the 250,000 US Army personnel stationed in Germany, an unknown soldier who was stealing documents that were then making their way to the Soviet Union via Hungary. Army Intelligence and the FBI's Washington Field Office have worked on this investigation for years, Al says. It was like trying to find a needle in a haystack, but finally the investigation led them to Clyde Lee Conrad for two reasons: the length of time he was stationed in Germany (most soldiers rotated out after a few years) and, more important, the fact that for much of that time he was the official custodian for the very G-3 Plans that had been leaking the Soviets' way.

But the story doesn't end there. By focusing on Conrad and using an undercover army agent named Danny Williams, investigators were able to identify Zoltan Szabo, a Hungarian émigré to the United States who'd won a Silver Star for valor in Vietnam only to turn traitor during his subsequent army posting to Germany. Szabo was the original Hungarian Connection. He'd been the first to peddle the documents via his onetime countrymen to the Soviets, and when he left the military, he recruited Conrad to succeed him as document custodian for the Eighth Infantry Division.

The undercover agent had also helped investigators tumble onto two Hungarian-born doctors, brothers Imre and Sandor Kercsik, who used their sacrosanct medical bags to transport the stolen documents from Germany, where Conrad was stationed, to Hungary. The brothers had been detained in Sweden, where they were living, and, under questioning from the Swedes with guidance from the Germans, had quickly confessed to their role in the Conrad spy ring. Now, Al says, they're under formal arrest in Stockholm. All of which is great, of course, but I can't help wondering what exactly the American investigators—INSCOM and the FBI—have contributed to this picture.

"How about Rod Ramsay?" I ask as we're pulling up to the terminal. "Where's he fit into all this?"

"Most likely, nowhere," Al answers. "Tens of thousands of people passed through the Eighth ID during the time in question, and maybe a thousand worked with or near Clyde Conrad. We're talking to all of them 'cause that's how we do things, but basically this case is over."

"Over?" I ask. He's out of the car by now, grabbing his bag out of the trunk.

"Yeah," he says almost over his shoulder, hotfooting it to make a flight to I don't know where. "Szabo lives in Austria. The Kercsik brothers are being detained in Sweden, where they live, and because espionage is considered a political offense in both countries, we can't extradite them. As far as Conrad, he was picked up by German authorities eleven hours ago—that's the 0400 hours Zulu in your teletype, right in the middle of his beauty sleep. It's up to the Germans now. We're out of it."

Al's short take on the matter sounds airtight, but something is bothering me—I just can't place my finger on it.

We promise to keep in touch if anything fresh comes up, and next thing I know I'm looking at Al's slumped shoulders racing for a gate.

For my part, I should be racing in the opposite direction, back to the office. I can't even imagine how high the paperwork is already stacked. Instead, I take three lazy passes around the terminal loop while I try to process what I've just learned.

One, this was at least a two-generation spy ring. Why is everyone seemingly so certain that Conrad hasn't recruited a third (or fourth, or fifth) generation of his own?

Two, if INSCOM and the Washington Field Office really have been on this case for half a decade, what's the big deal about spending another few months poking around while Clyde Conrad adapts to life behind bars?

But here's the thing I really can't get over: the fact (a) that collaring Conrad has been left to the Germans in the first place and (b) that, according to Al, the Germans are now running the show. In the Bureau it's an article of faith that if the US is the victim—the aggrieved party, the one that has suffered the insult—then it's up to us to make certain that the US prosecutes that individual, even if we have to be a little imaginative in getting the accused back on American soil. And even with sophisticated crooks, that kind of creativity isn't impossible to pull off.

I'm thinking for example of an operation I was in on four years earlier. The Mexicans had asked our help in running down Arturo Durazo, the former chief of police of Mexico City, who was wanted for corruption. By then, Durazo was sprinting from one Latin American country to another, seeking a safe sanctuary, and we were chasing him without a lot of success until, through Bureau sources, we identified his girlfriend and convinced her to sell lover boy on relocating to an island in the Caribbean, a crook's paradise where there's no extradition treaty with either Mexico or the US. A tall order? For sure, but so persuasive was she that Durazo eventually boarded of his own volition our undercover FBI twin-engine aircraft, with his girlfriend, his bodyguard, and a million dollars in cash. Unfortunately for Durazo, the island we did fly him to was under American jurisdiction: Puerto Rico, where we promptly arrested him and seized the stolen money on an international warrant, and shipped him back home for trial. If we can go to creative lengths on a case that isn't even ours, the Washington Field Office should have moved mountains to get Conrad back in the US.

Was it lack of vision, lack of will, or lack of balls that delivered Conrad to the Germans? Who knows, but I'm not betting against the missing cojones.

THE NEXT TIME AROUND the terminal loop, I follow the appropriate exit signs for downtown Tampa, but my mind is still looking backward, not ahead. Conrad was, as Al said, a needle in a haystack consisting of a quarter of a million military personnel who passed through the Eighth ID HQ in Bad Kreuznach, West Germany, in the late seventies and early eighties. But really, if you peel all the wrappers back, Clyde Conrad was a Day-Glo needle in a thin, dull-colored stack. The timing worked. He had access to the documents in question. Opportunity beckoned, almost begged.

Finding a co-conspirator among the ten thousand–plus people whom Al, I, and a host of others have been dispatched to interview— that would be the *true* coup. And by the time I get to the Bureau office on Zack Street in downtown Tampa, I'm beginning to think that an acne-scarred, dope-smoking, scrawny 150-pounder with an outsized intellect who happens to live right in my backyard might be looking like a prime possibility.

MY CAREER AS A campus cop had a lot to do with the FBI's hiring me, but counterintelligence is what hooked me on the Bureau once I was inside the door. CI was only part of the brief at my first posting, in Phoenix. There were drugs to run down, border issues, money laundering, just about anything illegal that crossed state lines—i.e., the whole overflowing banquet table of federal crime. But my next stop, in New York City, was all counterintelligence all the time: running double-agent operations, developing intelligence sources, and neutralizing spies assigned to the United Nations, which in the case of the Soviets was pretty much their entire UN workforce.

That was part of what I loved about New York—the spy action was nonstop. The other part was the special agent in charge of the Bureau: Don McGorty. He ran the largest CI program in the country, and he didn't take shit from headquarters because no office knew more or produced more than his. Don's dual approach to dealing with FBIHQ soon became my own: "Better to apologize than ask for permission," and "No one at HQ knows more about your target than you."

Puerto Rico, my next station of the FBI cross, introduced me to another legendary special agent in charge, Dick Held, and Dick passed along his own wisdom about dealing with Washington: "Do what it takes to get the job done so long as it's legal and ethical, and don't take no for an answer—especially from HQ." For me, though, Tampa was always the prize I had in mind. Not only had the Tampa office tried a disproportionate number of espionage cases; it moved me nearer to my expatriate Navarro clan, by now spread all over Southern Florida.

Another Tampa advantage: my immediate boss, Jay Koerner, a rising legend in his own right among those of us dedicated to CI, the kind of supervisor too rare in sprawling bureaucracies prone to eating their young. Jay has HQ's respect even though he has never served there. Just as important, he isn't falling all over himself to join the Bureau careerists who swarm to the Mothership like bees to a hive.

Unfortunately, Jay doesn't always feel that I am an equal blessing in return. Today is a case in point. He's on the phone when I barge into his office. As usual on these occasions, he fixes me with a look that says, "You can see I am on the phone, right?" Pretty much as usual, too, I set about straightening his desk—he's an office super-slob—

then start pacing back and forth right in front of him so he'll know what I'm about to say is important.

Finally, he gets the message and wraps up the call. "What?" he asks—although his New York accent makes it sound more like "Wat?" and his expression is pretty clearly saying "Hey, Navarro, do me a favor and drop dead."

"I just dropped Eways off at the airport," I reply, sitting down and loosening my tie.

"You're stomping up and down in front of my desk to tell me that?"

"Not really."

"Okay, how'd it go?" There's a bit of a sigh to his voice now. He seems to be bracing slightly, aware that I'm about to drop something on him.

"I want to initiate a full field investigation of this Ramsay character."

"Why, what'd he say?"

"Nothing much," I reply.

"Nothing much?"

"Well, he was cooperative."

"So that's what we're basing this full investigation on, then? His cooperative spirit?"

"No, his cigarette."

"Cigarette? Smoking's a federal crime now? I missed that act of Congress."

"Ramsay's cigarette shook."

Koerner cracks a smile. He knows I've spent a long time studying body language. He also suspects me of being a little nuts. "Are you fucking kidding me?"

"Not just once," I say. "It shook *three* times."

"Let me get this straight, Navarro. You want to open a full field investigation under the AG guidelines based on this interviewee waving his cigarette around?"

I've expected this. The attorney general guidelines were put in place a decade or so ago to curb the abuses of J. Edgar Hoover's reign.

The guidelines are exhaustively long, but simply put, they specify when a "full" investigation can be initiated and for how long, and they set the bar high, where it should be. A full field investigation requires reasonable cause to believe that a crime has been committed or that intelligence activity is afoot. Admittedly, a shaking cigarette, even thrice-shaking, is pushing the envelope a bit, but why give in on small issues?

"Yes," I reply, hands draped territorially over the edge of the chair arms. "That's exactly why we should open this investigation."

"You trying to get us all fired?" Koerner is shaking his head now.

"I think Ramsay is involved in this case."

"What case, for crissake?"

I'd forgotten that. From reading the original teletype, Jay knows no more about this case than I did seven hours ago. While I give him a quick fill on what I learned from Al Eways after our interview was done, Jay pulls an extra-large bottle of antacids from his top desk drawer. At least in Tampa, America's domestic protection is built on a firm foundation of Rolaids.

"Ah," he says when I'm through. "The army had this case, and now the Germans have it, but you want to open a separate investigation all on your own here in Tampa?"

"Correct."

"What about Washington Field Office? They have an open case?" This is an important question since we're clearly edging toward FBI jurisdictional disputes, which can get as nasty as two ferrets in a bag.

"According to Eways," I explain, "WFO has been helping on this case for years, but they have nothing to show for it, and besides, their case is now a German case."

"What do you mean 'nothing'?"

"You saw the communication that came in. Whatever WFO might actually know, they have absolutely nothing to offer us. But listen, Ramsay is somehow involved with the guy they arrested in Germany, and I want to prove it."

"How do you know that?"

"Every time the name Clyde Lee Conrad was mentioned his cigarette shook."

"Conrad?"

"The guy the Germans arrested with the help of the army. Ramsay worked for him."

"So just because Ramsay worked for Conrad and his cigarette shook, you want to open an investigation?"

"That's right. You got it. Congrats." I'm on my feet now, ready to get started on the paperwork, but Jay isn't quite through.

"You really are nuts, aren't you? I can just imagine the hearing. 'Yes, Madam Senator, I authorized the investigation of this American based on work proximity and a nervous twitch while he smoked.' Christ, Navarro, think about it."

I smile, thinking of Koerner squirming in the hot seat. "Nuts, maybe," I say. "You've suggested as much before, but I really do want to open the investigation, Jay." The "Jay" is important. I use his first name in conversation sparingly, only when I want to drive a key point home. "Ramsay was a bundle of nerves during the interview even though we told him we weren't interested in him. He exhibits enough antisocial traits and lifestyle issues to make me want to focus on him."

"Great, I can add that to my Senate testimony, just before I go to prison: 'Senator, he has had lifestyle issues.' Navarro, half the people on Earth have lifestyle issues. You, for one."

That stops us both cold.

"Listen," he says, after a long pause. "I'm sorry. That was unfair, way out of left field."

Koerner is a rangy six-three, with blond hair and a big mustache like one of those Oakland A's pitchers from the early seventies. He's got a reputation, locally and within the larger FBI, for not taking any shit. But he's got a heart of gold, and this is one of those moments that show it. My wife, Luciana, was born and raised in Brazil. She's still getting used to life in America. The fact that we've moved three times in the last seven years hasn't made it easy to build social connections either, but Jay is also aware that there are other issues at home.

I rarely venture far from work in our conversations, but Jay is my supervisor. He has a right to ask when he can see I'm too distracted by outside matters. He knows Luciana has had some health issues. On more than one occasion, I've also let on that Luciana has been complaining I'm not home enough, and when I am, that I'm not attentive enough to her or our daughter, Stephanie. Ask any agent: It's a common work hazard for those who aren't jockeying a desk all day long.

"Don't apologize," I say now. "Luciana is right. I'm going to work on that. But, Jay, I wouldn't ask this if I didn't think there was something going on here. I tested Ramsay to make sure. Three times that cigarette shook like a polygraph needle when I mentioned Clyde Lee Conrad."

"Oh, come on!" Jay is pushing his seat back, looking up to the heavens for guidance.

"I'm serious. Let me go back and talk with him a couple of more times just to see what he says. What if he was involved, what if he—"

Koerner cuts me off. "That's a lot of what-ifs—the AG guidelines are very specific. What does Eways say?"

"Nothing much. Ramsay flunked the piss test and that's about it. They don't have anything on him other than that he worked for Conrad."

"Christ almighty, Navarro!" Jay has given up on heavenly guidance, it seems. Now he's rolling his eyes in exasperation.

"There's one more thing. When Ramsay was getting ready to leave, I asked him if Conrad had ever given him anything. Yeah, he says, and he reaches in his wallet and pulls this out." I'm showing him the contents of the hotel envelope as I speak, but without letting him touch it.

"What is it?"

"Don't know yet—Ramsay said it was a phone number."

"And he carries it in his wallet?"

"Yes, but here's the thing. There aren't enough digits on the number to call anywhere."

"It's not illegal to have a phone number in your wallet, whether it's complete or incomplete. You know that."

"Jay, listen to me. Ramsay's dirty. I know it. I want to run that phone number, I want to check for fingerprints, I want to compare handwriting, I want to check the paper out to see where it originated, and I want to see if Ramsay has been in contact with Conrad and how. If he's dirty, I'll have a confession within ten interviews. Guaranteed."

"Ten?"

"Okay, five," which might just be over the top, but I'm running out of time. In fact, I just have.

"Out," Jay says. "Get out of my office—I have other work to do. Fortunately, some of the agents in this office are actually sane."

Jay is fumbling with the papers on his desk, messing up the neat piles I made fifteen minutes ago, anything to avoid looking me in the eye.

"Let me think about it," he finally says, but I notice Jay is already dialing HQ before I close his office door.

Mickey's big hand is on the nine and his little one is nearing six when Jay finally pops out of his door again. By my count, he has taken four calls and made five during the four-plus intervening hours. I've seen him cajoling, pleading, even in a few instances shouting—but who's monitoring?

He approaches my desk. "Do the paperwork," he says. "Open it up, but don't put anything in there about body language or shaking cigarettes. And interview him tomorrow. You've got ninety days. After that, I shut it down."

"Thanks, Koerner," I say, but Jay is already headed for the Bureau door, shaking his head like a moose that just lost its antlers.

*   *   *

I ARRIVE AT THE office promptly at 6 a.m. the next morning, Thursday, August 24, 1988, and am greeted as usual by the night agent finishing his duties and by the communications specialist, who hands me my envelope as he exits the vault. And by 6:02 I know there are going to be issues with this case. No, that's the wrong word; I know there are going to be *problems*, maybe very big ones.

Before leaving the office yesterday, I submitted by overnight mail the paperwork to open a full field investigation. I also overnighted the piece of paper Ramsay had given me to the FBI Lab, specifically the unit that handles espionage paraphernalia. My instructions were straightforward and simple: examine the paper and the ink, and their origins, and photograph the numbers and compare them with known samples. I also wanted the paper scanned for fingerprints and tested for drugs in case it had come into contact with cocaine or other substances. I thought all that would be prudent of me to do as an investigator. What I didn't expect was that the Washington Field Office—WFO, in Bureau-speak—would try to stop us from doing our job before we even got started. That's just what they've done, though.

I study the communication classified "Secret/ORCON" (for "originator controlled") over and over, thinking I must be missing something or maybe a word got dropped or a typo snuck in. Finally, I read the document from back to front—a good way to catch typos, by the way—but the basic message never changes: The joint FBI/Army-INSCOM investigation code named Canasta Player, we have now been officially informed, takes supremacy over all ancillary investigations, and thus everything involved in any way whatsoever with it has to be coordinated through WFO. Additionally, no investigative effort on our part should interfere with WFO's work.

Wow, I'm thinking to myself, *yesterday they needed me; today, not so much.* Indeed, not at all. The prohibition against "interference" is very inclusive, so inclusive that the only safe course of action seems to be to roll over and just do as they please. But why should I? We have every right to open an investigation if we can justify it, and I've done that in accordance with attorney general guidelines. Also, Conrad is *already* in German custody. What can I possibly spoil for them by trying to gather more of the truth?

Instinctively, my hand reaches into my top desk drawer for comfort, but all I can find is an empty Tums wrapper. Koerner isn't in yet, but his oversized Rolaids bottle never leaves and his desk is always unlocked. I find the bottle in its customary space, squeezed between an equally big bottle of Advil and his shoe-shine kit. Koerner is old school. Everyone in J. Edgar's day kept a shoe-shine kit close by, and God help the agent whose shoes weren't buffed.

I might raid the Advil later this morning, but for now, I dole out to myself three Rolaid tablets and settle back down at my desk to reread the Washington Field Office fuck-u-gram one more time. I went to bed last night thinking I had a great day ahead of me. Among the things I was looking forward to was partnering with Lynn Tremaine, an investigator with a bright future who would have done the initial interviewing with Al Eways yesterday if she hadn't been out of town. To be honest, I doubt Lynn would have picked up on the same clues I did. She's young—twenty-six, I think—and inexperienced in espionage matters, but, as I found out when we worked together on a case in Cape Canaveral, she has a great attitude, a rollicking sense of humor, and a fantastic work ethic. I've also noticed that she has an easy way around the younger guys in the office—she jogs with them, plays tag football, joins them for beers after work. From what little of Ramsay I've picked up on, Lynn would have the ability to get him thinking of her as his kid sister, the kind you like to have around.

As far as I was concerned, this was going to be a chance to have professional fun and do some mentoring in the process. Now it looks as though we'll be battling the WFO, and almost certainly FBIHQ behind it, all the way. No wonder steam is coming out of my ears when Lynn and Jay come through the door about half an hour later.

Koerner's hair is still wet from the gym as he grabs a pot of coffee, heads for his office, and promptly disappears behind the small mountain of paper that has come in overnight. Maybe two minutes pass before the top-secret communications custodian comes trotting in with the messages for which Jay has to sign individually. The custodian is just leaving when Koerner's disembodied voice comes booming out his office door.

"Navarro, you been in my desk?"

"Yes, sir. Rolaids."

"Can't you buy your own?"

"I could, but yours are cheaper."

"You're welcome," he shoots back as he slams his lower desk drawer. I don't get it—I handle that Rolaids bottle as if it were nitroglycerin, but somehow he always knows.

Lynn is ready for coffee, too, but not the crap the GSA supplies to the office. Instead, we head down to Perrera's, a little Cuban coffee shop that serves the best *café con leche* and Cuban toast anywhere around.

I'm ready to off-load on Washington, but Lynn is clearly looking at life from a rosier perspective. "Tell me all about the case," she says as we wait for our order in a corner booth, both of us with our backs to the wall. And so I do—from the teletype that would have gone to her had she not been on leave, to trying to find Ramsay, to seeing him scurrying naked, to the two interviews, one at the house and the other at the hotel.

Lynn takes my word for it that the shaking cigarette means something, even though she's been taught almost nothing about body language in the FBI. She's also almost as excited as I am about the piece of paper Ramsay handed us and points out on her own that the number "9" is written in the German way, like a "g." If I ever knew, I forgot that Lynn had studied in Germany and speaks the language fluently, another big plus if we can ever get this case off the ground.

By the time we're heading back to the Bureau, I've calmed down considerably. Washington is still bound to be a pain in the ass, but

Lynn is my kind of agent—eager to learn and ready to help out. As far as we're both concerned, the sooner we can talk to Rod Ramsay, the better, but there's yet another complication to that. Rod is under no obligation to talk with us. All he has to do is say, "I want a lawyer," and everything stops dead in its tracks.

I'm thinking hard about the best way to approach him when we walk back into the office and Sharon Woods, the squad secretary, solves the problem for us. "Roderick Ramsay called," she says. "He wants you to call him back."

SURE ENOUGH, ROD ANSWERS on the first ring. This call is important to him—he's been waiting by the phone. He starts out by wanting to clarify a few things he said the day before—a name here, a missed time sequence there. He's worried that I might have gotten the wrong impression of him because of where he was house-sitting.

"There used to be some occupants in that house," he explains, "who weren't the best kind of people."

"Does this relate to the gun in the cabinet?"

"Yeah," he says. "That and some other things."

In the end, it's all small stuff. I tell him I'll pass the added information on to Agent Eways. Then he asks if I've heard anything more from Germany. And with that I'm reminded of two things. The first is that while witnesses and victims make these kinds of calls all the time, I've had only one other suspect do this in my entire career. The second thing I'm reminded of is that that suspect was trying to find out where the investigation was headed and milk me for information. Maybe Rod is doing the same. Maybe he's just lonely and wants to talk about German prostitutes again.

"Tell you what," I say, "I do have questions I didn't get to ask yesterday. Can I stop by with my partner, Lynn, because Eways is gone."

"Sure," he says, "come on over. I'm at my mom's place."

"I'll be there in forty minutes," I say, knowing we'll be there in twenty-five. If Rod is setting some kind of trap for us, I want to spring it on our schedule, not his. Lynn and I spend our drive time going over safety issues just in case things do go kinetic. I also ask her to let me take the lead and to hide all appearances of being an agent. No credential-flashing when we show up. No writing materials once we're inside—if something important is said, I want Rod to give us the paper we make a note on. Since I was hoping to interview Ramsay today, I wore khakis and a polo shirt to the office—a big change from yesterday's blue suit. Lynn came more casual than usual, too, because she was expecting to spend the day catching up on missed paperwork.

All that will help keep Rod's guard down. Efrem Zimbalist Jr. rarely even loosened his tie all those years on *The F.B.I.* (Trust me, I know. I watched the TV show religiously even when I barely understood any English!) But in the real world of nuanced emotions, interviewees confronted with official-looking badges and starched shirts tend to batten down the hatches, the way Rod did when Al and I first confronted him yesterday.

Interestingly, Rod is waiting outside his mom's trailer when we pull up fifteen minutes early. He seems anxious but not on edge. Instead of lingering outside, he welcomes us quickly into the single-wide mobile home, pleasantly air-conditioned and even more nicely decorated. What I assume are his mother's touches are everywhere: pictures on the walls and an attractive centerpiece on the small, spotless dinette table in the kitchen.

"Your mother keeps a nice place here," I say.

"She does. She's very good that way," Ramsay replies.

"Yeah, very nice," Lynn chimes in as Ramsay leads us into the living room—so different than his behavior the day before.

Lynn, as I expected, proves to be a natural fit with Rod. On the way over, I asked her to be playful. A lot of male agents have trouble with that—they want to go Sergeant Joe Friday from Minute One. Not Lynn. She banters easily with Rod about traveling in Europe and everything else except what we're really interested in.

Not surprisingly, Rod is calmer, more relaxed and less tense than yesterday at his house-sitting gig, and thus he naturally opens up without prodding about where he's from and the places where he's lived—Japan and Hawaii for example, two more areas to explore.

As I had yesterday, and on my cue, Lynn pleads ignorant as to army things, and so I get to hear much of what Rod said repeated, and in fact, that's a large part of my goal for today: How Ramsay retells and summarizes these army tales will be a useful guide to both his memory and his authenticity. I also want to press him more on the note he claims Conrad gave him, but only a little harder. If he has been—or still is—involved in espionage, forcing the issue might send him straight into the arms of an attorney and might possibly screw up the larger investigation in Europe.

National security cases are difficult to prove—they tend to be laborious efforts that can fall apart in the blink of an eye. The more an investigator ambles toward the finish line, instead of sprinting, the likelier he or she is to get through the race, and by now, Lynn practically has Rod convinced the two of them are out on a date, and I'm the designated driver.

Ramsay is stretched out on the sofa, feet up on a coffee table, as he talks about his mom, Dorothy, and how she'd moved to Tampa after retiring, only to find work again as an archivist for a local company. He speaks of his love of reading, how he inherited it from his mother and how he went straight from high school into the military.

"Why not college?" Lynn asks. "Someone who loves books as much as you do—"

"It wasn't for me," Rod says, cutting her off mid-sentence.

The curtness tells me there's more to the answer than that, probably lots more, but I'm not going to take him anywhere he doesn't want to go, and besides, he's already telling us plenty with barely a push on our part—like that he has a brother (Stewart) and that his father had divorced his mother and Rod has had little contact with him over the years. There are other indications that the Ramsays aren't a Norman Rockwell–type family, but as I look around the mobile home, it seems pretty clear that Rod's mother has tried to carve out a normal life for herself and her stay-at-home son.

It doesn't take long for Lynn to pick up on Rod's high IQ, his knowledge of history, and his fluent German, and of course that pleases him immensely. He kids Lynn about her own German and how it's colored by her broad, flat midwestern accent. I don't know more than a dozen words of German, but Rod's own accent puts me in mind of those SS colonels dressed in long leather coats in vintage World War II movies. The two of them even manage to crack a few jokes in German—about me, I think, since they seem to be laughing at my expense.

It's not long either before Rod launches happily into the seamier side of his life in Bad Kreuznach—the heavy drinking, the visits to prostitutes (though he refuses to look straight at Lynn when he's telling this), and the drugs that were available, including acid, marijuana, and nitrous-oxide "whippets," which apparently could be bought at the post PX.

All this confirms for me Rod's moral apathy, his lack of self-regulation, and how easily others can influence him, but he also speaks once again with obvious pride about his work with the Eighth ID and how that fit in with V Corps and America's strategic interests generally in Europe. As if to prove his liberal-mindedness, Ramsay also notes proudly that an African-American general named Colin Powell took command of V Corps shortly after he left Germany, but fails to mention that the reason Rod wasn't there to greet the new commander was because he'd failed the by now famous "piss test"—more evidence that action and consequence are loosely connected in Rod's psyche.

Next thing I know, Rod has moved on to the document-keeping process and how riddled with potholes everything was.

"They had all these safes, all these procedures," he says, "but if somebody wanted to take something, all they had to do was put it in a burn bag and then pull it back out of the bag before they got to the burn facility."

"What do you mean, burn bag and burn facility?" I ask.

"That's the thing," he says, "you couldn't burn things where we kept all the documents. The burn facility was two blocks down and one block over. At the end of the day, we'd bag up the stuff they wanted destroyed and haul it over to be burned. Nobody questioned us when we were leaving our building or made sure that every document carried out was put in the furnace at the other end."

"That's a huge vulnerability," I say.

"Huge," he agrees.

I can't tell if Rod is dropping crumbs he expects me to follow or if he's simply in an expansive mood, but in this more relaxed setting, he's definitely smoking less, and the conversation seems to flow easily, especially from his side. Something else: Rod isn't playing all those smartest-guy-in-the-room games he played yesterday with Al Eways and later with me. All that's great, but after an hour or so, I decide it's time to narrow the focus and edge the conversation toward Clyde Conrad and that mysterious piece of paper with its six numerals.

"How about your friends in Germany," I ask, "the guys you hung out with?"

"Oh," he says, "they were mostly about my age. You know, drinking buddies, that sort of thing." The question clearly hasn't upset him, so I press on.

"I mean, did you guys travel around together? See the sights?"

"Sure, but once we left the base, a lot of them were dependent on me. I was the one who spoke German, and I was just about the only one with a passport as well."

Sounds like innocuous stuff, I know, but now I've learned something else. Most soldiers have only their military IDs to travel on, which means they're limited to countries under the status-of-forces agreement, but Rod's having a passport meant he could go anywhere he wanted without revealing that he was in the military.

Not all his friends were single, Rod goes on. Some of the married ones were allowed to bring their families over. They weren't running around with prostitutes all night long, obviously, and their wives were often good for a home-cooked meal.

"What about your boss, Conrad?" I ask. Rod's not smoking at that moment, and the timing is intentional. I want to test him in another way.

"He'd married a German national and lived off-base," Rod answers, pulling twice on his shirt collar—ventilating behavior that's as telling as a shaking cigarette.

"I guess you got to eat home-cooked meals at his house, too?"

"I did. Annja, his wife, is really nice and a great cook. Her schnitzel is the best." He looks at Lynn as he says this, as if only she can appreciate how good a schnitzel can be.

"Was it hard to live off of the economy?" I ask. We'd gone over this yesterday, but I want Rod to get back to comfortable ground before I move on to the paper he pulled from his wallet, and I'm curious to see if his response will be different this time around.

Ramsay laughs and says, "The dollar was strong at first, but then it declined. Some of the soldiers sold the rationed items on the economy to get by."

"Like what?"

"Cigarettes, Jack Daniel's, gasoline rations, stuff like that."

"Did you?" I'm rolling my eyes with playfulness.

"Mayyybeeee," Ramsay says, with the look of a naughty boy, just like he had yesterday.

I laugh back. "I'll take that as a yes." Then we all chuckle. One thing you don't do when you're interviewing with Al Eways is engage in a mass chuckle. Rod is feeling so comfortable that he pops to his feet and offers to get us a round of lemonade. I wait until he's served up the three glasses before moving on to the second subject I want to cover.

"By the way," I say, "that note you gave me yesterday—the paper feels weird, doesn't it?"

Ramsay carefully puts his glass down on the coffee table, then pushes his glasses right up onto the bridge of his nose and pulls once again on his shirt collar before answering. "I was with Clyde at a novelty store when he bought the paper."

"Ah, that explains it, then, because it doesn't look like regular office stationery."

"No, no, it's different," Ramsay says, coughing. "It's called flash paper. Magicians use it—they wet their hands and the paper dissolves."

"Yeah, I've heard of it," I reply, knowing Rod has just fed me grade A bullshit. I saw yesterday how deft Rod was at manipulating Al Eways, but that didn't guarantee he wouldn't make a mistake during an interview, and Ramsay has just demonstrated that. In fact, he's painted himself into a corner that I don't intend to let him get out of, but I'm going to wait for the forensics lab to tell me what the real story is with that paper.

For the moment, it's enough to know that the arm's-length relationship with Clyde Conrad that Ramsay described yesterday was a lot closer than that. Rod had gone to Conrad's house and enjoyed his wife's cooking. The two even supposedly went shopping together, to a novelty store of all places. Some investigators really go off when a subject lies to them. Not me. The more lies I hear, the closer I know I'm getting to the truth.

Rod seems to realize he needs to change the conversation, because out of the blue he asks Lynn what kind of gun she's wearing.

"None," she says (not true, by the way), "but the weapon I've been issued is a Smith & Wesson model ten-six revolver."

Ramsay's excitement over this news reminds me of the hum that always races around a classroom when we show schoolkids our weapons on career day.

"How about you?" he asks, turning my way.

"Sig Sauer two-two-six."

"Whoa, those are *nice* guns," he says, arching his eyebrows. "Made in Switzerland, right?"

"Yup," I answer, "and very expensive."

"Why do you get to have such a special one while she"—nodding toward Lynn—"has to make do with a Smith & Wesson?"

"Because I am a s-p-e-c-i-a-l agent," I joke, drawing out each letter.

Lynn jumps in. "He's not that special, trust me. But he's on the SWAT team—that's why he gets the Sig Sauer."

"Cool," Ramsay says, and I can tell that in his eyes my credentials have just been considerably burnished.

"Listen, we have to leave," I say, catching Lynn by surprise, "but before we go, that number Conrad gave you, what was the significance of that?" I'm keeping my tone of voice light, as if the answer barely matters.

"Not sure," he says, "just a number he wanted me to have."

"I see, but that's not his house phone number in Germany, right?"

"No, I know his number. I used to call him all the time."

"Right, well, maybe he was going on vacation, and this is where he could be reached," I say.

Rod just shrugs his shoulders as I take my empty glass of lemonade to the kitchen.

Lynn and I both thank him for his time and for the refreshments, and for the help.

"No problem," he says. "Call anytime," and he honestly seems to mean it. Just to put a cap on our chummy morning, Lynn and Rod make one more crack in German, probably about me again, that sends them both into temporary hysterics.

"WHAT WAS THAT ABOUT?" Lynn asks as we're buckling up. "Why end it so early? He seemed willing to keep talking."

"He definitely was. A regular chatterbox, and I want him to continue that way."

Lynn still has a puzzled look on her face as we pull out of the trailer park, so I explain further. "It's all about timing, about not pushing too hard, about pacing. By leaving now, we're convincing him that we believe what he's telling us, even the bullshit parts. Indifference at this stage is far better than pressing too hard for details. It's too early for that. Rod is giving us what we need."

"And what's that?"

"More reason to come back."

"So what was he bullshitting about?"

"There is no store he went to with Conrad to buy flash paper—that's just crap."

"How do you know?"

"Because after he answered that, his Adam's apple jumped up like a kid on a trampoline."

3

TIRED AND WIRED

On a bad night of flying surveillance, you're looking at a small object on the ground that you can't take your eye off for hours at a time while also maintaining altitude, avoiding other aircraft, adjusting for winds, orbiting around an erratically moving vehicle, coordinating with the spotter/observer you've been partnered with, and trying not to get too lost in your own thoughts. Trust me, it's not easy. Even though the plane is air-conditioned, I often end up with my backside completely soaked.

Tonight's not like that. For starters, I've got a copilot helping as we do three-mile-wide circles over Apollo Beach, just south of Tampa. While my flying partner monitors the traffic descending into and climbing out of Tampa International, I'm in the left seat, eyes fixed on the Gulf Coast home of a minor drug kingpin. We're waiting for him to fire up the Caddy in the driveway and head off on his nightly rounds, but he never does. Maybe the guy's a huge fan of *The Wonder Years* reruns. Whatever he's doing inside, at 9 p.m. the surveillance supervisor tells us to call it a night, but that doesn't mean the workday's over. By the time we land, park, refuel, and do the paperwork on the plane, it's almost ten o'clock, and I still face a forty-minute drive home.

Just shy of eleven, I tiptoe into the house, take a quick shower, hold my daughter Stephanie's face for a moment with my hands while she sleeps—I always do this, no matter how late—then slip into bed beside my wife. Luciana is thirty now, five years my junior, slender but fragile. Even though I'm half a foot taller than she, I used to marvel at how amazingly our bodies fit together in the middle of the night, when Luciana would snuggle her back into the curve of my chest and belly. I long for those days and pray for good health for Luciana—lately, she's had a series of medical problems.

There's a photo in a frame on my bedside table—Luciana, Stephanie (then three, now eight), and me on the beach at Culebra, a little island off the east coast of Puerto Rico, bright sun, sparkling water, all smiles. I keep it there as a reminder not of an idyllic past but of everything Luciana and I thought we were getting away from when I transferred from the San Juan office to Tampa. Puerto Rico did have its wonderful moments—the beach on weekends; walking with Stephanie to the park, her tiny hand cradled in mine—but the FBI was hunting terrorists there, the Macheteros I mentioned earlier, and, in turn, being hunted by them. Most of us agents carried not one gun but two. We checked our cars every day for bombs, and many of us spread talcum powder around the car-door handles and hood and trunk latches at night so we could see if they'd been tampered with while we slept. Luciana got a sense of how bad things were when the Bureau paid to have splinter-proof metal doors installed in our house and metal bars as well. The danger was further underscored when the office issued her and other spouses walkie-talkies just in case they came under siege when they were home alone. Trust me, Puerto Rico was no picnic, not for agents or spouses.

Tampa was going to be our reward for all that—not R & R exactly, but not a hardship post either—and for a while it was. The pace was slower. More evenings than not, I was home in time for dinner and almost always in time to read Stephanie a bedtime story. But the Tampa office, I soon came to realize, is a lot like Florida itself, a kind of early-retirement home for aging agents. Way too few can pass the physical exam for SWAT team duty, or even *want* to do so. Same with flying surveillance—poor eyesight, too many medications, etc.

Inevitably, the work piles up on those of us capable of doing it, and, consequently, home time, evening meals, and bedtime stories have been shrinking. Too often when I get home now, I want nothing more than a soft pillow to lay my head on. Tonight, though, like too many other nights, I'm "tired and wired," and try as I might, I can't get Rod Ramsay out of my mind.

A big part of the problem is the way I do my job. If I'm in charge of an interview, no one ever takes a note unless the subject hands us a piece of paper to write on. You miss too much when you have your head down, scribbling away. Notepads also put up a wall between you and the interviewee. So do tape recorders. They say Official Business, and they tell the person you're talking with to be very careful about his or her replies. I want to build rapport, not ramp up blood pressure, but there's a downside to my way of doing things: the FD-302.

Agents use this special form—a "302" we call it—to record anything that might be introduced in court in any way. You can go an entire career on a CI squad without filling out a 302 because so many intelligence matters never see the light of day, much less go anywhere near a judge and jury. But if Rod Ramsay has been aiding and abetting Clyde Conrad's espionage in any significant way, he's likely to face criminal charges, and when that happens the FD-302s Lynn and I are required to fill out after every interview session will become our sworn word to the court of what we observed—official documents, with our signature, distributed to both the prosecuting and defense attorneys.

Bottom line: We have to get the 302s right, and if you're not taking notes or otherwise recording interviews that can stretch for hours at a time, that requires prodigious acts of memory. Over the years, I've developed all sorts of mnemonic devices to help with that—mental filing systems, code words that will bring back half an hour of conversation as clearly as if I had the interview transcribed by a court reporter. If I've done the interview away from Tampa and have a long drive to get home, I can generally dictate all the key parts on the way back to the office and have one of the Bureau secretaries type up the FD-302 for my signature the next day. The real challenge comes when I pull back into the office expecting to have time to download my memory and get hit instead with some new shitstorm. Then I've got to put the memory circuits on pause and hope the mental systems don't crash in the meantime.

On the way back from our meeting with Rod yesterday, I was telling Lynn about all this: how to handle the 302s, and some simple memory tools she can start using right away. Jay wants me to use this investigation to mentor her, and keeping on top of the 302s will be a key part of that.

Here's what I *didn't* tell her, though: Memory isn't like a water faucet. You can't just turn it on and off at will. Once you get something lodged so well in your head that even, say, an intervening SWAT operation won't shake it loose, it's with you day and night for weeks, sometimes months, even years on end. And it's not just the words; it's everything that goes along with them and helps to make the words meaningful—a look, a nuance, that bony finger pushing glasses up the nose, a broken smoke contrail. That stays with you, too, and all that's what's going on now as I lie in bed, trying to align my own breathing with my wife's. Rod Ramsay is living inside my head.

Christ, I'm thinking, if it's this bad now, after only two sessions, what's it going to be like if this goes on for another six months or more? I'll be possessed by a demon!

ANOTHER VOICE HAS JOINED the chorus, too—a more comforting one but not worry-free: Al Eways.

Al was happy to hear from me when I ran him to ground at his hotel in the Baltimore area, just before heading to the airport for my evening surveillance. Although he was reluctant to give details on a nonsecure line, he did manage to let me know that Conrad wasn't talking, and he reminded me not to expect anything from the Kercsik brothers. As for Szabo, Patient Zero of all this spying, who knows if we'll ever catch him.

One more thing, Al said: The search of Conrad's house in Germany had turned up a shortwave radio and some camera and video equipment. Al seemed to think that could be important, but I have serious doubts from a prosecutorial standpoint. If you arrest every German who owns a Grundig shortwave radio or a Leica camera with a macro lens, you are going to need a lot more prisons. Besides, the Germans are notoriously lenient with spies. Court sentences on average are measurable in months, not years. Shaving six weeks off a six-month sentence isn't going to give someone like Conrad much incentive to cooperate.

Here's what I keep coming back to, though: Why did they haul in Conrad in the first place? And if there's a case to be made, why are American authorities leaving that up to the Germans? It's not just the embarrassment of letting another country do your job— although that's a big deal in the Bureau. The real issue is now that Conrad knows we're on to him and is keeping his mouth shut, and the Kercsiks are doing the same, and Szabo is in the wind, we're likely never to find out just how many documents have been purloined and just how much our national security has been compromised— unless, that is, we can find some other back door into the whole mess. Someone like Rod Ramsay. But Conrad's arrest has likely fired a warning shot across his bow as well.

Snafu—that's the word playing through my brain when I finally fall asleep: Situation Normal, All Fucked Up. No wonder I'm sleep-deprived. On the bedside table next to my head, the night-glow clock reads 12:35. The alarm is set for the usual wake-up call: 4:55.

4

CLARIFICATIONS
AND EVASIONS

August 25, 1988

At 4:55, the alarm drags me out of a nasty, repetitive dream—a critical exam at the FBI Training Academy at Quantico that I've forgotten to study for, being held in a classroom I can't find, in a building with stairs that keep climbing to dead-end hallways. The ring of the alarm coincides exactly with the last ringing bell at the Academy, the one that says: "Test rooms closed and secured."

By five-thirty, I'm shaved, dressed (casual, in the expectation of seeing Ramsay again), and sitting down to a bowl of yogurt, a big helping of Florida fruit, and a homemade *café cubano* that seems to blur the line between liquid and solid. On the breakfast table in front of me is the ever-growing to-do list prepared for my attention by my sleeping wife upstairs. What yanks at my heart are all the activities and events coming up for Stephanie—events I'll miss and already regret not attending.

I'm on the road a little before six, and by the time the Tampa Bureau building heaves into view, about six-fifteen, I'm once again feeling strangely optimistic. Sure, the Washington Field Office is trying to screw us. No doubt about it, WFO is much closer to HQ's ear than we are down in the semi-tropics. Granted, something about the way this whole investigation has gone down to date is starting to smell a little like a three-day-old armadillo squished along the side of US 41. But like Annie sings in the movie, "The sun'll come out tomorrow."

Fortified by a fistful of Tums—I raided my home stash, rather than risk Koerner's Rolaids wrath—I positively bounce into the office at six-thirty, and by 7:05 everything has gone to hell in a handbasket.

LYNN MUST HAVE BEEN looking on the rosy side of life, too, because she bounced into the communications vault at the same time I did, 7:05, and seemed equally frustrated that there was nothing for either of us regarding Conrad, the mysterious piece of paper I'd sent to the lab people, the enigmatic six-digit short number written on same, or anything else that might give us the least leg up in loosening some semblance of the truth from Rod Ramsay.

Koerner is just settling into his office when Lynn and I storm through his door.

With Lynn's tacit approval, I cut to the chase. "We haven't received shit from WFO."

"Christ, Navarro—I haven't had my coffee yet."

"We're doing another interview today, and we have nada, nothing, zilch."

"Give 'em a few days, guys," he tells us. "You know how it is. They get—what?—three, four, five thousand of these requests for examination a week, and all are priorities: rapes, murders, cases going to trial. I mean, look, the main suspect here is in jail already, for crissake."

"And . . ."

"And?" Koerner is looking at me a little strangely, sort of the way people in the movies look at ticking time bombs. Am I about to go off? "Just get it off your chest, Navarro."

"I know we're a small office and HQ all but ignores us, but this isn't another smudged fingerprint from a goddamned bank robbery.

This is an espionage case, and you've always taught me that nothing trumps espionage. What's more, in case no one has noticed, it now involves three countries that we know of and, according to Eways, the defense of Western Europe. So, yes, *I* am pissed, and"—turning to Lynn, who nods in agreement—"*we* are pissed that it takes the lab so long to get this processed."

"Are you done?"

"Jesus, Jay, you know I'm goddamned right!"

Jay looks up, seeking either saintly patience or one of those famous Gulf Coast lightning bolts that occasionally strike a person—hopefully me.

"What do you want?"

"I want you to get them off their ass and treating this as a priority, just as we have. Lynn and I are pushing this as hard as we can. All we're asking for is their support."

Koerner ponders this for a minute or so, with fingers steepled under his chin, then slips into his supervisor's voice. "Well, let's see what you guys get today, and hopefully we'll hear tomorrow from Washington or the army. Who knows? Maybe both!"

"Will you call?"

"I will. Now get the hell out of my office."

Truth is, I probably would have said the same thing in his position—we weren't the only brushfire that needed tending—but still, it's frustrating. I always want things done *now*, not ten minutes later. That's a weakness, I know, but I'm feeling an urgency with this case, and "Well, let's see . . ." just fans my flames.

Lynn and I clear our desks, head to Perrera's, and over the always-excellent coffee agree that this time *she'll* call Ramsay and arrange for us to get together. But for the second day in a row, he's beaten us to the punch. While we're out, he leaves a message for us to call him. Lynn is ready to dial as soon as we're back in the office, but I tell her to wait. First, I don't want Ramsay thinking we're needy. More important, if he's done this twice, he's either terribly lonely or really worried about something. I'm betting on the latter. No harm in letting him stew a little longer.

For the next fifteen minutes, Lynn paces back and forth in front of my desk the same way I would do to Koerner. Finally, I give her the high sign to start dialing, and as I might have predicted, Ramsay picks up at the second or third ring. In short order, he and Lynn are right back where they left off yesterday—gabbing in German and apparently cracking jokes about stodgy old me. Whatever Rod said has Lynn almost rolling on the floor, and she seems to mean it. As soon as she hangs up, she flashes me a thumbs-up.

"Eways asked him a question, and he wants to clarify what he said. I told him we'd be there within the hour."

"Fine by me," I tell her, "but we'll want to stop by Perrera's again on the way out."

"More coffee?"—thinking maybe that I'm wired enough already.

"No, sandwiches to go. Spies always travel on their stomachs." And in fact, the first thing I do when we get to Rod's mother's trailer is to hand him a bag with three still-warm Cuban sandwiches nestled inside. The smell of the roast pork and ham drifts over the living room like some heavenly cloud. Rod's pleased, I can tell; he's maybe even more pleased with the cold Diet Coke that Lynn fishes from her purse for him. We'd noticed a pile of empties in the garbage bin on our previous visit.

"How is your mom, Rod?" I ask, settling down at the end of the couch like an old pal.

"She's fine," he says as he hands out paper plates, but the way he bites the right corner of his lip suggests otherwise. "She's worried I'm in some kind of trouble."

Lynn plays her part perfectly, fixing Rod with a look that says "Why would your mother ever think *that*?" I take a big bite of my sandwich, give it a good chew, then follow Lynn's lead.

"Listen, Rod, I can promise you're definitely not in any trouble. How could you be when you're helping us and the Germans? Mothers always worry, but you can have your mom call me if she's concerned, and I'll put her worries to rest. In fact," I say, pulling out a business card and jotting some numbers on the back, "tell her if she has any questions, to call me day or night. Or she can call Lynn. These are our private lines."

I'm not particularly worried about Mrs. Ramsay, at least not yet. Rod seems enough of a mama's boy that he wouldn't be initiating these visits if she really has a bug up her ass. But wherever the alert barometer should be set, we've dealt with the issue up front and without hesitation (if not entirely honestly), and I can see that Rod is relieved.

"This is really good," he says, digging into his sandwich.

Lynn: "You never had one before?"

"No, this is my first."

Me: "What? You've been here how long and you haven't had a Cuban sandwich—that's a sacrilege! It's an insult to my people!"

Rod smiles, takes a few more bites, then gets down to business.

"Have you heard from Al?" he asks as he adjusts his seat slightly side to side.

Interesting, I'm thinking. He's willing to ask the questions, but he isn't comfortable doing so. He'd fronted his mother's concern the same way—some fidgeting here, some lip-chewing there. Now that that issue is out of the way, he's moving on to the second item on his agenda and, I'm guessing, by far the more important one. I wonder if, like me, Rod stayed up half the night poring over what little he'd learned about Conrad's arrest and strategizing how he was going to get inside our heads. I've been cutting our sessions too short for his liking, and I intend to keep things that way.

"No, not really," I finally answer. "The investigation is all but closed on the army's part—it's now in the hands of the Germans."

Ramsay is leaning back in his chair, savoring the last of his sandwich and finishing off his diet soda, when Lynn jumps in. "What was it that you wanted to tell Mr. Eways, Rod?"

"He asked me if I'd ever seen anything that might be construed as suspicious."

I remember the question, and not particularly liking it at the time. "Suspicious" conjures a hundred different things to a hundred different people. Policemen, CI officers, wives who worry their husbands might be cheating on them, classroom teachers, teenage girls—they all interpret the word according to their own place in life, their own experiences. God knows, Rod must have found it "suspicious" when Al and I showed up at his house-sitting door two days ago. Truth told, I've been finding him "suspicious" ever since. It's one of those words that means nothing and everything, but Rod has clearly been pondering the question and wants to make a clean breast of something. Except the set of his jaw tells me he isn't quite ready to go there yet.

To distract him, I point to a heavily lacquered doll on the coffee table.

"Is it authentic?"

"Yes," he says, "I got it as a gift for Mom in Japan." The deep breath he takes in just then tells me he's trying to calm himself. "It's really nice, isn't it?"

"Nice?" Lynn says. "It's beautiful!"

"Really beautiful," I add.

"They're worth a lot now," Ramsay says, swelling a little with pride. Lynn picks up on his more relaxed state and forges ahead.

"So what did you want to clarify for Mr. Eways?" she asks, as I briefly wander off to dump some crumbs in the garbage can in the kitchen. I want Ramsay to think I'm not interested in whatever he might have to say on this subject. A lifetime of studying TV detective shows would teach you exactly the opposite—everyone leans into the suspect when the sweat starts pouring down his brow—but in the real interview world, the key thing is to distance yourself at these moments, to lessen the psychological pressure on the suspect and let him or her talk free and clear.

"There was a girl stationed in Germany—Caroline. I wanted to date her really bad. But she wasn't that into me."

Rod's looking at me, not Lynn, when he says this, so I shoot him back a look that begs to know if this Caroline was a looker. "*Really* good-looking," he says back, understanding me exactly.

"So what happened?" I asked.

"I wanted to spend more time with her. So I hinted to her that I was involved in something and wondered if she wanted to take part." Lynn and I can't help ourselves; we both lean in before we catch ourselves and pull back again.

"And?" Lynn asks.

"She turned me down."

"That's it?"

"We were selling gasoline coupons on the black market. I was trying to see if she was willing to give us hers." Rod's studying us as he talks, to see if we believe him.

"Honest, that's the truth," he says, trying to convince both of us but doing the reverse: Truthful people *convey*; the dishonest try to convince.

"I see," says Lynn.

"And were you also mayybeee looking for something from this Caroline other than just her *time*?" I ask, getting back to the playful tone of yesterday.

"Mayybeee," Ramsay says, sheepishly strumming his fingertips together.

"I'll take that as a yes," I say, and he smiles. Score ten points for Navarro for keeping the subject relaxed and talking.

"So why are you concerned about Caroline?" Lynn asks, bringing us wayward boys back to the straight and narrow.

"Eways might talk to her eventually, and I don't know what she'll say went on from that time period. I don't want Eways to think I was trying to get Caroline involved in something that Conrad has been arrested for. I was just trying to get her interested in me, that's all."

"So did she ever cooperate with you?" asks Lynn.

"No."

"I take it she didn't become your girlfriend either?" I ask, looking askance.

"We were good friends and that's all. I know what you're hinting at and the answer is no, I didn't bed her."

"Hey, just wondering."

"We were just friends."

It's Lynn's turn to jump in: "You two—you sound like you're in junior high, I swear."

"Important things need to be clarified," I say, to which Ramsay agrees with a solemn nod.

"Boys!"

"Well, I don't think you have to worry. It's not like you asked her to take documents or anything like that," I say, treading lightly.

"No, nothing like that," Ramsay answers, as his face contorts slightly around the corners of his mouth, a sure sign of psychological distress.

"So it was strictly something you thought up to spend more time with her, and it merely involved the black market?"

"Yes, it had nothing to do with Conrad or selling information," Ramsay says. This is the second time he's avoided using the word "espionage." Why is he distancing himself with the words he uses? I wonder if Lynn has caught that.

"Gasoline was expensive. A lot of soldiers could make some nice side money selling their coupons. There were also the cigarettes. You could make a fortune selling American Marlboros on the black market. They're a different tobacco mixture than what's sold in Europe."

"What kind of money are we talking about?" I ask.

"You buy Marlboros for about eight dollars a carton at the PX and sell them for twenty dollars or even twenty-five dollars. Germans love the real American cigarettes—not the stuff they sell on the store shelves."

Lynn whistles appreciatively at the markup.

"Then there were the CD players. You could buy a nice one—a Sony, say—for about a hundred bucks at the PX and sell it for three hundred dollars, and the Germans would still be coming out ahead."

"Wow!"

"Yeah."

"You sound like you know all about that," I throw in.

"Kinda-sorta-mayyybeeee," Ramsay says.

"I'll take that as another definite yes. By the way, was Conrad involved in the black market?" I throw in.

The abrupt change doesn't seem to faze Rod. "When I first got there, I didn't have a car, so he asked me for my coupons and we worked out a deal."

"Well, I guess if you didn't need them, what's the harm?"

"Exactly, everybody was doing it," Ramsay agrees.

"It's like that at every base, isn't it?" I say.

"It is."

The larger point is this: Ramsay and I have found a way to connect. Like I said earlier, every person communicates differently. Some come out and say what they mean, others circle about, still others want you to say it for them, and then there are the ones who don't want to say anything at all. Finding the way early on is key because when you get jammed up later—and you always do—you have something to fall back on, common ground to get the conversation back on track. If Ramsay wants to play coy, that's fine by me so long as he's talking.

Today we're getting a more complete picture of what went on in Germany, about the value of money and how Ramsay and Conrad viewed criminal activity—which in Rod's case was pretty much "Everyone else is doing it, why not me?" The Big Question still to be explored is what other schemes the two of them combined on. For Rod, were black-market Marlboros a kind of gateway drug to espionage?

Superficially, at least, it isn't hard to connect the dots. Conrad had been in Germany for over a decade, so he had to know everyone. Ramsay, for his part, seems as if he can get up to no good in any environment—he's a thrill seeker. Add brothels, prostitutes, and drug use to the mix, and the vectors point down predictable paths. But soldiers have been chasing skirts since time immemorial, and ever since the dark days of Vietnam, drug abuse has been a reality for many soldiers serving overseas, and still, very few have taken that further step of selling out their country.

The easiest approach for Lynn and me, of course, would be the most straightforward. Jolly Rod along for a while, trade some cheerful banter, then when he least expects it, hit him between the eyes with the question we ultimately want answered: "Did you commit espionage?" But there are three possible responses to that—well, maybe four if you include "Define espionage"—and none are satisfying. He might say "No, and I want an attorney," and that would be it. No further interviews and no case—all the evidence is in Moscow. Or he could say "No" and not request an attorney. We'd still be playing the same game, but he'd know exactly where the finish line was as far as we're concerned, and start doling out information (or non-information) accordingly.

Or he could scream "Yes," pull his hair out in bitter self-recrimination, and otherwise become the sort of drama queen that he doesn't seem to be. But even then—even if he swears on a stack of Bibles that he's committed treason against his country and begs the judge to send him to the gallows—we *still have to prove the case*, still have to provide corroborating evidence that Rod was where he said he was on the tenth of who knows when, meeting Dimitri Ispyalot, a secret agent he claims to have met, and passing along the documents he's accused of supplying to America's sworn enemies. Crazy, huh? But that's where the investigative abuses of the sixties and seventies have landed us, and a guy as smart as Rod Ramsay isn't likely to be dancing in the dark on that subject.

Better by far to circle around what you *really* want to know—thus all this talk about food, gasoline, cigarettes, taxis, snacks, movies, CD players, restaurants, wine, bread, prostitutes, marijuana, smack, you name it. Anything but—horrors!—espionage. Besides, every new little revelation helps to fill in the larger puzzle of just who Rod Ramsay is and what he's capable of.

My goal today has been to get just enough for us to chew on without satisfying in the least Rod's information hunger, and after about two hours, I think we're there. We've logged enough time— particularly because this little mobile home community is going to start buzzing like a beehive if Rod keeps spending hours inside every day with two visitors who, dress down as we might, stand out like sore thumbs every time we pop by.

Sure enough, as we're getting into our car, one of the neighbors is out watering his lawn and staring straight at us with a giant question mark on his face. To answer it, we wave at Rod and give him a big smile as if we've known each other our entire lives, and Rod smiles and waves back just the same.

5

TRIUMPH AND DESPAIR

August 26, 1988

"**W**ake up!"
         I shout it loud enough to raise the dead, so loud in fact that I see Koerner's head shoot up over the sloppy towers of paperwork in his office across the way. Even Lynn seems startled, and she watched me dial.

But raising the dead might be just what's needed because Rod, at the other end of the line, sounds half dead himself. Maybe he's hungover or sleeping fitfully (a guilty conscience?), but when he finally responds, his voice is full of gravel and an octave lower than usual. The words "What's up?" sound as if they're coming from a crypt.

Me, as chirpy as I can be: "Something came in from Germany this morning. Lynn and I were wondering if you had time for us again today?"

Rod, pepping up slightly: "Sure. Give me time to—"

"Yeah, I know. Don't spell it out."

"Okay," he says, almost normal.

"We'll see you in an hour. Want some coffee?"

He doesn't even bother to answer.

TRUTH IS, MY HEARTY cheerfulness was a bit forced. Last night's surveillance duty had been a bear. It was midnight when we were

69

told to stand down, and one-thirty in the morning when I briefly cradled my daughter's face in my hands. I set the 4:55 a.m. alarm back to 6:00 a.m. before climbing into bed, but Rod Ramsay was standing in the doorway, blocking my way to Dreamland. Worse, the communications vault this morning has been no more yielding than yesterday. We've received nothing at all from HQ, the Washington Field Office, the army, or the legal attaché in Bonn who is (supposedly) assisting the Germans with leads.

I spent the first couple hours of my workday crafting the FD-302 for yesterday's interview and vetting it with Lynn. By 9:30 a.m, we were both sick of inaction and decided to go on the offensive. That's when I called Rod—the ear-shattering "Wake up!" was sheer inspiration. And it seems to have worked.

Rod's neighborhood is clogged with people waiting by their mailboxes—a mystery until I remember that today is Social Security payday, virtually a public holiday in the retiree-rich Sunshine State. By now, people close by Rod's trailer have seen Lynn and me often enough that they wave when we drive by. Lynn gives them her best Queen Elizabeth half wave back, while I (creature of habit) check their unoccupied hands for lethal weaponry. Happily, there's none, and Rod, showered, with hair slicked back and bags under his eyes, is waiting to greet us.

I hand him his coffee and, this time, a bag of Cuban toast (Cuban bread slathered with butter and pressed on a grill), and we both dive into it together. Lynn finished her share on the way over, but I wanted to make sure I'd be Ramsay's eating companion.

"We hate to bother you," I finally say, with a sheen of butter glinting off my chin, "but our attaché in Germany sent us a question." Lynn keeps her face vacant although she knows this is bullshit on my part.

Rod breaks off from his mouthful of bread, gulps greedily on his *café con leche*, and at long length favors us with: "Shoot."

"They're wondering whether you know if Conrad ever visited the United States after he retired."

"He did—back when I was in Boston, before Tampa."

"Oh, I thought you moved here right out of the army."

"No, I lived in Boston for a while before my mother moved down here."

"I see," wondering why this hasn't surfaced before. "So what was Conrad doing in the States?"

"Visiting family in Ohio."

"How about you. Did he stop off in Boston?"

"Just a courtesy call, that's all."

"Courtesy call?"

"That's what he called it. I remember him saying it that way."

"And what's a courtesy call look like?"

"Not much. We caught up on what was going on in Germany and on the base. And then he left. He was between flights."

"Just talked shop?"

"Yeah, pretty much. We were reminiscing about old times."

Another question mark: Does the WFO know about this visit? If so, were they intending to mention it to us? But then of course they haven't told us jack-shit about anything so far.

Me: "When was this?"

Rod: "Can't say exactly, but you know, after I failed the *piss test* [same ironic tone] and before Mom and I came down here. Maybe the spring of '86?"

Conrad had been in WFO's sights for years by then. What an opportunity that would have been to grab him on American soil so he could be tried in an American court. Crap.

"Did he come alone?"

"I think so. At least, he didn't have any family with him when he came to see me."

"How about gifts—did he bring you anything?"

"He gave me a little cowbell, the kind that they sell at the airport and tourist shops in Germany."

"A cowbell? Weird."

"No, not really. People go to France, and they bring back a little Eiffel Tower. In Germany, it's a cowbell. Same idea."

Lynn chimes in, in German, with what I take to be something like: "He's right; I've got a shelf full of them myself." The only words I can really pick out our *da*, *mein*, and *glocke*, like the glockenspiels in high-school marching bands. Whatever Lynn actually says, though, it's enough to lighten everyone's mood, mine included.

"See?" Rod says with a smile. "Lynn knows. She's seen a little of the world"—in a tone that implies my knowledge of the world might cover a hundred square blocks of downtown Tampa, Florida.

"Okay, okay. I give," I say, holding my hands up in surrender. "This bell—what did you do with it?"

"I still have it. Want to see it?"

"Yahhhh," Lynn answers before I can say yes.

"Let me get it."

"Uh, you don't have a gun back there by any chance, do you?" I ask, not that he'd tell me if that was what he had in mind.

"Naw," Rod answers. "I left my Sig Sauer in the glove compartment."

Ha-ha.

At any rate, he's back in thirty seconds with a crummy little fake-brass bell that Conrad probably bought in bulk on discount at the base PX.

"Any significance other than a memento?" I ask, gently shaking the clapper against the bell casing.

"No, not really," answers Ramsay, cracking his neck joints to the left.

"Would you mind if I take it for a few days, just so I can send a photo to our folks in Bonn? You never know what's going to be important," even (though I don't say it) this piece-of-crap souvenir.

"Sure, I don't need it. Keep it."

"Thanks," I say, handing it to Lynn.

"So after Conrad visited you, he left for Ohio?"

"That's where he said he was going."

"More specific? Cleveland? Toledo? Cincinnati? Do you remember what airport he was flying into?"

"Didn't ask, and he didn't say that I can remember."

"Did you hear from him again?" I'm thinking Rod's an information freak. Wouldn't he ask where Conrad was headed next?

"No, and I haven't heard from him since."

"No letters or postcards?"

"Nope, nothing," Rod replies, cracking his neck again. To some this might seem like ordinary stretching. To me, the neck cracking is a sign of how uncomfortable he is with his own answer. Why, I don't know, but at least I've confirmed that Ramsay and Conrad were closer than I imagined on that first interview. Did the army or WFO not have any idea of that either?

Back to Rod: "I meant to ask you the other day, what kind of games did you guys like to play over there?"

"Video games. *Donkey Kong* was a big hit"—a groan from Lynn—"and *Hydlide*"—bigger groan—"stupid stuff mostly."

"Anything else?"

"*Dungeons and Dragons*."

"What the hell is that?"

"Boy, you *are* old," Lynn jumps in.

"Seriously, I've never heard of *Dungeons and Dragons*," I say, smarting just a bit. Old? Me? "What is it?" And to my deep regret, for the next twenty-seven minutes, Ramsay proceeds to describe in pedantic, mind-numbing detail this apparently wildly popular fantasy game that has flown completely beneath my radar.

"Did Conrad play?" I ask when Rod finally takes a breather.

"Nah, he was like you—old-fashioned."

"Old this! Who else played?"

"Everyone, all the guys in the barracks. We'd play for hours, sometimes days at a time."

"Get out."

"No, it's intoxicating. Once you start a game, you can't stop. I have a whole book on *D and D*. You want a look?"

"Sure," I say, "let me see it," thinking that there can't be anything else to learn on the subject after Rod's dissertation, but he's back from his bedroom in a jiffy with a thick hardcover book full of illustrations. I thumb through while Lynn and Rod trade *D&D* stories, but the charm is still lost on me. Is this something young people do when they're stoned or just bored out of their minds? (I have trouble imagining Lynn being either.) Or is there something here I'm just not seeing—a *Key to Rebecca*–type thing, maybe, to help decode secret messages? The best codebooks often hide in plain view, which is why the Bible is often as useful to spies as it is to priests. In any event, I figure I need to do a little deeper dive into this.

"May I take this and read it?" I ask Rod, holding the book high.

"Sure," he says, "I *want* you to have it." And just like that I've got another puzzle piece in my hands. Why's he giving me all these things? I wonder. Maybe he's just generous, or impulsive more likely, but there's also a good chance he's testing me in some way I can't quite understand. Whatever's going on, I figure it's time to change the tenor of our session.

"Do you like to read history?" I ask.

"Herodotus, of course. Napoleon."

"What about Clausewitz?"

"Sure."

"Sun Tzu?"

"Yes, he was a near contemporary of Herodotus." Is that right? I better check.

"Machiavelli?"

"What do you think? Of course. Why?"

"I just wondered if you only read shit like *Dungeons and Dragons*." I intended to be harsh—Rod's snotty tone is getting out of hand again—but even as the words are coming out, I know I've gone over the top. For a moment, I worry that I might have really offended him. Instead, Rod seems to decide that it's game on.

"Have you ever read about Theodora?" he asks, slipping into a higher gear, as if he wants to put me in my place.

"You mean Justinian's wife?"

"Justinian *the First's* wife," he clarifies. "I'm surprised you know that."

"I really don't know that much about her," I concede, although I'm not exactly ignorant on the subject.

"Well," Rod says, "she was a whore before she became empress." He gives Lynn a quick glance to see if she's shocked, but Lynn just shrugs.

"I'm not sure she was so much a whore as she was peddled by her mother," I say. "Later, she became an actress."

"She was a whore."

"Whatever, she ended up an empress," I say through clenched teeth. "Now, Justinian the Second—"

"Slit-Nose?" Rod has gotten way up on his high horse. Maybe so have I.

"Boys, boys, boys." Lynn wisely intervenes, shaking her finger at both of us. "What am I going to do with you two?"

"Matters for discussion next time," I say.

"You bet." Rod's beaming now, almost glowing with excitement. This is clearly the kind of contest he thrives on. For my part, I think I better bone up on the Byzantine Empire, in a hurry. But as I keep saying, face time is what counts in this business, and if that means adding late-night history sessions to the rest of my schedule, so be it.

"Well," I say, rising. "Bonn's waiting. We better get all this to them. It's got to be what time there?"

"Four-forty-two," Rod chimes in, almost before the question is out of my mouth. I don't see a clock or watch anywhere in sight. "P.m.," he adds, just in case I'm a dope.

I'm halfway out the door when I remember my manners.

"The book," I say, waggling my *D&D* primer. "Thanks."

"And for the bell," Lynn adds, giving it a little shake.

"No problem," Rod says airily, like a philanthropist being thanked for giving alms to the poor.

I'm practically to the car when I remember Rod's mom.

"Did you talk to your mom yet? Did you tell her what I said—she can call Lynn or me anytime?"

"I did."

"And we're okay?"

"We're good."

"Later, then."

This time, the neighbor watering his grass in front of the trailer across the way doesn't even bother looking up from his hose as we drive away.

"Nearly lost it back there, didn't you, Navarro?" Lynn says once we're back on main roads.

"That, Agent Tremaine, was calculated."

"To achieve what?"

"To shake Ramsay out of his comfort zone."

"By the way, how do you know about this Theodora?"

"Justinian I was a grand spymaster. He's the one who covertly sent two monks to China to obtain the secrets to silk production. They returned with silkworms and white-mulberry bush seeds hidden in their walking staffs, thus permanently shifting the silk trade from China to the Byzantine Empire and permanently weakening China's balance of trade."

"How the hell do you know that?"

"I'm into books, just like Rod."

MY BLOWUP ASIDE, I'M pleased with our morning session. By seizing the initiative, we've managed to take a day that started out as chicken shit and turn it into chicken salad. What I don't know is that a five-course chicken feast will be waiting right inside the Bureau when we return.

Koerner can hardly contain himself when we walk through the door.

"My office," he says, almost breathless as he grabs each of us by the elbow, pulls us through his door, and all but pushes us into the two chairs opposite his own, across the vast paper mountains of his desk.

"Look at this," he orders, reaching behind him, grabbing a sheet of paper for each of us, and shoving them in our hands. "It came in just twenty minutes ago."

"Holy shit!" is all I can blurt out of my mouth as I read. Lynn is more decorous: "Damn!"

"I gotta hand it to you, Joe," says Koerner, who uses my first name as rarely as I invoke his. "You were right all along. This changes everything."

Does it ever.

The message is from FBIHQ, with copies to our legal attaché in Bonn and of course to the Washington Field Office. The FBI lab processed the note Ramsay gave me. The paper, the lab report says, "is consistent with the paper used by East European intelligence services"—a "water-soluble paper that dissolves instantly when exposed to water or saliva." The kind of paper, for example, useful to a spy anxious to get rid of information quickly by throwing it in a toilet or placing it in his mouth. Not quite the same thing as the novelty-store magician's paper in the story Ramsay ginned up on the spot.

But there's more, and even better. The number written on the paper is the known "hello" number for the Hungarian Intelligence Service in Budapest. Every spy network has something similar, an emergency contact number. You call it, someone answers "Hello," and then you deliver a coded message via a prescribed menu. "Is this the pharmacy?" might mean an operation has been blown or someone in the network compromised. Hello numbers are common currency in espionage, but why does Rod Ramsay have one? And why did Clyde Conrad give it to him—if Rod is telling the truth about that?

Oh, and as for the six digits, that's part of the price for living in a Warsaw Pact nation. Technology is so backward in Hungary that the country has yet to go on the seven-digit system standard in Western Europe.

"What are you going to do?" Koerner finally asks.

"WFO is going to have to step up to the plate and help us now. They can't ignore us any longer," I say. "We have to sit down and start putting together all the leads we want covered, everything, and we need to put together a plan for moving forward. The cat is out of the bag—we need to start thinking prosecution."

Koerner concurs. He still looks a little shocked that all this has fallen into place so quickly.

"I mean, there is so much more we need to do here," I say. "I want to arrange for a meeting in DC to coordinate matters and to meet with the folks handling the Conrad case, including the Internal Security Section. We've got leads that should have gone out yesterday, others that can wait, but we've got to start prioritizing, and we need to review everything to date and where we want to go next." Lynn is taking notes as fast as I'm spitting things out.

"Are we going to talk to Ramsay again?" Koerner asks.

"Of course, but we may have to wait a day while we coordinate all this," I say. "We need to make sure the army, the Germans, and the Swedes are all on board. If the Kercsik brothers can give us more background, that's going to help us climb the ladder with Ramsay. Information is power. We can't play this dance-around-the-campfire routine forever. I need to know more. I need to know the whole case—front to back."

"Remember," Lynn cautions, "tomorrow is Saturday. Nothing will get done until Monday." Maybe so, I'm thinking, but so much for R & R, and the long, sleepy two-day break and family-bonding (okay, re-bonding) events I'd been planning. My mind is going to be racing a thousand miles an hour all weekend long.

HAVE YOU EVER HAD one of those spurts when you just love your work? When you wake up inspired and go to bed inspired? When you feel that what you do in a day really counts? That your life and work are truly consequential? It's not that the work is easy—anything but—but worlds are opening up into even larger worlds. There's purpose. There's direction. A light waits at the end of the tunnel.

That's what the start of the week is like for me—a workaholic's nirvana. Lynn and I put out dozens of leads. We plot strategy, set up timelines. Both of us go back and read the FD-302s over again. We've each got lists longer than our arms of the follow-up questions we need to ask and flowcharts of where the various possible answers to those questions might lead us next.

We do go back to talk with Rod again, pretty much at his invitation. Our few days away from his mobile-home park have him missing us, or so it seems, but we talk about nothing important, just maintenance chatter while our leads are being covered.

And then, right at the height of our working high, the pushback begins. I want to set up a meeting with WFO so we can talk about the information everyone has and what we're missing, but I'm reminded that the Washington Field Office holds the reins on this case, not Tampa, and I'm told in no uncertain terms to mind my place.

I remind everyone up the chain of command of what has occurred down here. Rod Ramsay, I say, is obliquely cooperating, but we need to know more about the case itself so we can ask the right questions. Instead, I'm told to slow things down—Ramsay can wait.

Then I make the horrific mistake of asking about the crime scene. "Crime scene? What crime scene?" they ask. "Well," I answer, "the one from which the documents were stolen." But WFO, it turns out, hasn't conducted a crime scene investigation, and that's when it dawns on me that things aren't as bad as I thought; they're far worse.

On August 31, 1988, I get a call from Rod Ramsay's mother, wondering if he's in trouble. I'm touched that she's called, and we have a nice long chat during which I assure her once again that only Conrad is in trouble and that her son Rod is being very helpful to me and to the Germans. She says an attorney friend of hers has told her Rod really shouldn't be talking to anyone. That would be true, I say, *if* Rod were the focus of our investigation, but that's Conrad, not him. She thanks me for reassuring her, and I put the phone down feeling, well, a bit deceptive. I mean, what kind of man lies to a fearful mother? After reflecting on the conversation, I tell myself that some mistruths are more justifiable than others. Still, it bothers me to be leading Rod's mom down a primrose path. Maybe it's my Catholic upbringing, but this kind of dissembling feels like something the nuns wouldn't have approved of.

Then the next day, September 1, Washington Field Office case agent Bill Bray contacts me and asks me to stop talking with Ramsay.

"Stop?" I say. "In the middle of an investigation that's just getting started? That's nuts." Within a few minutes, someone from HQ does a follow-up call with the same request, and I give the same response: We've opened an investigation in accordance with FBI and Justice Department guidelines, and we will pursue said investigation with scrupulous attention to same.

Then at roughly two o'clock that afternoon, I get a teletype from high up the FBIHQ chain of command informing me that the asking phase is over. Just nine days after first interviewing Rod Ramsay and after working so hard to get him comfortable talking with us, my partner and I are ordered not to talk with Rod Ramsay again, under *any* circumstances.

6

WORK-AROUNDS

In the Bureau, as in any large organization, there are orders and there are *orders*. *Orders* are the ones you better obey lest you end up five rungs down the career ladder, transferred to a permanent post in Resume Speed, Idaho, in the middle of winter. Orders, though, are more like directives, often issued—in the FBI's case—by HQ people who have their heads so far up their asses they haven't seen sunshine since they were promoted. After stewing for several days about being pulled off the Rod Ramsay case, Lynn and I decide that what's been issued is, in fact, a directive, a not-to-be-taken-*too*-seriously order, and that the best way to deal with it is mostly to ignore it. Besides, there's too damn much to do.

The Kercsik brothers, for example. They're not telling all, but they are being more helpful than expected. They were the ones who confirmed that the six-digit number Ramsay handed me was, in fact, the Hungarian Intelligence Service's hello line. If they're willing to go that far, I figure, maybe they'll go a little further and tell us if they've ever seen Rod themselves, so I put in a call to Jane Hein, one of the very good people at HQ and among the few with whom I have a long and pleasant history.

Jane and I worked together in New York (she was Jane Chenowith then), where we chased down the same targets, mostly UN attachés from the Warsaw Pact nations and their friends. Like me, Jane is at heart a spy-catcher. Now she's at the Mothership, working CI matters, and I've just learned that she has been assigned to the Conrad case. Jane is on a short leash with limited authority, but better a hobbled friend than a fully empowered enemy.

"How you been, Joe? Long time!" she says to greet me when I finally track her down through the HQ maze. "To what do I owe this high privilege and honor?"

"Spies."

"Really?"

"Yes, the real deal. Listen, Jane, I need help with this case I'm working—I keep running into roadblocks."

"HQ roadblocks?" Jane knows where the trouble usually comes from.

"HQ and Washington Field Office."

"Let me hear it," she says, "and by the way, I'm fine. Nice of you to ask."

Okay, I haven't observed the niceties, but Jane is used to how obsessed I get when I'm onto something big.

"It's the Conrad case—one of yours, I'm told," I say. "My partner and I have been interviewing a guy who worked with Conrad in Germany, Rod—"

"Whoa!" she says, cutting me short. "Who has authorized this?"

"Koerner," I say. I don't have to identify Jay further. Jane and all of HQ know who he is.

"But where did that come from? We already have a pending investigation on Conrad."

"I know, I know. Washington Field Office. The army. INSCOM. The Swedes. Everyone is in on this investigation, here and overseas, except us poor cousins down in Tampa, even though we probably have the only American who'll ever see a trial here in the States. Conrad's treachery ultimately benefitted our archenemy the Soviet Union, but never mind, he's going to be tried by the Germans. The Germans, Jane. The Germans, not us—that's just not right. Worse, there's no guarantee that he'll be convicted, and even if he is, he probably won't get diddly-squat by way of a sentence."

"Let's not assume."

"Come on, Jane, you know how it is over there. Günter Guillaume gave the East Germans and the Soviets access to the most sensitive NATO secrets and destroyed Chancellor Willy Brandt's career, and still got only thirteen years."

"Joe . . ."

"Besides," I go on, rolling right over her interruption, "this is no longer a CI matter. It's a criminal matter that needs to be expedited. We want to aggressively go after Ramsay. And that, Jane, is why I'm calling." I'm shouting a little, I admit, by then.

"Calm down, Navarro."

"I know—I'm worked up. But listen—"

"Joe."

"Okay. You're right. Sorry. The last thing I want to do is piss off my friends. I've got plenty of enemies just itching to be mad at me."

"So, what can I help you with?"

"We want to see if the Kercsik brothers ever saw Ramsay and can pick him out of a photo lineup. Look, I know HQ needs to sign off on something like this, and it takes time, and WFO is going to balk because they are in the let's-wait-to-see-if-the-planets-all-line-up-by-the-turn-of-the-century mode. I also know how long it would take to go through State Department and the Justice Department to get the necessary letters rogatory, but, Jane, we don't have months to wait—we need to know now."

"We?" asks Jane, knowing what's behind this.

"Okay, I want to know."

"Joe, I hear you, and I appreciate how you feel, but the Kercsik case is in the hands of the Swedish Security Service, not ours. It's SÄPO's investigation, and SÄPO represents a sovereign country."

"And Sweden is supposed to be neutral, I know that also, but they have in their hands two individuals who conspired against the United States, and I want access to them, now, not six months from

TEN MINUTES AND ONE bathroom break later, I'm walking around the office with Rod's army ID photo—the one piece of help we've gotten from INSCOM—and gathering FBI ID photos from anyone who looks enough like Rod Ramsay (thin face, pointy nose, under age thirty) to be included in a photo lineup.

I'm helping Lowell, the office photographer, lay the mug shots out in some kind of plausible random order when I hear one of the office managers, Shirley (not her real name, for reasons that will soon become apparent), calling my name.

"Joe-o!"

The very fact that Shirley has risked doing this is significant, since the last time we chatted I gave her the same look I give to criminals who call me names when I arrest them. Shirley, though, is clueless to nonverbals and plies happily on with whatever her singular pursuit of the moment happens to be. On that occasion, about a week ago, Lynn and I were running maybe fifteen minutes late for one of our maintenance sessions with Rod—not a big deal, but I expect punctuality out of everyone I deal with, myself included. Shirley had other priorities.

"Joe-o," she said as Lynn and I were racing for the office door. "You can't go right now. We're having the raffle."

"Raffle?" For a moment I wasn't sure she was speaking English, or any language I understood.

"Yeah, you know," Shirley said, "our annual raffle. You've got to stay here for that. What if you win?"

"Win, Shirley? Win?! I've had four hours of sleep. I've got a full day ahead of me. I'm fifteen fucking minutes late for an interview, and you want me to stop doing whatever I'm doing because there's a raffle?"

"Well," she said, "everybody has to be here for the annual raffle—that's what the front office wants."

Just as I was thinking to myself, *This is how you end up in a hospital, with a stroke or a heart attack or a nervous breakdown,*

Shirley pivoted on her little spiked heels and went looking for another victim.

"Steve! Oh, Steve-o . . ."

This time it's not a raffle. The annual raffle won't be happening again for 358 days, thank God. This time it's an official form, something that has to be filled out every month, or day, or hour—at the moment, I can't quite remember which.

"Joe-o," Shirley is saying, "you haven't turned in your PM form for your car."

"Preventive maintenance?"

"It's the *fourth*, Joe-o. PM forms are supposed to be submitted on the *third*. You're a day late."

Technically, of course, she's correct. Preventive maintenance forms are due on the third, and today is the fourth, but to fill out my PM, I'll need the mileage from my car odometer—the exact mileage, to the tenth of a mile, not an estimate, not an annual average divided by twelve, oh, no, *exact*—and the Bu-Steed is parked two blocks away in the Bureau garage. Just listening to Shirley makes my stomach leak acid.

"Tomorrow, Shirley?" I say. "Lowell and I, we're right in the middle of getting this photo lineup together, and I've got to get it off to Washington in the overnight—"

"But by tomorrow, Joe-o, you'll be *two* days late."

"All right! All right!"

Outside it's steamy hot, and an afternoon thunderhead looks to be about twenty minutes from breaking open. I could run to the car, but if I do, I'll be drenched in sweat by the time I get back to the office. If I don't run, on the other hand, I'm likely to be drenched in rain. In the end, I opt for a trot. I'm within sight of our office building door—mileage safely memorized—when the skies open up, and I have to sprint for safety. My shirt is still clinging to my skin when I hand Shirley the PM.

"Aren't you forgetting something?" she says after a quick glance.

"Forgetting?"

"It's the fourth, Joe-o. You were due for an oil change *yesterday*. Oil changes are a critical part of PM."

"Let me get this straight, Shirley," I say, "because I'm a slow learner. Do I look un-busy to you? Do I look like I'm fanning my ass? I'm working on an espionage case, and I need to get something to head-quarters by tonight, but you, Shirley, you want me to drop everything and go get my oil changed because . . ."

"Because PM is important, Joe-o . . ."

"And tomorrow . . ."

"Tomorrow, you'll be two days late."

By now, though, I notice Shirley has put a desk between herself and me. A smart move, but only temporary. The Shirleys of the world never go away because bureaucracies always seem to attract and then reward them.

7

TAKING STOCK

September 20, 1988

Here's the way the FBI works: Every agent has to complete a file review every ninety days—no ifs, ands, or buts about it. The reviews help supervisors and case agents evaluate the progress of ongoing investigations. But over the last decade-plus, I've learned that if you wait that long, the work overwhelms you. Instead, I do my own file review every month, just to put a fence around the cases, the flying, the training, the SWAT operations, and everything else that comes up.

That's what I'm doing right now—timelining the Ramsay case.

8/22/88: TELETYPE ARRIVES OVERNIGHT, instructing FBI Tampa to locate and interview one Roderick James Ramsay.

8/23: Ramsay located and interviewed by Agent Joe Navarro (me) and Al Eways, INSCOM, first at third-party house where Ramsay is house-sitting, later at Pickett Hotel. Before exiting, Ramsay hands over note with number allegedly written by Conrad.

8/24: Ramsay calls FBI Tampa office on his own, asks to speak with Agent Navarro regarding previous occupants of house where initial interview took place. Navarro and Agent Lynn Tremaine respond to Ramsay's mother's trailer, where he has been living.

8/25: Ditto. Ramsay calls again, wants to clarify comments made to Eways regarding female associate at HQ Eighth Infantry Bad Kreuznach, Germany. Agents Navarro and Tremaine respond.

8/26: Ramsay interviewed a fourth time, at mother's trailer, by Agents Navarro and Tremaine. FBIHQ lab reports that paper Ramsay handed Agent Navarro 8/23 is consistent with water-soluble type known to be used by Soviet Bloc intelligence operatives. FBIHQ further reports that six-digit number on paper is hello number for Hungarian intelligence service. (Kercsik brothers confirm.)

9/1: Agents Navarro and Tremain directed to have no further direct communication with "Subject Ramsay."

9/8: Jane Hein contacted at FBIHQ. Agrees (eventually) to Agent Navarro's request to do photo lineup in regard to Subject Ramsay if State Department, Justice, Swedish Intelligence (SÄPO), Kercsiks, etc., agree.

9/9 (early): Photo lineup and formal request transmitted to FBIHQ (transmittal delayed by oil change). Apparently I wasn't the only one who forgot because a long queue was waiting when I got in line.

9/9 (later): Agent Navarro is informed (by usually reliable source) that Washington Field Office has learned FBI Tampa has opened full investigation into Subject Ramsay and is upset.

9/12: First real evidence of FBI-WFO interfering in case. Information from Austria, regarding Suspect Szabo, sent to WFO, which sat on it instead of forwarding to FBI Tampa as requested.

9/14: Second evidence of FBI-WFO interference. Request for Agent Tremaine to go to Sweden to interview Kercsik brothers turned down by FBIHQ at request of WFO. In similar circumstances, such requests routinely granted. Interference is unprecedented.

9/19: John Martin, head of DOJ/ISS (Department of Justice / Internal Security Section), meets with Agents Navarro and Tremaine and Supervisor Koerner in Tampa. Very complimentary of our efforts but in essence tells us to back off. The Germans and WFO have this now, Martin tells us. (Really? They didn't even know about Ramsay.) Koerner tells me not to get "too upset with Martin," but since when does the head of ISS travel to a small office to derail an investigation by patting us on the head and then telling us to let others handle the case?

9/19 also: We find out from the army that Rod's IQ score is shockingly high—in fact, it's the second highest *ever recorded* on the basic Army Intelligence Test. This is information you think might have been available to us sooner, but I know how these things work. First, Rod was one of thousands of people interviewed in the grand sweep after Conrad was arrested, and Al Eways was sent out with the same information all the other investigators started with: name, date of birth, years of service, and nothing more. Second, retrieving military information is a lot like retrieving treasure in *Raiders of the Lost Ark*, without the finer Spielberg touches. First the right building (of many) has to be found. Then miles of dank, cobweb-ridden hallways have to be negotiated by pasty clerks who rarely see the sun. These fetchers must find their way to the right section of the corridor, the right shelf of boxes, the right box, and the right part of the right box.

Fact is, I feel very fortunate to now have this information, or rather this confirmation of what had been pretty obvious to me from day one: Rod Ramsay is one smart son of a bitch. And I guess the truth is that knowing I'm *not* dealing with some run-of-the-mill stumblebum makes me even more determined not to buckle to HQ, WFO, DOJ, and every other chickenshit acronym trying to pull us off this case.

9/20/88. THAT'S TODAY, AND LYNN and I are in my Bu-Steed, sitting in a strip-mall parking lot along US 41, reviewing the statutory requirements of Title 18 United States Code Section 794, especially subsection (a), before our 10 a.m. meeting with Rod Ramsay. Actually, it's more of a tutorial on my part. You can waste an awful lot of interview time in criminal espionage cases if you don't keep your eye on the prize.

"You understand, don't you?" I'm saying. "We're not going after a confession."

"What else is there?" Lynn asks, somewhat surprised.

"Have you ever worked an espionage case before?"

"No, but I helped on one."

"Don't feel bad. Out of fifty-nine field offices in the FBI, only six have ever prosecuted an espionage case. Tampa is one of them."

"So what are we going for?"

"We could aim for a confession, but that may never happen. We need admissions."

"To . . . ?"

"To whatever satisfies the espionage statute, and I know that isn't covered in basic agent training."

"No, it's not."

"That's why we have to focus on what is important: small admissions that add up until they satisfy the statute."

"Go on."

"Seven ninety-four requires that we prove that the subject acquired classified material, that the said material was knowingly conveyed to somebody or some entity that had no right to be in possession of it, and lastly that it would do grievous damage to the United States of America."

"Doesn't seem that difficult."

"That's what I said on my first case. But try to get a suspect's words to track with the requirements of the statute and you'll see how difficult it becomes. That's why each admission is so critical."

While Lynn is processing this, I run into a Cuban bakery I'm fond of and pick up some guava-filled *pastelitos* for Rod.

As I get in the car, Lynn smells the bag.

"God, that smells good," she says, eyeing the bag as I strap myself back in the Bu-Steed.

"Sooo good, and sooo fattening," I tell her as I hand her one fresh from the oven.

"I have a lot to learn about espionage, don't I?" The flaky pastry has thrown her into a temporary, dreamy ecstasy.

"We all do, Lynn. Every case is different, and they're never easy."

ROD, IT TURNS OUT, is fond of the *pastelitos*, too. He's practically inhaled two of them. I'm waiting for my turn to dig in when Lynn looks at me with a slight smirk and tells Rod to finish the bag.

"Really?" he says. By now, the corners of his mouth are cherry-red from the guava filling.

"Really," Lynn says. "Our treat."

Ha-ha. But no sense being sore about it, especially since I've already had my fill.

"Rod," I say, getting down to business, "you told us before that the base in Germany was pretty loosey-goosey. I mean, it sounds like there was hardly any adult supervision at all in the documents section where you worked."

He's licking his chops like a two-year-old and nodding his head.

"Can you give us some more on that? The army people know they need to tighten security over there. Your experience and insights would really be helpful to them."

Rod looks at me for a moment as if trying to decide just how much I'm bullshitting him—a good deal, in fact—but I'm betting that he can't resist giving a little tutorial of his own, and that's what happens.

"Basically," he begins, "with the documents, there was no supervision at all."

"So take us through the process."

"Yeah," Lynn adds, "pretend we're idiots."

"Pretend?" Rod's in a playful mood today. Good.

"Well," he says, "it was kind of a cradle-to-grave operation. The documents arrived, and we logged them in. While they were there, we kept track of who had their hands on what, and when the documents were no longer of use, our job was to destroy them and sign off on possession."

" 'Our'? Who are we talking about?"

"The document custodians."

"And who were they?" Lynn chimes in.

"Me and Clyde." And with that he just lights up like a Christmas tree. "It was up to us, do you see?"

"In what way?" I ask, playing the eager learner. "Tell us more."

"Okay," he says, slipping into the present tense as if he still is an Eighth Infantry document custodian, "we have these big heavy burn bags, and everybody just puts the documents in there. Then we seal them up with tape and truck them out, and, you know, when the burn facility's working, we put the stuff we're destroying in there. Basically, it's like this giant pig-roast thing, a big wire-mesh contraption. You dump the documents in there and then turn it like you do a pig. It can be really messy and dirty, and it takes hours."

"And who watches over this while you're doing it?"

"Well, no one," Rod says. "It's just us, of course, the custodians, Clyde and me. Who else would there be?"

There's almost a smirk to his face as he says this, as if the question is beneath his consideration. In other circumstances, I'd waste no time cutting him down a peg or two at this point, but this isn't an interrogation. Really, it's not even an interview. This is an *elicitation*. I just need to keep Rod talking and wait to see what hints he drops as to what actually went on in Bad Kreuznach roughly three years ago, in the mid-eighties, before Rod peed cannabis and the army said goodbye.

Instead of confronting him, I shrug my shoulders, mutter something about "stupid me" to a general chorus of approval from Rod and Lynn, and move on to what I hope will be a rich field to dig in.

"Okay," I say. "I've got it. You and Clyde seem to have pretty much ruled the roost." A confirming nod from Rod, mostly Lynn's way. "What else did you do together?"

"We'd go out for a beer. We'd go on terrain walks."

"Terrain walks?" This is Lynn.

"Yeah, sure. You know, we'd be looking at the topography, the lay of the land. One of our favorite walks was the length of the Fulda Gap, the place the Red Army tanks were going to come storming through if the Kremlin ever decided to set up a substation in Bonn. Napoleon—"

"I know. I know," I say. "Battle of Leipzig, retreat, et cetera." I don't want a history lesson right now, especially when it sounds as if Rod is heading somewhere interesting.

"The Gap was what pretty much all the ops plans that passed through Documents talked about—if the Soviet tanks do this, we do that. If they do that, we do this. I mean, there couldn't have been a lot of time in the Pentagon to strategize about anything else. It was like a living video game. Clyde and I would walk along the high side of the Gap and pretend we were each in charge of a tank division— one Soviet, one NATO. You fuck with my head here; I'll fuck with your head there. Oh, and also destroy your people."

Lynn is shooting me a glance about now that says, "Unbelievable!" He's admitting that he not only logged the ops plans in but read them, carefully, and I'm doing my best without taking my eyes off Rod to signal telepathically to Lynn that this is just what I was talking about in the car an hour ago. Ramsay isn't your traditional spy. This guy knows what's important, he knows the tactical and strategic value of documents, and he and Conrad were basically the unsupervised librarians for those documents.

"Sounds like you guys had some real fun together," I say to Rod, taking all the tension out of my posture, settling back into my chair for a good gab. Lynn picks up on my cue and practically sprawls at her end of the trailer sofa.

"Oh, yeah," Rod answers, stretching his legs out on the coffee table, next to the lacquered doll. "And not just fun. Clyde was a smart guy, you know. He'd sit there and read a book, and he'd tear the pages out as he read and throw them away. I still read the same way."

Me: "Weird."

Rod (with a laugh): "Yeah, I mean think about it. Why carry around the weight of those already read pages? If you're done with them, you're done. I learned lots of things from him, and he was always testing me."

Lynn: "Like school tests? Exams?"

"No, not school tests," Rod says.

"What are we talking about, then?" I ask.

"Well, for one thing, Clyde wanted to know how far I'd be willing to go in bending the rules."

"Rules?"

"Yeah, he had lots of them. The first rule was that you always had to be indispensable. I remember he told me one day, 'If your superiors think you're indispensable, they'll leave you alone.'"

"Meaning?"

"Meaning they'll never look in on what you're doing; they'll never check on you."

At this point, I'm thinking two things. One, Rod and Clyde are absolutely right: Indispensable people make the best embezzlers, for example, because they're never supervised; and two, if you don't need to be supervised, then you can do anything you want, like copy classified documents and steal them from under the noses of people with some of the highest security clearances going.

"Any more rules?" Lynn asks. "You said that was the first one."

"Sure," Rod says, ticking more rules off on his fingers: "Always look busy. Always look like you're in a hurry. Always have something in your hand. Always be the first person in the office and the last to leave."

"Wow!" I say. "Why all that?"

"Well, just think about it," Rod answers, settling back into his professorial mode. "If you always look busy, always have something in your hand, always rush from this place to that, and are always the first person everyone sees in the morning and the last one they see in the office at night, then . . ."

Rod pauses here to let us complete the sentence, and Lynn and I both do so at pretty much the same time and in the same words: ". . . you can do anything you want!"

Rod is beaming at us, as if we're star pupils, and I'm beaming back, not because I've guessed the answer but because Rod has just told us how to operate in the open, without having to sneak around during the day or risk breaking into the facility after hours or before the morning bell. None of this rises yet to the level of actionable information, but Rod is building our case for us, one small admission at a time, and I want to keep his roll going.

"Well," I say, "just between us girls, did you ever get the impression that Clyde might have been up to no good?"

For a long time, Rod just sits there with a smile on his face. I have no idea what's going on in his head, but I don't see any of the usual body language of fear or anxiety—the hand to the mouth, the bouncing Adam's apple. Then, as if this trailer park living room is full of people and he wants to speak only to us, Rod leans forward in his seat, waits for us to lean in toward him, and says almost in a whisper: "That was part of what he was testing me about."

"Bending the rules?"

"No, more than that. He was always testing my morality—testing it in all these ways."

"Well," I ask, "why would he do that? You guys were friends, pals."

Then Rod gets this sheepish look on his face, leans in even closer, and whispers still softer: "Because he had this business going on."

"Oh," I say, leaning back into my chair, trying to take some of the tension out of the moment, "a business, huh? Like those black-market cigarette coupons you were telling us about? It doesn't sound like he was stretching your morality too far with that one."

Lynn has leaned back as well. Before long, Rod takes the cue and pulls back himself. You can almost feel the room filling back up with air again.

"Clyde," Rod starts to say, then pauses for a beat or two, gathering his thoughts or maybe parsing them in advance to make sure he doesn't give away too much. "Clyde was a conniver, a schemer. He always had something going on, and you know, some of it was a little out on the edge."

"Like what?" Lynn asks.

I follow up with "Yeah, give us an example."

"Well," Rod says, "what if, hypothetically, Clyde wanted to set up a video-rental business?"

"Pirated copies, you mean?"

That gets a little smile from Rod. "Hypothetically," he adds.

"Of course," I answer. "Purely hypothetical."

"But what if this 'hypothetical' video-rental business," Rod continues, "wasn't really about renting videos?"

"Well, I don't know," I say. "What else, hypothetically, might it be about?"

"Information?" Rod answers, twisting the word into a question at the last moment. "Information, he used to say, was everything. What if, hypothetically, Clyde really wanted to use the video-rental business to get information from the soldiers who came in?"

"What would he do with it?" Lynn asks. "Hypothetically."

"Hypothetically," Rod says, "he could maybe sell it."

I'm dying to say, "To whom?" but Rod has been intentionally talking in "hypotheticals." He's playing a game with us, teasing us with hints and probably satisfying his own risk-taking needs at the same time. Odds are, if we ask him to be any more specific, he'll decide the game is over and clam up. Instead, I nod toward the bathroom and ask with my eyes if he'd mind.

"Sure," he says. "Go right ahead."

Inside, I flush the toilet and splash some water around in the sink, to make it sound real. I'm hoping that Lynn will take over in my absence and that maybe, without me in the room, the talk will loosen up, and that seems to have been the case. As I'm leaving the bathroom, I hear Lynn asking about Clyde's other buddies—a good question, one I was heading toward myself. By the time I settle back into my chair again, Rod is making a distinction between Clyde's "poker players" and his "poker-poker players."

"Whoa," I say, "I get 'poker players'—stud, five-card draw, all that. But what are 'poker-poker players'? Are these the guys who play for really big stakes?"

"No," he says, "poker-poker players are Clyde's really good buddies. They do all sorts of favors for him."

"Like what?"

But Rod doesn't answer that one.

"How about you, Rod?" I say. "Were *you* a poker-poker player?"

"Maayyybbbbeeeee," he says, stretching the word out as long as it will go, then disappearing behind his grin. And that's when I know we've done all the good we can do here today.

Lynn is still slipping back into her shoes when I put my hand on the front doorknob.

"Look, Rod," I say, turning around, "this has been incredibly helpful once again. You're really giving us a great sense of how things went down at Eighth Infantry HQ. I'm going to talk today with our people in Bonn and see what else they need, but I'm sure we'll be calling you soon to see if we can stop by again."

"Tomorrow?" Rod asks in a hopeful voice. He has enjoyed today's gamesmanship immensely. That's obvious. "I'm free. How about it?"

"Maayyybbbbeeeee."

BEING DIGNIFIED PROFESSIONALS, AGENT Tremaine and I wait until we are well out of the trailer park before celebrating the day's progress with a high five—or as high as you can five in a

Bu-Steed, which in this case happens to be a 1983 Chevy Malibu. No, we don't have a confession in hand, but we have something far better as far as I'm concerned—a ladder of admissions that, when we finally get to confession or even if we don't, will allow us to build the kind of rock-solid criminal case that can stand up against the toughest defense.

Rod Ramsay has fessed up to bending the rules, to having his morality tested by what we soon hope will be a convicted spy, and to being tutored and influenced by same. He has also willingly spread hints of nefarious activities on Clyde Conrad's part and of intimate knowledge of those activities and some of the "poker-poker players" who were possibly Conrad's co-conspirators. Conrad and Ramsay are tight and unsupervised, and this is the kind of story a jury will buy.

Not a bad haul. I'm happy for Lynn, who has proved herself an able partner and quick study despite her tender years. Most of all, I'm happy for Jay Koerner, who has more to lose than either of us—more salary, more time invested, more upside potential. (My upside potential is going to sink to zero if this war with Washington keeps up.) Koerner gave me ninety days. That's all anyone could ask under the circumstances. And in less than a month, Lynn and I have built a case that justifies his faith almost to the maximum degree.

"By the way?" I say to Lynn as we swing around a fender bender on Kennedy Boulevard. "I want to thank you."

"For what?"

"The way you've handled this case, the way you've handled Rod. Most agents wouldn't be able to do that."

"Ya think?" she says with that unmistakable Midwestern accent.

"Yeah, I do. You go with the flow. I call an audible and you're there, ready to catch. I really appreciate it."

"Thanks. That means a lot."

"Jay was right—you're a good agent. But more important, Rod likes you."

"Yeaaaah, he kinda does," Lynn responds. It's a credit to the way she purposefully shows delight with anything Rod has to say, but I also suspect that he appreciates *any* female giving him her attention.

"Good," I say, "let's keep it that way. And one more thing."

"What's that?"

"I can't wait to interview that goddamn weasel again!"

"Me, too, Joe," Lynn says. "Me, too."

Lynn would never get the chance. Nine days after our September 20 interview, the Kercsik brothers pick Rod Ramsay out of the photo lineup we sent and confirm he was involved in the Conrad case. The next day, FBIHQ once again orders us to break off all contact with Ramsay—an all-caps ORDER this time, the kind you can't ignore. By the time I'm again allowed to talk with Rod Ramsay, 357 days later, Lynn Tremaine is married and gone from the Tampa office, and the case against Ramsay has gone cold as a Russian winter.

8

MY YEAR IN THE DESERT

Washington, DC—October 29, 1989

Good news: I have permission to talk with Rod Ramsay again!
Bad news: The Ramsay investigation pretty much sat on the shelf for twelve months and eight days—but who's counting? And who spent every day of those twelve months tormented by the fact that he couldn't officially pursue a guy who he was sure had done America great harm?

Maybe worse news: Storm clouds are gathering, not outside the windows of the Eastern Air Lines Ionosphere Club, here on the second floor of the main terminal at Washington National Airport, but in more ominous places. Rod has been getting calls from ABC News. Maybe someone has tipped one of Ted Koppel's *Nightline* producers to Rod's possible connection to Conrad; maybe the *World News Tonight* staff is just doing due diligence, following up on last March's piece about Conrad in the *New York Times*. Worse-case scenario but also the most likely: James Bamford is sinking his teeth into the Conrad case. National security types were leaking substantial information to Bamford even before he wrote *The Puzzle Palace*—his international best seller that pretty much stripped bare the National Security Agency. Now that he's (a) famous and (b) heading up ABC's Washington-based national security investigative team, the intelligence crowd is falling all over itself to get on his good side, and the Clyde Conrad case seems to be doing the trick.

I understand that the press has a job to do and Bamford is just doing his. But I've got a job to do as well, and I have a lot of concerns. Rod is a twenty-seven-year-old nervous mess with a pins-and-needles mother. I want him chilled out when we get back to serious interviewing, not glancing at the phone with every new query and thinking of the lawyer his mom has lined up. (And you can bet your last dollar Rod has the lawyer's number stored for instant recall in his prodigious memory.)

Around me, guys in suits, ties loosened at the neck, are standing over fax machines or hunkered over the club's new IBM PS/2 computers, complimentary highballs at their elbows. Some of these wayfaring businessmen and lobbyists are maybe padding their expense accounts or exaggerating their success at getting in to see Congressman X or Senator Y or even Speaker Foley himself! More likely, they're just filling out and filing whatever corresponds to an FD-302 in the corporate or lobbyist world.

I'm dressed in a suit, too, but my tie isn't at half-mast, and there's a soda water at my elbow, not a Jack Daniel's and ginger. Also, I'm working on a legal pad, not a computer screen—old-fashioned, just like the Bureau, where computers are still wood-fired and faxes a novelty. I've got two and a half hours stretched out in front of me— the 6:29 p.m. flight to Tampa was full. The next one doesn't leave until 9:00. I figure it's a good time to make sense of a nonsensical year, and for me, paper and pen is the best way to do that.

COLUMN ONE I HEAD "HQ/WFO" (aka Shitstorm Central), and here I list all the roadblocks, all the obfuscations, the outright lies, the bureaucratic swamps, and petty, niggling warfare that has dogged our investigation of Rod Ramsay from day one and particularly since last year's edict not to talk to him or get near him again.

Example One: The October '88 decision prohibiting us from dealing directly with INSCOM and the army in this matter. Instead, we were told that all communication and information exchanged with the army would come through the Washington Field Office, which meant it would arrive weeks late or not at all. (Fortunately, we were able to figure out a partial work-around. Incredibly, the army has been more helpful to us than our own people.)

Another example: The headquarters meeting about the same time at which the WFO's Dale Watson and Bill Bray—respectively, the squad supervisor and agent handling the Conrad case—told Koerner and me in an ever-so-patronizing tone that this was just "too big a case" for a small office like Tampa. (And yet somehow too small for WFO to make any effort to investigate it properly?)

Still another one: The way HQ and WFO fought tooth and nail to keep Lynn from going to Sweden to talk with the Kercsiks and to Germany to investigate the crime scene, and then, when they finally *did* let her go, barely let her open her mouth and wouldn't allow her to investigate a damn thing.

Recalling Lynn's thwarted crime scene investigation reminds me of how incredibly slipshod the geniuses in our Washington Field Office have been about the most basic forensic details. We know that highly classified documents from the Eighth Infantry Division headquarters at Bad Kreuznach somehow made it into Hungarian intelligence hands. We know that such documents are frequently copies of original documents. We know what copiers Clyde Conrad and Rod Ramsay most often used in their capacity as document custodians for the Eighth Infantry HQ. And, critically, we know that every copier in the world has its own unique fingerprint—scratches, blurs, markings of whatever kind that are mostly undetectable to the naked eye. So why hasn't WFO collected "fingerprints"—"exemplars" in FBI lab-speak—for every copier that the two men were known to use or might possibly have used, just on the off chance that a recovered document or two falls back into our hands? You don't have to be Dick Tracy to come up with that idea.

(I can tell I'm getting frustrated. My handwriting is growing bigger line by line, and I'm pressing down harder and harder.)

Then there's the crime scene itself: Bad Kreuznach, the Eighth Infantry HQ, the Document Section where Conrad and Ramsay worked, the safe they used, the burn pit where they destroyed documents. You'd think investigators serious about getting to the bottom of what happened would have photographs, schematics of where everything was, not just for investigative purposes but to eventually show a jury. But no, that would take *work*, not sitting on your ass, buffing your résumé. And perish the thought that anyone—WFO, the army, our people in Bonn—would actually do anything to secure the crime scene, just in case, say, a confederate of Conrad wanted to remove an incriminating piece of evidence so far undiscovered. There's no other way to say it—this is a shit way to conduct an investigation. Period.

Also, let us not forget the article I mentioned earlier, the one that appeared in the March 10 *New York Times* and reported everything then known about the Conrad case, including these memorable paragraphs (I carry the clipping in my briefcase, but I've pretty much got it down by heart by now):

> The F.B.I., which investigated the Conrad case with the Army and West German officials, is now investigating as many as five Army associates of Mr. Conrad who are believed to have assisted him, according to American officials and Sven Olof Hakansson, the Swedish prosecutor who handled the Kercsik case . . .
>
> The assistance included help in copying and transporting stolen Army documents to the Hungarians, according to officials. A spokesman for the F.B.I. said the bureau would have no comment on the case.

Note particularly that last sentence: ". . . the bureau would have no comment on the case." Very interesting, I remember thinking at the time and still think, since the only way the *Times* could have gotten the full story was if someone inside the FBIHQ or WFO sang like a canary to reporter Jeff Gerth. What's more, the only reason I could think of (and still can think of) to sing so richly and completely was to derail the ongoing investigations. Of the "five Army associates of Mr. Conrad" mentioned in the article, the only one leading this investigation into uncharted waters is our very own Roderick James Ramsay. He's also the one most likely to have been so spooked by the article that he finally called that lawyer and will never say another word to us again.

Suspicious? I guess I am, but usually for good reason.

6:45 P.M. TIME ISN'T exactly flying. I arm myself with another club soda, this time with a piece of lime trapped below the ice, and write "USSR" at the top of a new page. The Soviets, after all, are the end buyers of Conrad's (and, in my mind, Ramsay's) product. What's been happening in the People's Paradise? Well . . . lots.

That virus the Soviets unleashed last November on the Pentagon, SDI Research, and a half-dozen American universities is way beyond my pay grade—I still think of the flu when I hear "virus"—but the way all computers are connecting with each other and taking over the world, these electronic viruses could become a major counter-intelligence threat.

More disturbing news: The Soviets have conducted nine nuclear tests since the Ramsay investigation was put on ice—nine!—most in the northeast corner of Kazakhstan and one within a week of Mikhail Gorbachev's much-celebrated can't-we-all-get-along goodwill tour of America. Nukes have burdened me with dark thoughts ever since the Cuban Missile Crisis, when trains ran twenty-four hours a day past our Miami duplex apartment, delivering war materiel to nearby Homestead Air Force Base. But nukes in the hands of the military in a country that's looking closer and closer to collapse make those thoughts more vivid, even terrifying, and there has been plenty happening of late to put Soviet generals even more on edge.

Estonia, for example, has announced that it's now free of Soviet influence in its internal affairs. Journalists in Yugoslavia are clamoring for more freedom. Things have gotten so precarious in Czechoslovakia that the Soviet-proxy cops there have arrested Václav Havel—a writer, for God's sake! It's been almost five months since Lech Walesa's Solidarity Party came to power in Poland. Only two weeks ago, the East German Communist Party seemed close to collapse—unthinkable!—and just last week there was news that surely made Soviet politburo members' blood pressure soar: Hungary has declared itself an independent country.

Most analysts I've talked with think the NATO countries can ride out this storm so long as those Pershing II missiles in West Germany are staring down Moscow's throat, but desperate empires do desperate things, and the commissars in the Kremlin wouldn't be the first tyrants to try to save their skins with a convenient war—one begun by, say, sending a thousand tanks roaring through the Fulda Gap. Or something even worse.

AS I STARE DOWN at my legal pad, I try to cheer myself with optimistic thoughts. FBIHQ staffers behaved somewhat cooperatively at my meeting at the Mothership earlier today, and the Justice Department seems to be ginning up some interest. Also, the Germans put through a request at the start of October to use Lynn's and my FD-302s in building their case against Conrad—that was a real morale booster.

Best of all, not only do I have permission to talk with Ramsay again, but we were actually able to find him, and believe me, that wasn't easy given how long this case has been on the shelf. We can't keep tabs on people just because we think we *might* want to collar them someday. J. Edgar Hoover got away with that kind of stuff, but those days are long gone. Also, surveillance like that requires a good deal of expertise. You don't want it being done by amateurs who are either going to lose the subject constantly or be so heavy-handed about following him or her that the subject bolts for cover.

We began the Rod-hunt with multiple phone calls across every shift at the Bob Evans restaurant out on Highway 60, his last known place of employment. The stories were always different: Rod's mother was sick; his car was fixed and ready to pick up; etc. But Rod was never there, and we got the sense that most of the people we talked with had never heard of him. So we sent one of our youngest agents out there, pretending he was a long-lost friend, and that at least netted us the information that Rod had quit months ago and was maybe driving a cab in Orlando, eighty-five miles to the northeast.

I used that thin piece of intelligence to pay a visit to Rod's mother, Dorothy, and I'm glad I did. ABC News had been calling her, too, and she was worried that Rod's being mentioned on air in connection with the Conrad case would somehow expose him to danger.

"Rod was *assigned* to that job, Mr. Navarro," she reminded me. "He didn't seek it out. You can't be held guilty just because you worked with a criminal."

I liked Dorothy immediately. She was full of energy and clearly had a big heart. In fact, she reminded me very much of the librarian in my junior high—a woman who always treated antsy seventh- and eighth-grade boys with a smile and was quick to forgive our many behavioral excesses.

It was a miserable afternoon. A driving rain had swept in from the Gulf and found a hole in Dorothy's metal roof. A plastic bucket sat on the kitchen floor, slowly filling up. The drip-drip was background music to the tea and cookies Dorothy insisted I share with her.

"Rod won't talk to his father or his brother," she told me, "but the three of them are a lot alike, all smart as whips. Unfortunately, back when Rod was in high school, the family fell apart. Rod's father went one way. Stewart went another. And Rod and I were left with each other," she said, her face betraying how much she wished things had been different.

"Rod," she went on, "at least found the army. I'd hoped it would settle him, but, oh, the marijuana. It's always something with him."

Perhaps a good deal more "something" than she could imagine, I thought, but how do you tell that to a mother?

"Maybe he'll settle down," I said. "Some people just take longer to find their niche."

"Maybe," she agreed, but I didn't hear much hope in it.

We talked on for another twenty minutes or so, a calm moment in the usual storm of my day, and in the end Dorothy was able to confirm that Rod had relocated to the Greater Orlando area and was driving a cab, but exactly where he was living and which company he was driving for were mysteries to her as well.

"You know," she said as I was preparing to dash through the rain to my car, "Rod is a rolling stone. He moves around a lot."

No doubt about it, Dorothy is a nice lady, doing the best she can in tough circumstances and more than willing to help us, but knowing that Rod was in Central Florida driving a cab these days still left us with a big challenge. Thanks to Disney World, Epcot Center, SeaWorld, and a dozen other lesser tourist destinations, Orlando probably has as many for-hire car services per capita as any place in the United States. The sheer number of possibilities forced us to send in a dozen undercover agents. We were just about out of faces young enough to make the cover credible when we finally glommed on to the right cab outfit and were able to ID Rod coming in the next morning to pick up a car.

Even now, though, we still have to walk lightly. We already know that ABC News is sniffing around Rod. If he senses that the national media and the FBI are both about to come down on him, who knows what he might do. This is a guy who lacks the normal range of inhibitions.

*   *   *

IT WAS ABOUT A month before making this trip to DC, on September 26, that I finally got to see Rod Ramsay again, after our twelve-month forced separation. No other way to put it: The guy was a complete mess.

Not that I expected a lot out of the meeting. I just wanted to reestablish contact while we assembled a support team that could meet the demands of every agency that had skin in the game: from the National Security Council to the Department of Justice. The real interviewing was to come.

When I first reached Rod by phone at the cab office, he told me that he couldn't talk freely, but he did manage to let me know that he was living in a camper with a woman, although not very happily. According to Rod, she had another boyfriend who regularly stopped by and kicked him out of his own camper. When that happened, he wound up sleeping in his car. What a life!

We agreed to meet at seven-thirty in the lobby of a hotel in Kissimmee, near Disney World, but I got there early and waited upstairs so I could see Rod coming in without his seeing me. Once I confirmed that he had nothing in his hands that might go Bang! in the night, I approached him from the back and surprised him. Even from behind I could see that he looked disheveled, but once he turned around, I was almost shocked. A lot of weight had dropped off his already skinny frame, and it was way too easy to tell that he hadn't bathed in days. The first thing he did after we shook hands was to take out a comb and try to make sense of his tangle of greasy hair.

Either this guy is a volcano about to explode, I found myself thinking, *or he's on the edge of collapsing into his own sinkhole.* Whichever the case—and maybe it's some of both—Agent Navarro is going to have to be Dr. Navarro, Nurse Navarro, Headshrinker Navarro, and Father Confessor Navarro, too, if Rod Ramsay is going to become the asset I know he can be.

* * *

DOES ALL THIS AMOUNT to progress? Well, in an up-and-down way, yes. The people at headquarters don't seem to hate me as much as I thought. The door to Ramsay has been cracked open again. If I wasn't packing heat, I might even order a Cuba libre with Bacardi rum. Instead, I ask for another club soda, this time with bitters. The bartender is just sliding it my way when *ABC World News Tonight* pops up on the TV behind him . . . and the shitstorm begins anew. Clyde Lee Conrad is the lead story. "Goddamn it!" I say loud enough for the three people sitting nearby to hear me.

"ABC News has talked to investigators, had access to investigative documents, and talked to self-admitted participants in the suspected spy ring," the broadcast begins. "Our national security correspondent John McWethy has the story."

McWethy does indeed have the story, all of it: Zoltan Szabo, the Hungarians, Conrad's suitcases stuffed full with top-secret documents—"everything but the nuclear go-codes, the codes that could actually launch the nuclear weapons," McWethy reports, citing one admitted spy-ring participant. There are even mini-interviews with Conrad's wife, Annja, and his son. But it's the close of the segment that has me almost gasping for breath.

Conrad was the only one arrested on that day in West Germany. Since then, a massive US investigation has been launched—one of the largest espionage probes the FBI has ever handled. Sources say there were many others working in the spy ring. What began with Szabo in 1967, then expanded to incorporate Conrad in the mid-1970s, eventually included a whole new group of people, a third generation of spies that sources say Conrad himself recruited in the mid-1980s.

Government sources claim the FBI now is keeping track of more than a dozen of these suspects. ABC News has learned that one of Conrad's recruits continued to work for Conrad back in the United States, illegally exporting hundreds of thousands of advanced computer chips through a dummy company in Canada to the Eastern Bloc.

According to the man himself, who asked not to be identified, Conrad
paid him to make the purchases.

Want to guess who the Conrad recruit is who got involved in the computer-chip scheme? My guess is it's a skinny guy who doesn't recognize the difference between right and wrong and who now is or very soon will be shaking in his boots. (Actually, I'm almost certain who this is since Rod's mother told me that ABC people had been calling him specifically about computer chips.)

Want to further guess who fed all this to John McWethy? Probably the same person who force-fed Jeff Gerth at the *Times* more than seven months ago and now has upped the stakes with even more insider knowledge. And unless I miss my bet, that has to be one of the very people I met with today, someone who sat through that entire four-hour session secure in the knowledge that however much progress I might have felt I was making at HQ, *ABC World News Tonight* was going to torpedo the whole damn investigation before the day was through.

Condemned men get to make one call, so I make mine to Jay Koerner as I finish off my now flat club soda:

"Jay," I say, "who at headquarters is working for the Communists? Someone up here is trying to derail our investigation."

We have an adage in the FBI that perfectly captures how so many of us in the outposts feel about HQ: "Only the guppies get eaten, never the sharks."

9

SHE-MOODY

I mentioned earlier that Lynn Tremaine had gotten herself hitched during the year FBIHQ red-lighted us on Ramsay. Ironically, Lynn met the INSCOM agent of her dreams while in Germany running into a lot of Ramsay case brick walls. Good for her but bad for me. Now I need to find another partner.

And it can't just be anyone. I need to find someone who is sharp, works hard, and will have my back. If I get stuck with the wrong person, it will make *both* of us miserable. Believe me. I speak from experience.

When I first entered the FBI, I was assigned to work with someone I'll call Frank in the Yuma, Arizona, office. The first thing he said to me when we shook hands was "You don't look like a spic." Naturally, I replied, "You don't look like Efrem Zimbalist Jr." Things went downhill from there. Not only was Frank a slob and morbidly obese—the polar opposite of the trim and natty Zimbalist on all those *F.B.I.* shows—he also had about as much personality as an iguana. Pedantic, nitpicking, paranoid, distrustful, and permanently unhappy, he resented just about everyone, and he especially abhorred Mexicans and the Native Americans who lived on the reservations that surrounded us: i.e., just about everyone we had to deal with on a daily basis.

I promised myself way back then that I'd never work again with someone like Frank. So far I've lucked out, but the agent pickings in the Tampa bureau are thin, and the Ramsay investigation, I'm hoping, is about to break wide open.

"How about Terry Moody?" Koerner is saying. We're sitting in his office, late in the morning, and my boss is playing nice with me. He knows I'm still fuming over the ABC news broadcast two evenings ago. Terry Moody is one of the bones he's throwing my way.

I like Terry Moody. Koerner knows that. Terry is the latest addition to our SWAT team—just last month I was teaching him how to rappel off of a forty-foot tower dangling by an eleven-millimeter rope. Terry's tough, a quick learner, and funny. There's just one problem.

"What I need is a *female* partner, Jay, a woman."

Koerner responds by shaking his head.

"C'mon, Jay! Rod loved Lynn. She had him eating out of her hand. I don't know if he has a mother complex, or a sister one, or if he's just one horny son of a bitch, but I need a female partner—that's what this case needs."

"I *know* that, Navarro." Koerner has stopped shaking his head. In fact, he's smiling as if he's trying to coax, oh, say, a five-year-old toward understanding. And then it dawns on me.

"Oh!" I say. "*She*-Moody?"

"The very one."

This requires a moment of explanation. We have two agents named Moody in our office: Terry Moody and his wife, Terry Moody. The odds against this are probably astronomical, but there it is. Terry Halverson was already an FBI agent when she met and married fellow agent Terry Moody, and they became agents Terry and Terry Moody. To keep them straight, we refer to the former Miss Halverson as She-Moody and to her husband as He-Moody. Koerner was obviously setting a trap for me when he sprung "Terry Moody" on me, and I fell right in. Now my job is to extricate myself as gracefully as possible.

"Christ, Koerner, She-Moody is a first-office agent. She's never worked counterintelligence before—never ever. She's been all criminal. It's not the same thing. You know that. I don't want to train another agent—I don't have fucking time."

But even as I'm trying to talk my way out of She-Moody, my mind is talking me into it. Terry is tall and, frankly, beautiful, and Lynn already proved that looks go a long way toward opening up Rod Ramsay. What's more, Terry has a disarming smile and laugh, and she's humble to the core and a pleasure to be around. If this investigation is headed where I want it to go, we're going to be spending, literally, hundreds of hours together, maybe thousands, doing interviews that might stretch up to half a day, and that's just the interviews, not the parsing and dissection—and endless FD-302s!—afterward. Even a little friction between partners can quickly grow into big rifts, even open feuds, under those circumstances.

In that sense, at least, I know she'll be easy for me to work with, but partnering is a two-way street, and word has gotten back to me that I'm not anywhere near high-man on She-Moody's favorite-fellow-agent list, maybe because I'm a little, um, hyper, while Terry seems more laid back—not lazy, mind you, just more inclined to smell the roses occasionally.

"So?" Koerner has his phone in his hand. I can tell he's getting ready to punch in She-Moody's extension.

"Well," I say, "we *have* worked together before, on a Title III, when we were short of personnel."

"And?"

"And she was fine. Good, in fact. Sharp. But that was a wiretap, drugs, not CI. Also . . ."

He's rolling his eyes by now.

"Yes, Navarro, what else?"

"Also," I say, shifting uncomfortably in my seat, "our personalities might not match up all that well."

"Yeah, she's nice," he says, stabbing away at her extension number. "Now get the hell out of here."

"Yes, boss!" I say. "And . . ."

"And. And. And. It's always something else with you, Navarro. And what?"

"And let me know what she says," but he's already talking with She-Moody.

WHILE I'M WAITING TO hear from Koerner about a new partner, I try to piece together a surveillance team on a shoestring budget. Finding Rod after our year in the desert was hard enough. Keeping tabs on him now that we have him back in our sights is going to be harder still.

For starters, these days Rod is driving a cab—and not his own. Every day he picks up a vehicle that he may or may not ever have driven before and spends up to twelve hours or longer behind its wheel, much of that time at Orlando International Airport, waiting in a long queue to pick up whoever happens to be at the front of the line when he gets there. Once he has a fare in the backseat, he goes wherever the customer directs, in a yellow cab identical from the air or ground to perhaps two thousand other yellow cabs working the streets of Greater Orlando.

Put a bug in Rod's cab? Which one? Make sure all his fares are our agents? Just imagine how many man-hours would be consumed standing in cab queues at the airport, not to mention the expense for the perpetual fares. And how would you ever time things so our agent was at the head of the line every time Rod's turn came up? (God forbid that one of the agents might need to take a piss and screw up the entire cab-rank rotation.) This isn't TV surveillance. This is the real thing. And you've got to be on your toes at all times because it's easy to detect surveillance if you know what you're doing.

And don't forget: The stakes are double on this surveillance job, maybe triple, depending on how you look at it. One, the world hasn't gotten any safer since I made that list at National Airport two days ago. At some point, the KGB is going to say enough of this freedom shit, and who knows what might happen then, and not just behind the crumbling Iron Curtain. Two, ABC News has been harassing Rod almost nonstop since airing the Conrad segment on October 29—or *would* be harassing him nonstop if they knew where he was. As it is, they're harassing Dorothy Ramsay almost nonstop, trying to find her pride and joy, and Dorothy, God bless her, is harassing me in turn, or at least harassing as much as an inherently nice and decent middle-age lady can bring herself to do. Three, most important, I don't know for sure what secrets Rod might have to tell, but if he spooks and bolts, we're likely never to learn any of them.

Every CI agent in the FBI has memorized—or should have—the cautionary tale of Edward Lee Howard from a few years back. Howard was already suspected of providing classified information to the Soviets when Vitaly Yurchenko walked into the American Embassy in Rome, defected to the US, and fingered Howard and Ronald Pelton as KGB assets. Things got confused when Yurchenko redefected back to Russia in November 1985—had he been a double agent? or was he now a redoubled one?—but the case against Howard remained strong enough that the FBI got permission to tap his Santa Fe, New Mexico, phone and set up a twenty-four-hour-a-day surveillance operation on him.

That's what they were doing in September 1985 when Howard and his wife, Mary, returned home from dinner out. As Mary slowed to round a corner, Howard leapt from the car, leaving a stuffed-clothes dummy topped with an old wig in the passenger seat to dupe the agents who were tailing them. Back home, Mary called a number connected to an answering machine and played a message her husband had prerecorded to fool the wiretap. The next thing anyone knew, Edward Lee Howard was knocking on the door of the Soviet Embassy in Helsinki and carrying all his secrets with him.

Screw up our surveillance, overplay our hand, spook Rod Ramsay too badly, and we'll end holding the same empty bag—with, to my mind, even bigger secrets unrevealed. That's what's been haunting my sleep these last few nights, along with the teletype from HQ kindly letting us know that the Swedes, the Germans, and the Austrians are all in a lather because Washington is making them look bad and they don't appreciate the news leaks. *They* don't? What about us? We have to investigate with the intention of prosecution, and we're being thwarted at every turn!

First things first, though. Ramsay is a lot less likely to go to ground if we can stabilize his life even a little bit. And since I still don't have a partner, "we" in this case is a substitute for "I."

I reached Rod this morning in the office where he picks up cab keys, and we agreed to meet after his shift. She-Moody and Koerner are heavy in conversation, door closed against the world, when I knock on his office window to let him know I'm leaving. Neither of them bothers to look up.

HERE'S THE ALARMING THING: Rod's life is an even *bigger* mess than I realized. Not only is he still getting thrown out of his camper regularly so his "girlfriend" can get it on with her ex-beau; Rod, I learn, is also getting screwed (not quite so literally) by the outfit he's working for. The first $75 he makes each and every day goes to the cab company no matter how his day goes. Some days he breaks even, he says; other days he actually loses money and has to dig into his own pocket to pay off his daily obligation. It's the rare day—when the tourists are pouring into Orlando International and in a generous tipping mood—that he actually turns anything close to a decent profit.

Images of Southern tenant farmers trapped in their miserable lives float through my head as he talks. No wonder Rod is, even by his own high standards, jittery as a frog in a frying pan. I wonder for a moment if he's on speed. I can see a vein throbbing like a disco light along his right temple. But I finally convince myself that this is just what life of late has done to him.

I learn all this, by the way, as Rod and I lean against my car, munching on ranch-flavored Doritos and downing Busch Beer in the parking lot of a 7-Eleven near the campground that Rod now calls home. Sounds like a dump, doesn't it? Well, it should—it *is* a dump, but it's also a perfect place for what I want to accomplish tonight.

Interviewing? Forget it. Interviewing is nuanced. It requires enormous advance planning, and in Rod's case, it helps greatly to have a feminine presence to grease the skids. What we're doing tonight is lots simpler and utterly necessary: an old-fashioned man-to-man, under the stars—raw, basic, simple. Nowhere is the human condition more on display than in a convenience store parking lot, after dark, on the back edge of civilization. Everyone out here has a story, and each new one is sorrier than the last. As Rod enumerates his problems, I point out others in the passing parade who are beyond any doubt worse off than he: slouched, emaciated, even maimed. One guy has a truncated limb that looks as if it might have been picked clean in a thresher.

Dastardly? Yeah, sure, and calculating. I want Rod to see where he could end up, or sink to, if he doesn't make some effort to get his act together—and of course I want to be a key part of that reversal of fortune. But this isn't entirely cold-blooded on my part. There's also something about Rod that screams out "Help me! Help me!" And as I said before, he can be winning in an almost childlike way.

When I ask him if he'd like to meet again tomorrow night for dinner at the Embassy Suites on International Drive, his face splits with what I think is the first smile I've seen all night. I can't imagine when Rod had his last square meal. When I tell him (with fingers crossed) that my new partner will be joining us, the smile widens into a grin.

"Is she nice?" he asks.

"Nice," I answer, "and beautiful."

Check that: a shit-eating grin.

"But, Rod," I add as he settles back into his car, "she's a lady—like Lynn. Clean up a little for her, okay?"

"Okay," he says. "Definitely okay!"

ROD KEEPS HIS WORD the next evening. I don't know where he showered, but he looks almost presentable. I keep mine, too, in part. We have a big dinner—steak, baked potato, salad, the basics—and Rod seems to down half of it without even chewing while I fill him with a combination of fatherly advice (stand up to the son of a bitch who's screwing your girl and throw her out of the camper while you're at it) and motherly cautions (brush your teeth twice daily, eat a balanced diet, don't wash up only when I'm coming to see you). But the most important part of the promise I made to Rod, I can't keep. Yes, I do have a partner—She-Moody herself—and she's a stunner. But, no, she's not able to make it. She's on another case at the moment. Truth is, it's probably best that Terry and I have a night to get over the time we spent together earlier in the day.

THE DAY BEGAN UNPLEASANTLY enough with a new missive forwarded on to us from the Austrians regarding the ABC News report. In yesterday's installment, they were merely lathered. Today, they were royally pissed, largely because they'd managed to contact Zoltan Szabo only to find out that he now feels the FBI can't be trusted and will have nothing to do with us. Really? Just because someone high up leaked the whole story to the media? Picky. Picky. But this is also deeply troubling because I know that at some point I'll have to visit the Austrians in furtherance of my investigation. A warm welcome doesn't seem in the cards.

Koerner's first words to me didn't do a lot to lift the cloud.

"She-Moody would rather not work with you," he said, leaning against my doorjamb and cradling his morning cup of coffee. "In fact, she'd rather work with anyone else but you."

"Really, anyone?" That hurt a little. We have a couple of real jerks in our office.

"Pretty much."

"What's the issue?"

"She knows about your work habits, and she just doesn't want to be driven crazy by your demanding nature. But . . ." He hesitated here as if delivering news he'd rather not be bearing.

"But?"

"But she'll do it because she knows we need this."

"Aw, don't worry," I said. "We'll get along fine."

"Seriously, Navarro, be kind. Let her come up for air. Not everyone is comfortable working at warp speed."

"I'll keep that in mind."

I might be wrong, but I think the dagger look Koerner shot back at me was completely unwarranted.

A FEW HOURS LATER, I saw Moody descending the stairs from her office on the floor above ours and walking my way. Her smile said "I can do this," but everything else about her screamed "What in the hell have I gotten myself into?" so I took her into one of our small conference rooms, where I could brief her on the case in general and then get down to the details of how we'd work together. She barely said a word until I got to the details part.

"Two things you should know at the outset," she declared, holding up her hand like a crossing guard. "One, I'm not going to drive myself into the ground if that's what it takes to keep up with you. If this gets out of hand, I'm gone."

"Okay, it won't. And two?"

"I'm pregnant."

"Fine."

"Fine? I tell you I'm pregnant heading into a major case, and all you can do is say 'fine'?"

"What do you want me to say? I can't undo it, although I got to say that I'm worried you'll name this child Terry. Then we'll have He-Moody, She-Moody, and Wee-Moody."

That at least got a smile from her, a real one.

"But listen, I'll take the lead in the interviews, and I'll do all the FD-302s, at least for now. Those wore Lynn into the ground."

"I know."

"She told you so?"

"Many times. And much more. Your reputation, Navarro, does precede you," she said with a knowing smile and confident face.

And then, as if to prove her point, I launched into the meat of this get-together: how we were going to work together. And as I went on, I couldn't help but notice that her genuinely warm smile was slipping increasingly into incredulity.

"Item One, when we first meet Ramsay, I'll keep him on my right, so stand to my left as we walk in. He has to look through me to see you."

Right? Left? She was locked into my eyes, but somewhere behind those powder-blue orbs, I could see her brain saying *Huh?*

"Two, you and I must be in complete synchronicity at all times except when it comes to humor. You want to laugh, laugh. I'll control what I do depending on the situation.

"Three, Rod will try to divide us. He did this with Lynn, and we can't let it happen. If I jump down his throat, it's because he's getting out of hand.

"Four, don't wear anything that would make you look like an agent. Jeans are fine, but no skirt, no business suits. On most occasions, I'll be wearing a polo shirt with khaki pants, and for the record, my weapon will be concealed, as will yours."

This got an eye roll—engagement was good.

"Five, no note-taking. We have to memorize everything Ramsay says, and it has to be accurate. I don't know how long the interviews will last, but the shortest one so far has been two hours."

A Moody question: "What do you guys talk about?"

A Navarro answer: "Everything. Rod's going to talk about women, the army, his mother, history, the Peloponnesian War, physics."

"What do I say to that?"

"Thank him. Have him educate you. Hang on his every word as if he's a gifted professor, but don't shut him down and don't criticize him."

"What if he's full of shit?"

"He probably won't be. The guy is incredibly smart. But even if bullshit is seeping out of his every pore, don't say anything . . . that is, until we're ready, and I'll signal you when we get to that point."

"Six?" I'd lost count, but she was obviously ticking this off.

"Six, use your smile."

"Use my smile? I hope you and Jay don't think I'm just going to sit there like a doll for this guy's entertainment."

"Moody, this is acting, and your role is important. You'll play by the rules of comedy and improvisation: Never say no. You agree, you contribute something positive, you link to something useful, but you never say no or disagree. This rule cannot be broken—it's about flow. Don't go doing a Joe Friday on me. Whatever you learned at Quantico about how to handle interviewing, forget it—we need to get inside his head. Right now. Lastly . . ."

"Seventhly," Moody corrected. "My smile was item six."

"Okay, seventhly, we'll meet every day for breakfast and choreograph how we'll sit, what we'll talk about, what evidence we'll present or leads we'll pursue, and we'll do everything in our power not to deviate from that. I want a confession within a week—one week. We need it."

"You ask a lot."

"Of myself and everyone else."

"Anything else?" in a tone that suggests, hopefully, there couldn't possibly be.

"Yes. Ramsay is never to sit higher than either of us even if we have to change the furniture or cut down the legs, I don't care. We walk into the room first, then he comes in. We ask if he needs something to drink, and we regulate when he goes to the bathroom and what and when he eats. You and I are the parental figures, you understand? He'll look to us for direction, and we'll accommodate him, but he has to come to us first.

"Any chance Ramsay will have a gun?"

"Who knows? He hasn't yet, but I'll check him every time—an *abrazo*, a guy-hug. If you want to give him a little hug, fine, but always feel for the small of his back. That's probably where the gun would be. And for God's sake, if he does pull a gun and we're struggling, don't hesitate, don't try to aim, just shoot him in the head. Are we clear?"

"Clear as day. Tell me, Navarro, are you like this at home?"

"No, at home I make them recite back what I just said."

Moody looked at me not knowing if I was lying or telling the truth. In fact, I was doing a little bit of both. The reality of this new assignment was hitting her—I could see it on her face.

"Let's take a ten-minute break," I said.

"Good, I need to go powder my nose and ask myself why I agreed to work with you."

NINE MINUTES AND FIFTY seconds later, She-Moody turned up at my office door looking not only relieved but amazingly refreshed. Her hair, which had started to come undone in the conference room, had been pulled back. Her face had a ruddy, scrubbed glow. She had a pad and pen in one hand and a water bottle in the other. I was impressed—at least she'd come back.

"So where do you want me to start?" she asked, clearly thinking I was going to hand her a file.

"You see the four-drawer cabinet over in the corner labeled 'Navarro Eyes Only'?"

"Yup," she said, following my eyes. "There it is."

"Begin with Volume One, Serial One. That will help you get started. Then keep going."

"Everything in the cabinet?"

"Everything," I confirmed as we relocated by the file cabinet.

"And that would include . . . ?"

"Serials," I said, sliding open the top drawer. "They're not going to mean a lot to you at first." I began paging through one of the files, showing her a jumble of messages, communications, photos, other bits and scraps of paper. "CI is a different world than Criminal. You've got a whole new language to learn: 'liaise,' 'false flag.' "

"Sounds doable."

"What's a letter rogatory?" I threw at her.

"A letter what?"

"Letters rogatory are formal letters or requests that a recognized nation state sends to a corresponding nation state and in particular its justice department, asking for help with something criminal, such as an opportunity to talk to someone, conduct a deposition, or ask questions."

"Got it, letters rogatory," she said, writing it down. She maybe wasn't liking my tutorial, but at least she was willing to learn.

"Usually, the receiving nation states do the query, and that can vary from average to poor because they're not vested in the case, and if you don't ask the specific question, it won't get asked. Plus, if the suspect says no, there's no follow-up. It's the most shitty way of conducting interviews . . ."

"Shitty with two 't's?"

That was funny! But I was in another mood.

"Letters rogatory—note the plural, like 'attorneys general'—are what has been relegated to us by diplomats. You get a host interviewer, generally an attorney who doesn't like us because it took too long for his family to get a visa to the US, and the attorney will either do a for-shit job or do it so far in the future that it will no longer matter.

This is why the FBI maintains and always has had legal attachés in foreign embassies, even before the CIA existed, to conduct liaison and to make sure these things get handled, sometimes by other methods, such as persuasion or over a drink."

"Got it."

"Do you? How about PHOTINT? HUMINT? SIGNINT?"

"I've heard the terms."

"What's a 'barium pill'?"

"Okay, you got me there," she said, shrugging her shoulders.

"You've got to know this stuff!" Boom, boom, boom—I could actually hear my blood pressure climbing into the ozone layer. I didn't have time to be teaching, but I also didn't have any choice.

"A barium pill is something that can be traced because of a particular micro-stain—indentations, scratches, markings, maybe a micro-tear, maybe a particular word within each document or a word intentionally misspelled deep inside the document. Why? Because we can then trace the document's origin, vector, and/or provenance. Example: If you and He-Moody are equally but separately suspected of espionage, I would give each of you the same letter or document to pass on, but on yours I might use a comma on the eighth line and on his I might use a semicolon. Most people wouldn't notice, but if the document shows up where it shouldn't be, we can ask an asset to see if there's a comma or a semicolon on the eighth line—a low-risk proposition, but we can trace back from there and identify the culprit. We use barium pills all the time."

"Okay," Moody said. "I get it. By *when* do you want me to have this file cabinet read?"

"Well," I said, checking my watch. "It's just a tick before noon. I'm headed out to lunch. Then I want to take a run down by the Bay. And this afternoon I need to spend some time with an asset I'm training to pass himself off as a disaffected spy. We're going to run him against a hostile service in the Soviet Bloc to see if they're still interested even though things are crumbling all around. I'm guessing

I'll be back here between five and six. What do you say you have the file cabinet memorized by then?"

"Navarro?" There was an edge to Moody's voice.

"What?"

"Where does it say that in the FBI manual?"

"Say what?"

"That you have to be an asshole."

10

THE EDUCATION
OF NAVARRO

The trip from downtown Tampa to International Drive in Orlando takes eighty-five minutes on Interstate 4—not a lot of time, but time is precious right now. Moody and I have been partners for two weeks, but she had a lot of old cases to clean up. We've been working side by side only for the last two days, and this is my last chance to get her ready for her first meeting with Rod Ramsay. I'm not wasting a minute of our drive time.

"How are you going to shake hands with him?" I ask as the tread flies off a truck tire in front us.

"Navarro!"

"I mean it. How are you going to do it?"

"Well," she says, "since you haven't yet mentioned that he lacks a right arm, I'll probably reach over with my own right hand, give him a firm grip, and look him square in the eye. And then maybe I'll briefly cover his hand with my left hand to reinforce how glad I am to meet him."

"No."

"No?"

"No!" I say, more emphatically than necessary. "You never do that. You're not entitled to cover somebody else's hand with yours. Politicians do that because they're idiots, but everybody else hates it. You are, however, entitled to shake Rod's hand and touch him on the elbow, but don't do it today."

"Why not?"

"Because *Rod* is not entitled to it. He hasn't earned that extra touch from you yet."

"Oh, for crissake . . ."

"I want this first handshake sterile, you understand? Eye contact, sure. A firm grip. The FBI way. But nothing more than that. If he's good and gives us information, then you can touch him some more."

"Where?"

The pause that follows this question is frankly a little unnerving. The look on Moody's face makes me wonder if she's reconsidering her career choice—maybe even considering rolling out of the car if we hit a traffic jam. Finally, she sighs, takes a deep breath, and looks at her watch.

"We're meeting Ramsay at six o'clock, right?"

"Correct. The Embassy Suites on International Drive."

"But we're going to get there in, what, maybe fifteen minutes?"

"Yep," I confirm, checking my watch. "We should pull in at just about four-forty-five."

"So, what are we going to do for the hour and a quarter before he arrives?"—this in a tone that suggests she might not want to know the answer.

"Rearrange furniture and, if we're lucky, one more rehearsal."

This time Moody just sighs and waits for me to go on. I'm thinking, however, that a little quiet time might be best considering the circumstances.

ROOM 316 TURNS OUT to be pretty much what I anticipated—a midsized suite with adequate sitting space in the front, and with the rolling swivel chair I requested waiting in the center of the room. We slide the sofa over, so Rod will be sitting within a few steps of the door, and relocate an end table and lamp so the light won't be shining directly on him. We could be here for three, four hours or more. That light would be way too distracting for him. Then I reposition the one easy chair in the room so Moody will be sitting at a slightly oblique angle to Ramsay.

"Sit down," I say as I plop into what will be Ramsay's position.

"Why?"

"Because I want to be certain your eyes will be higher than his, and they will be," I say, popping up again, "so long as you don't slouch."

I'm adjusting the height on my swivel chair when Moody drags the coffee table over and positions it just in front of the sofa.

"Move it farther away," I tell her.

"It's a coffee table. Coffee tables are for putting things on."

"Not this coffee table. At some point during the interview, I'm going to say to Rod, 'Do you want something to drink?' And he's going to say, 'Yes,' because by then he'll be thirsty. And I'll say, 'Why don't you get up and get it from the table.'"

"But if we move the coffee table out here," Moody says, "you'll be closer to it than he is. Why not just be a nice guy and hand him the drink?"

"Because I'm establishing the father-child relationship. When he wants to go to the bathroom, he has to ask me for permission. If he wants a drink, he has to wait for me to offer it, and he has to get it himself. And it's got to be the same with you. Nothing free. Nothing easy. That's why he'll be sitting in the lowest seat in the room—so he has to physically look up to both of us. I'm the father. You're the mother. Don't forget it."

"From everything you've told me about Ramsay, I don't want to be this guy's mother, okay?"

"Moody," I say, "CI is theater on a world stage. We have to get this right, not for you, not for me, not for the Bureau, or the Germans, and certainly not for the Washington Field Office. We do this because this is what we get paid to do—a job that's not for everyone. If this were a destruction-of-government-property case, no one would care. But this is espionage. We have everyone from the SAC to the Director to the CIA looking at this case. Oh, and did I tell you that David Major on the National Security Council staff at the White House is aware of this case and has been briefing those above him, and so is State Department?"

I can't tell if David Major, our FBI representative to the National Security Council, rings Moody's chime or not, but I do know that I've got her attention.

"So while you may not want to play mother, and I don't particularly care to play father to someone who doesn't share my values, those are precisely the roles we're going to play. And I don't give a rat's ass what you were taught at Quantico about interviewing. We have to get into this guy's head, and we have to dominate it. And to do that I need for you to kindly do as I request and not question my methods when we're twenty-one minutes away from touchdown."

Moody's silence might indicate that she's processing what I am saying or just loathing me further. I send up a small prayer for the former.

"One last thing: You and I were handed a turd. Conrad will never talk, the Kercsik brothers can't be trusted, nor can we use their testimony, and HQ is doing everything possible to get in our way and derail this investigation. So in the end, we—you and me, She-Moody and Navarro—are the only game in town."

THE NEXT TEN MINUTES pass in silence—if you discount the veins pulsating loudly along both our temples. I'm thinking of Trappist monks when Moody finally breaks the quiet.

"So what's next—if I dare ask?"

"We have to rehearse how we're going into walk in the room."

"Walk into the room? It's an interview, Navarro. Not a wedding." She's still resisting but not as much.

"They're both processions; they're both rituals. There's a right way and a wrong way to do everything. We have to establish psychological dominance and hierarchy, and that starts before we enter this room."

Moody is rolling her eyes in a way that must have driven high-school boys nuts back on the midwestern plains of her well-spent youth but to me is sending up yellow warning flags.

"You don't own a dog, do you?" I ask.

"No, I don't."

"Here's why I ask. You never let a dog go in the door first or exit the door first. You make him sit until you decide what is permissible—otherwise the dog thinks he is in charge. With humans it's more nuanced, but essentially no different."

"They told me you liked to play mind games, Navarro, but I swear to God, I had no idea how true that is."

"I wish it *were* a game. You don't lose sleep over a game."

I spend the next seven minutes indoctrinating Moody in the Navarro Way of entering a room—she first, me second, Ramsay last—and of sitting down once inside: Ramsay first, but not until we invite him to do so and exactly where we tell him to sit; then Moody in the easy chair; then me on my rolling swivel seat. I went through all this fourteen months earlier with Lynn Tremaine, but Lynn wasn't an utter stranger to counterintelligence. Moody is a CI babe in the woods, I'm thinking, and the woods could catch fire at any moment.

TWELVE MINUTES LATER, AT 6:09 p.m., Terry Moody and I are standing in the lobby of the Embassy Suites, off to the left side of the main entrance, studying surveillance angles. Just as I remind her that we'll be taking Rod directly upstairs and that she's to follow my lead in all matters, Ramsay walks in and cranes his head up toward the landing where I was standing two days before to watch him enter.

"That him?" Moody says to me.

"It is, but let him find us."

Moody, though, is already walking toward him.

"You must be Rod Ramsay," I hear her saying as I close the space between us. Moody has her hand out, a firm grip, good eye contact. "I'm Agent Moody, Agent Navarro's new partner."

Rod looks a little stunned, in all honesty, but not unhappily so.

"But why don't you call me Terry. 'Agent' sounds so—"

"Formal?"

"That's it, formal."

Rod's stunned look, I notice, is softening into a major smile.

"Rod," I say, slipping between the two of them, "thanks for—"

"Agent Navarro," it's Moody again, edging me off to the side with a surprisingly strong hip check, "if I could just have one more moment."

"Rod," she says, staring him straight in the face, "you'll pardon a mother's instincts, I hope, but what have you had to eat today?"

Now that she says it, I can see that his face is even more gaunt than it was two days ago.

"Kit Kats," Rod answers, suddenly studying his shoes.

"Kit Kats?" Moody has a finger under Rod's chin and is raising his face so they can talk eye to eye.

"Two of them," he says, "and a Pepsi."

"That's all?" Moody asks.

Rod nods sheepishly as Moody does a spin and, this time, stares straight at me.

"Well, Agent Navarro," she says, "that does it!"

"Does what?"

"We're feeding this young man dinner before we sit down to talk about anything. And Rod . . ."

That shit-eating grin is back again.

"Yes, Terry?"

"You *are* going to eat *all* your vegetables, even if I have to feed them to you in little bitty pieces."

If I had to use one word to describe Rod Ramsay at that moment, it would be: bliss—and over vegetables, for God's sake!

I SHOULD BE READY to jump down Moody's throat by the time we get up to the room—somehow the words "I will take the lead" have flown completely over her head. If she'd screwed up the room-entry sequence, I definitely would have demanded that Koerner take her off the case. But she lines up just as we'd rehearsed and pauses once we're inside as if looking around for her purse (it's over her shoulder), until Rod is in place, before taking her own seat. Her eyes, I note, are a good two inches above Ramsay's—just right—and she's sitting up straight, while Rod is kicking his shoes off and settling into his corner of the couch. (If I hadn't insisted the coffee table be where it is, his feet would be on it right now.)

Also, I have to concede that dinner first might not have been an awful idea. I was planning on ordering burgers and fries up to the room if Rod was being at all forthcoming, but dinner downstairs gave him some unpressured face time with Moody, and she made the most of it, including cajoling him into ordering a salad, even one with a healthy dressing—"No, Rod, oil and vinegar; it's better for you than all that gooey French stuff"—and then, amazingly, getting him to choke it all down. By the time we get up to Room 316 and Rod lights his first cigarette of the evening, he looks genuinely content. Moody, I notice, is about to take issue with his smoking, but I jump in before she can get started. We don't want to be altering too many bad habits at one time.

"Rod," I say, "I know you and I have been over this Germany stuff before."

"You and I and Lynn," he corrects me, with a what-are-we-going-to-do-about-him look at Moody.

"Yes, of course, Lynn, too. But Agent Moody—"

"Terry?"

"Right, Terry, is new to the case—"

"Obviously."

"Yes, obviously," I concede with as much grace as I can muster, because I suddenly have an urge to toss Rod off a third-floor balcony. "And since you're in a humoring mood, perhaps you would humor me by giving Agent Moody—"

"Uh—"

"Terry, that is. Perhaps you would be kind enough to give *Terry* a quick rundown on your relationship with Clyde, how things worked in Germany, all that, just so she's up to speed."

"Why, of course!" Rod answers, beaming Moody's way. "I would be glad to." And with that he lights another cigarette, stretches his stocking feet and legs out on the couch, and launches into a mono- logue notable for its detail, depth, breadth, and preening narcissism— which in some ways is Rod Ramsay to a tee.

Rod begins by telling Moody how Conrad had been a mentor to him, a father figure. With an offhand gesture, he dismisses his own father as "someone I never really knew . . . a man I couldn't talk with." Clyde, he says, was different. The two worked "elbow to elbow all day long," sharing responsibilities. They even spent their time off together. In fact, Rod says, he'd often go to Conrad's house to have dinner or snacks with the family.

I heard some of this last year, of course, when Lynn and I were getting to know Rod, but now I'm wearing my prosecutor's hat along with my investigator's one, and Rod basically is doing our job for us. Frequency and duration of contact often define relationships. Rod is handing us that. Prosecutions also are a form of narrative: Eventually, if this goes where I think it's headed, we'll need to tell the jury a convincing story of how Ramsay came to commit espionage. As Rod expounds, he's unconsciously, or maybe *consciously*—you never know with him—filling in plot, character, and context. The little Bic pen in my brain is scribbling notes like mad.

Without any prodding from me, Rod moves next to exactly where

I hoped he'd go: what it was like to work with Conrad in the G-3 Plans Section and what their responsibilities entailed. The officers, he says, were all "short-timers." Clyde was the steady (if thieving) rock in Documents, well respected by the brass who relied on his knowledge of war plans to assist them in their own work. I've heard this before, too, but repetition is a form of confirmation, and as Rod talks, he begins to reveal both his own intimate familiarity with the war plans that passed through his Documents section and what seems to be an encyclopedic capacity to retain that information.

Moody seems to have processed my earlier messages better than I thought. She's looking devotedly on, eye-locked with Rod, which leaves me free to study Ramsay's body language for signs of emphasis, something liars never get right. The arching of the eyebrows, the way thumbs pop up from interlaced fingers, a subtle knee raise—these are all gravity-defying behaviors that we tend to use only when we're confident about what we're saying, and even sociopaths are most confident when they're telling the truth.

At this point, with everything happening so fast, I'm not sure even Moody is fully aware of where we're headed. She's looking so raptly at Rod as he lectures that I find myself worried that this isn't artifice, that in a matter of hours she's become a Ramsay acolyte, just what I don't need. Maybe Moody senses what I'm thinking as well because out of the blue she stirs herself, smiles warmly at Rod, and interjects herself gently into his torrent of words.

"But, Rod," she says, "you seem to know so much about these— what are they?—G-3 Plans. I thought you and Clyde were just the custodians, the ones who kept them safe and secure."

"Well," he says, "we did, of course. But we also copied them on request."

"Copied? But how does that explain it? I mean, didn't you just see the text for an instant?"

"I read fast," Rod says with unapologetic pride.

"But how much can you retain?"

"I retain everything."

"Well, for heaven's sake," Moody says, and I have to agree with her. It's one thing to copy or photograph a document and pass it on to a hostile intelligence service, but it's another to have what Rod seems to be claiming: a photographic memory. Copies get passed along, however obtained. But with a photographic memory, you're the copy, an infinitely more dangerous and threatening situation. Now you can travel overseas and say, "Hi, folks, here I am. Turn on your tape recorders, fill up my Swiss bank account, and I'll do a data dump that will blow your fucking mind."

Do I necessarily believe everything Rod is saying? No, of course not—but the only way to validate it in the short term is to balance it with his body language, and that measure is working right now in truth's favor. In the end, though, everything must be corroborated.

Frankly, I'm not even certain there *is* such thing as a "photographic memory." Maybe it's one of those myths we keep telling ourselves because we want it to be true—like "the Sasquatch." But I do know that for a guy with so little formal education, Rod clearly knows one hell of a lot and has the vocabulary to go along with it. And as I've now witnessed twice before, with two different partners, he loves to hold court, and the more beautiful the audience, the heavier he pours it on. Witness: now.

Rod has segued, fairly gracefully I have to admit, from G-3 Plans to the larger history—the *very* larger history—of military planning generally. Thucydides and Sun Tzu have already rolled off his tongue. Hannibal snuck in there, too—"Elephants!" Moody piped up. "Only *part* of the story," Rod answered, "and de minimis, at that." Clausewitz, Rod hardly paused at. "So conventional warfare!" Instead, he has moved on to Caesar's *Gallic Commentaries*.

"All Gaul," he says majestically, "is divided into three parts."

"Really?" Moody replies, but there's something a little off about her tone of voice. Rod hasn't noticed; he's too busy being professorial. But I have—she wants me back in the game.

"See what I mean?" I interrupt. "Rod should be teaching at the university level." Rod smiles indulgently at me, as if I've laid a tribute at his feet. Moody seems grateful as well—probably from my having saved her from having to write up everything he might have said about Gallic history. I have another motive for jumping in, though. We've been at this for two hours, and Rod frankly looks a little squirmy in his seat.

"Would you like a bathroom break?" I ask. "It's just over there before the bedroom on your left." I'm pointing with my palm in the vertical position like a traffic cop, making sure he follows my directions.

"Well," Rod says, "since you mention it . . ." But his feet have already started following my hand signal toward the bathroom. Subconsciously, Rod is taking my lead.

MOODY WAITS UNTIL WE hear the click of the bathroom lock before mouthing me a word: "Interesting." In return, I quickly pantomime climbing a ladder, and she nods in agreement. This is something else we'd talked about on the way to Orlando. Rod, I said, was going to be most comfortable talking about topics that really didn't threaten him. That's only natural, and everything to date falls into that category. We can use all this stuff about Conrad and reading the documents the two of them had copied as telling background in preparing a court case. Even his boasting will help demonstrate (a) that he has accurate recall and (b) that he presents a clear and present danger to the security of the United States. But at some point, I told Moody, we're going to have to vector closer to the real issue at hand—i.e., Title 18 United States Code Section 794, aka the espionage statute. And that time, I now silently indicate by pointing to my wristwatch, is now.

Moody is nodding in agreement as Rod clicks open the bathroom door and theatrically reassumes his place on the couch and his devoted attention to Agent Moody. I've been standing by the window as he does this, seemingly studying some commotion in the parking lot below but in reality waiting for him to sit before I resume my own seat. I've just settled back in my chair and swiveled toward Ramsay when Moody picks up the cue.

"Rod," she says gently, "I think Agent Navarro has something to say."

"Yes?" Rod says, turning to me and wary for the first time this evening that I've noticed.

"The last thing I want to do, Rod, is embarrass you, but in preparing for this interview, Agent Moody—"

He starts to correct me, but doesn't.

"Agent Moody noticed on your military record that you had been discharged for cause. Could you explain that to her? I'm sure you can do a better job of it than I could."

I can see the relief flooding over Rod as I finish.

"Oh," he says, filled once again with bonhomie and the milk of human kindness, "the piss test! Well . . ."

And we're off again on a rollicking, Rod-centric tour of drugs, sex, rock 'n' roll, and petty black-market swindling Eighth Army Infantry Division–style à la HQ Bad Kreuznach, Republic of West Germany, etc. By now, I've heard this often enough to put my mind on cruise control.

Listening with maybe half an ear, I'm still astonished to hear Rod speak of drug abuse as if he's talking about having a glass of milk. Here, I keep telling myself, was a guy with top-secret clearance—the same access to classified information that most of the NATO military commanders had. What in the hell is going on? I keep thinking. This whole saga is a case study in the damage a really smart person can do to critical organizational structures, but the problem is we aren't sitting in some business-school classroom, chatting about possibilities. We're in an Embassy Suites suite and Exhibit A is sitting across from me, with his fucking stocking feet once again spread out on the couch.

Moody, meanwhile, is playing my perfect foil . . . or maybe "playing" isn't the right word. Maybe she's just doing what mothers do with wayward offspring. "Weren't you concerned about getting caught?" she keeps asking. Or "Rod, you didn't actually do that, did you?" To the average person, this might sound like maternal banalities, but in fact, Moody (I realize reluctantly) is helping to establish that Rod didn't give a damn about rules or laws. For him, these indiscretions were points of pride, not an embarrassment. Like any good predator, he was happy to be working a target-rich environment.

So am I, frankly, but time is short, so after another minute or two of Rod's blather, I decide to cut to the chase.

"Rod," I say, "Agent Moody and I, INSCOM, the FBI, Al Eways, you name it—we all thank you for your cooperation, but you and I and Agent . . . Terry . . . simply can't ignore that ABC broadcast of four days ago. Your mother saw it. I'm sure you saw it. [Rod nods yes as I'm speaking.] Agent Moody saw it. [She nods yes, too.] Hell, most of Washington, DC, saw it."

"The computer chips?" Rod asks as he swings his feet back on the floor and shakes another Camel Filter out of his pack.

"Yes, Rod," I say, wheeling my swivel chair toward him and leaning in from his right, opposite Moody's angle. "The computer chips. I keep going back over this in my mind. I might not have the wording exactly right, but it went something very close to 'ABC News has learned that one of Conrad's recruits continued to work for Conrad back in the United States, illegally exporting hundreds of thousands of advanced computer chips through a dummy company in Canada to the Eastern Bloc. According to the man himself, who asked not to be identified, Conrad paid him to make the purchases.'"

"Actually," Rod says, "that would be exactly the right wording. I'm impressed."

"Thank you, but what gets me is that the only person I can think of who could possibly have been ABC's source for this would have to be . . ." I pause to let him fill in the blank.

"Me?"

"You, Rod?" Moody chimes in, just when a little sympathy seems due. "But why would you . . . ?"

"That producer, Jim Bamford, he kept bothering my mother. She was getting very upset. I thought if I just gave him this one little story, some bullshit, he would go away."

That much, at least, even I can sympathize with. Dorothy of course already gave me a fill on how upset she was, but neither she nor Rod had any idea that someone at HQ was clearly channeling sensitive information to Bamford, filling in the bigger background, of which the computer chips were just a small part.

"Besides," Rod goes, "it was just a hypothetical."

The last place I want to go right now is Hypothetical World, but Rod seems ready to open up, and if what-ifs help him get there, I'll play the game.

"Hypothetical? What do you mean?"

"Well," Rod says, "I mean it's not a crime to just talk about doing something, is it? Terry?"

Moody, though, knows better than to get involved in this. She simply nods silently my way.

"Joe?"

"I'm afraid you're going to have to get a little more specific, Rod. We're talking a lot of variables here."

"For example," he says, "what if, hypothetically, two guys in a foreign country were to discuss buying computer chips and selling them to another country. Could they be prosecuted?"

My turn: "Are the two hypothetical individuals in this foreign country American citizens?"

Rod: "Perhaps. Does it matter?"

Me: "It may, depending on a few other things."

"Like what?"

"Well, are they just talking about it or do they intend to do something in furtherance of that?"

"Hypothetically [air quotes], it was just talk."

"Hypothetically [my air quotes], would they have been violating the law to do so?"

"Hypothetically, yes, I suppose," Rod says with that impish smile he can't keep off his face when he talks about his own wrongdoing. "But remember, this was just a hypothetical conversation about hypothetical computer chips."

Moody: "Hypothetically, I'm getting a little lost here."

Rod and me: "Ha! Ha!"

And then it's my turn again: "So hypothetically [more air quotes], nothing was ever bought in the United States with the intention of selling it to an embargoed country, correct?"

"Hypothetically, no," Rod says with great satisfaction, but in fact we are tiptoeing through a very dangerous legal minefield.

The truth of the matter is that conspiracies can be prosecuted if any party takes a step in furtherance of a crime, whether the actual crime is committed or not. To meet the prosecutorial threshold, all the parties have to do is agree on the crime to be committed and how to carry it out. But if I tell Rod that, he's going to crawl back into his shell just as he's beginning to emerge from it. On the other hand, if I assure him that he can't be prosecuted, which is what he clearly wants to hear, I'll be issuing, in effect, a prosecutorial waiver, which I have neither the right nor the standing to do. In the end, I opt for what I hope is a middle ground more likely to satisfy the needs of the moment than Koerner's review the next morning.

"Well, Rod," I say, "I'm not an attorney, but I don't see how anyone could be hypothetically prosecuted if nothing was purchased or transmitted to an embargoed country."

Ramsay takes this in quietly, so I jump in again.

"Look," I say, "hypothetically, one of the individuals involved would have to testify against the other or have a recording of their conversation, and someone would actually have to go out and at least buy the computer chips with the intention of selling them or transmitting them to an embargoed country. According to ABC News, they were only going to."

An even longer pause this time—so long that even Moody begins to look uncomfortable—but finally Rod decides to reenter the world.

"I will tell you about the computer chips," he says, "if it's absolutely true that I can't be arrested for just talking about it."

By now, this whole hypothetical back-and-forth has consumed more than thirty tortured minutes. For me, that's more than enough time.

"Rod," I say, "the only absolutes in life are death and taxes. For crissake, just tell us what happened. No more hypotheticals—let's deal in reality because my head is spinning. My boss needs to know if something really did take place and computer chips were sold to the Warsaw Pact. So please," I say, leaning in, my palms up in supplication.

"But first," I say, rolling my chair back until I'm next to the coffee table and sliding the top off the small cooler we've had sitting there all along, "how about something to drink? Why don't you help yourself?"

ROD'S FIRST PULL FROM the Pepsi bottle goes poorly, probably because his throat is tight with nerves and tension. He tilts the bottle back too far, sends half the drink down his windpipe and the other half up his nose, and the next thing I know he's coughing like a madman and wiping snot away with his hand. Moody, thank God, is on top of him in seconds, pulling a wad of tissues out of her purse, dabbing at the spill on his shirt collar, and rapping him gently between his shoulder blades. Watching her, I'm struck by how few times I've even been around to wipe my little girl's nose and comfort her coughs.

Rod is just getting his composure back when Moody returns from the bathroom with a moistened towel for cleaning his hands and a glass. She's pouring the rest of the Pepsi into the tumbler—"a little easier to drink from," she explains—as Rod launches into his story.

The first mention of computer chips, he says, came when Conrad stopped by Boston in 1986, on his way to Ohio (or wherever he was really going).

"So it *wasn't* just a social call?" I ask.

Rod shakes his head and looks down, seemingly embarrassed. "No, it was more. I wasn't really working much then, and Clyde thought it could be a way for both of us to make some serious money."

"Give us some details, Rod. Moody and I need to understand this."

"Well," he says, settling into his professorial mode, "there are computer chips and there are *computer* chips. The more advanced ones were embargoed from sale to the Soviet Union and Soviet Bloc countries. If we could obtain these in large numbers, Clyde said, he could think of a country that might buy them from us for somewhere in the seven-figures range."

As he says this, Rod raises his eyes at both of us, to let us know what a viable and clever idea this was—never mind, of course, the various illegalities involved. Those are never high on Ramsay's priority list.

"What country might that have been, Rod?" I ask.

"Not the Soviets," he answers. "They play rough. Maybe someone more like the Hungarians. They're a lot more civilized."

And exactly how would you know all that? I'm wondering, but I simply say, "I guess that would be my choice also. Hungary, after all, would be easy to access through a third country such as Austria."

At this, Ramsay's face positively lights up with joy that I'm getting the efficacy of picking a country like Hungary. Maybe he's thinking that I'm not so dumb after all. More likely, he's thinking what a first-rate person he is to be able to explain these things so well.

"So what happened?" I ask, ready to bring this evening to a close.

"Nothing."

"Nothing, Rod?"

"Turns out," he says, "this was a lot tougher to do than you might think. One computer chip would have been a snap, even a dozen or two. The advanced ones are about half the size of a credit card. You could hide them inside a stuffed animal and take them anywhere you wanted to. But hundreds? Now you've got to deal with a lot of questions from the retailer about who you are and why you need so many. What is your company name? Where are you registered? What's your tax ID number? Do you intend to use these abroad? All that is pain in the ass enough without the packaging issues and significant up-front costs."

"And, Rod, just to put a lid on the evening, how do you come to know so much about this?"

"I know this because I, hypothetically [air quote, air quote, air quote], looked into it."

"So ABC News got it wrong?"

"It never took place. It just couldn't be done."

"Well," I say with a big sigh, meant to push the burden back on Koerner again, "I'm sure glad to hear this. I was worried that something was afoot that we had to investigate. Our boss is going to be relieved to hear it was all talk and bullshit."

"And you, Terry?" Ramsay asks, turning her way.

"Oh, Rod," she says, "I never doubted you for a moment."

What a beautiful answer, I tell myself, without, of course, giving it away.

ROD, I'M GUESSING, IS back in his camper, snuggled beside his lover [air quotes] with visions of Agent Moody dancing in his head, by the time we get the furniture moved back in place.

I'm already thinking of how Shirley the Office Scold will question why I have to do these interviews in a hotel room when, as she so often says, "the office interview room is absolutely free. Why do you have to keep interviewing people at the Waldorf-Astoria?" As if the Embassy Suites were the Waldorf-Anything. I could cite for Shirley plenty of evidence that Bureau offices have a chilling effect and are far more likely to drive a suspect into the arms of an attorney, but I'm reminded of Mark Twain's wisdom at times such as this: "Don't try to teach a pig to sing. It annoys the pig, and it wastes your time."

Moody snaps me out of my reverie as we're waiting for the elevator.

"What do you think, Navarro?"

"About what?"

"What else? About how it went."

Three fingers immediately pop up.

"Yes and . . . ?" Moody asks just as two tourists in Panama Jack floral prints walk by with ice buckets in hand, headed for the ice machine around the corner from the elevator bank. I wait to answer until the elevator doors slide open and the ice cubes around the corner begin clattering on plastic.

"One, we've garnered a huge conspiratorial admission. Ramsay basically told us that he and Conrad were very comfortable with each other talking about things that could potentially break laws and get them prosecuted. And what's more, they were both willing to do these things. We also learned that either Ramsay or Conrad had a means to get the computer chips into the hands of a buyer from an embargoed country. That kind of connection just doesn't appear in the phone book; most likely someone already existed who could facilitate this."

"Ditto. I thought the same thing. Two?"

"Two, my ass is going to get raked over the coals tomorrow."

"For the hypothetical prosecutorial stuff?"

"You noticed that, too?"

"I wasn't sure where you were headed, or where he was headed, but I think you're right. This is going to be an issue of clarity, but—"

"But?"

"For the record I'm on your side on this one. I don't think you overstepped any bright lines, and I do know that we wouldn't have learned what we did if you hadn't taken the risk. He asked and you tried to answer, and you did preface it by saying you weren't an attorney."

"Thanks. I appreciate that." I'm incredibly glad I threw in that bit about not being an attorney—hopefully, that will save me. I'm also more and more impressed with Moody's performance tonight.

"And three?"

"Three, we're just scratching the surface with this little shit. He has tons more to tell us, and I think he's ready to—"

"Unburden himself?"

"Maybe that," I say.

"And maybe what else?"

"Impress you even more."

We've crossed the parking lot by now and are just pulling out on International Drive when I feel the need for a little unburdening of my own.

"Point Four."

"Four?" Moody says, with what might be mock surprise. "There's still more?"

"Yes, Point Four. You were right. There's nothing in the FBI manual that says I have to be an asshole."

"All of the time?"

"That's right," I say, "all the time."

"Well," Moody says, leaning back into her seat and clasping her hands under her slightly swelling belly, "that's a Big Friggin' Relief."

11

SMARTEST GUY
IN THE ROOM

November 6, 1989

Jay Koerner takes my accidental venture into the prosecutorial waiver minefield much better than I expected, which is to say he doesn't come flying over his desk at me with both fists pounding. He has every reason to be upset, but he also knows that this is for the legal minds to sort out now. Moody is in his office with me when I break the news, and Jay is old-fashioned enough that he likes to play the gentleman when a lady is around. Besides, Moody has done a damn good job of standing up for me when she could have left me twisting in the wind.

"It was all hypotheticals," she keeps reminding Koerner. "Nothing specific was ever promised. Joe was answering his questions as they were asked, and he did throw in that caveat about not being an attorney."

I'm grateful for her support. And as I look at my other fellow agents trickling in before the 8 a.m. start of the day, I'm having trouble picking out many others who would go to bat for me in a situation like this. In the end we all agree on a game plan. We'll go ahead with this evening's interview as scheduled. I'll keep my big yap shut if any more hypotheticals are thrown at me or if the subject of prosecutorial anything comes up again—She-Moody looks absolutely giddy at the prospect of enforcing this stricture—and tomorrow morning I'll go see my pal Greg Kehoe, the first assistant at the United States Attorney's Office in the Middle District of Florida. Greg will be prosecuting the Ramsay case if and when it comes to that—"as now it likely will," Koerner reminds us, "if Agent Navarro hasn't fucked the whole business to high heaven—with apologies," he adds, with a penitent look toward the demure Mrs. Moody.

Now Moody and I are seated at the far left end of the counter at the Zack Street Sandwich Shop a short block from the Bureau office. Fact is, I don't like the place. It's filled with fellow agents, for obvious reasons, and the only one who seems entirely comfortable with seeing Moody and me huddled together is the other Terry Moody— He-Moody—who waves cheerfully from a booth all the way at the back of the room, where he is holding court with his white-collar-crime buddies. Almost worse, the coffee is unforgivably watery. I've been trying to talk She-Moody into doing these morning briefings at Perrera's, but she claims the Cuban coffee there is so strong that her unborn baby will be kicking all day long and probably grow up with three different kinds of attention deficit disorders.

"Nonsense," I tell her. "Cubans are the most laid back, mañana, no problema, take-it-as-it-comes, play-it-as-it-lays people on the face of the Earth."

"Like Fidel during one of his four-hour speeches?" she says.

"The exception that proves the rule."

"How about Ricky Ricardo?"

"Ohhh, that's low, Moody—even for a first-office agent."

"What about you, Navarro?" she asks with a big grin, knowing she's getting under my skin.

"I'm laid back. Haven't you noticed?"

"The only thing laid back about you is that photo in your office." She doesn't have to say which one. It's the only photo there: My daughter is eighteen months old, fresh out of the pool. I'm reclined, holding her to my chest underneath a beach towel. I keep it on my desktop. "Everything else about you is a tempest, Navarro, and I'm being kind because I'm in a maternal mood."

"Really, I don't see myself that way."

"That's because mirrors don't stand up to hurricane-force winds."

"Noted. Can we talk about something serious?"

"I thought we just were."

"Something serious that *I* want to talk about. Something serious about the *case*."

The words are out of my mouth before I can even think about them, and for a moment there's a look of such pity on Moody's face that I want to take them all back.

"Okay, Joe," she says after a long pause, her voice somewhere between resignation and curiosity. "What's this serious thing *you* want to talk about? This serious thing about the *case*?"

"The language of interviewing. The words we're going to use and not use this evening."

"Ah," she says with what sounds almost like relish, and I think she really means it. I'm not much for socializing with my colleagues— that much is obvious, I guess—but I can mentor all day long, and Moody seems willing to hear what I have to teach. She's like Lynn in that regard. She knows she has a lot to learn in a Bureau that is mostly male and still very biased against women, and I'm sure she feels she has to work harder than her male colleagues just to prove herself. Not with me, though. Most of my Bureau partners have been women, and none has let me down, and I don't expect Terry to be the first.

"Espionage," I say.

"Espionage?"

"That's a word neither of us is going to utter at any point when we're talking with Ramsay for as long as we're interviewing him."

"Why?" she says, but not in a challenging voice. "If I'm interviewing a suspected bank robber, at some point I've got to raise the fact that a bank was robbed, that money was taken. Same thing with a murder or any crime."

"This is different," I tell her as our waitress, Linda, done up today in a lopsided hairnet, slops down a plate of eggs sunny-side-up and four halves of pre-buttered whole-wheat toast that already look cold and defeated. "With a bank robbery, solving who did it and getting a confession—or at least enough probable evidence to build a case— is the whole point. Same thing with murder: You find the body or enough forensic evidence to identify the body as well as the manner and means of death. You create a defensible link between the suspect, how the crime was committed, and the victim, and you file the charges.

"With espionage, the crime in a sense is only the threshold of what we're after. Even if we can establish beyond a reasonable doubt that espionage was committed in this instance, we're never going to recover what Conrad and Ramsay, if he was involved, sold to the Hungarians or the Soviets. There's no putrefying body, probably no bag of hundred-dollar bills hidden behind some false wall either. In-stead, there are secrets, some highly classified, circulating among our enemies, and until we know what those secrets are—what was copied and stolen and sold—we have no way of knowing how badly our national security or the security of our allies has been compromised."

"And this has exactly what to do with uttering the word 'espio-nage'?" Moody, I notice, hasn't yet touched her fruit and yogurt. My eggs, meanwhile, are starting to look petrified.

"And," I go on, "it has to do with the fact that the very first time we name the actual crime he has committed and force him to confront at a conscious level the judicial shitstorm that lies ahead of him, including always the perceived possibility of execution (see Rosen-bergs), Rod Ramsay will call an attorney or otherwise clam up, and we'll never know just how much damage he and Conrad have done."

With that, Moody signals the waitress for a fresh cup of tea and dives into her expectant-mother breakfast special while I nibble warily on one of my toast halves. I'm just thinking that maybe I've overdone it again when my partner finishes off her last strawberry, gives the tea bag a slight squeeze against her spoon, and turns my way with a let's-get-down-to-business look that's about all a mentor could ask for.

"So, how are we going to play this?" she asks.

"We're going to walk him right up the ladder again—past where we got to yesterday, until he tells us that he committed espionage without any of us saying the word and how he committed it and with whom, and then the son of a bitch is going to start telling us what he stole in infinite detail."

"And how, Agent Navarro," Moody asks with a wry grin, "are we going to accomplish all these wondrous things?"

"By making Rod feel just like what he certainly will be—the smartest guy in the room."

WE MEET ROD AT the same place we did the previous evening, but this time with advance notice. Rod's admission that he and Conrad had at least talked about conspiring to sell sophisticated computer chips to a foreign power has given me enough oomph to call in minimal surveillance. I have a guy waiting in the Embassy Suites parking lot, armed with Rod's photo and a description of the rust-crusted Dodge Aries he drives when he's not behind the wheel of a spanking-clean Yellow Cab. I don't think Rod is a risk to bolt at this point—and one guy on surveillance couldn't prevent that, at any rate—but I do want to know where our suspect goes when he leaves us at night. Back to the camper to endure more humiliation? Someplace to load up on his beloved cannabis? Or maybe he still has some kind of foreign minder hanging around—although if so, there is no apparent financial benefit of the arrangement accruing to Ramsay's lifestyle. Also, it's just really nice to know when someone you're waiting for is only steps away from the lobby entrance, and two beeps on my pager takes care of that.

Also like last evening, Moody is immediately concerned about someone's weight, diet, and health, but to my great surprise, it's me, not Rod, that she's focusing on.

"Do you see what I see?" she says to Rod, holding him by the elbow.

"Of course," he answers, with no idea of what she's talking about but pleased as punch to be in the hands of a take-charge woman.

"When did you first meet Agent Navarro—a year ago?"

"More than fourteen months ago," Rod corrects, "with Agent Eways."

"Right," Moody goes on, not skipping a beat, "and how much would you estimate he weighed then, compared to now?"

They're both looking me over top to bottom now, like maybe I'm a side of beef hanging from a slaughterhouse hook.

"I would say fifteen more pounds at least," Rod ventures. "He's wasting away."

"Exactly," Moody says, with a radiant smile his way. "And what do we do with people who *haven't* been eating carefully?"

"We buy them a big dinner . . ."

"And?"

"And we make them eat their salad."

"Even if . . ."

"Even if we have to sit there all night long and feed them leaf by leaf."

And thus, fifteen minutes later, at the same table where we sat last evening, I'm tucking into a twenty-eight-ounce medium-rare Porterhouse, baked potato (without the sour cream), and a salad so lightly coated with oil and balsamic vinegar that a rabbit would feel right at home at our table. But Rod, I notice, is eating exactly the same thing, this time without any encouragement from Mother Moody.

This woman is good, I'm thinking, and maybe right, too. I'm not a clothes horse, but I try to be a neat dresser, and things have been hanging a little loose off me of late. Fact is, I'm running out of holes on my belt to tighten it around what is no longer a size 34 waist. For whatever reason, those two eggs and three toast halves I left on my breakfast platter this morning are how too many of my meals end up of late, half or more uneaten while my brain races ahead to the next day's work, chasing the clock while my body tugs the other way, crying out for more sleep.

WE'RE IN SUITE 416 this time, not the floor directly below, but otherwise things are identical. Moody and I have relocated the couch, her easy chair, the coffee table, the end tables and lamps to where they were when the three of us first walked into the room last evening (and this time without our little contretemps about the coffee table), and I've got what seems to be the same rolling swivel chair waiting in the center of the room.

Showtime, I'm thinking, when Rod nervously shakes a cigarette out of his pack, lights up, and throws us an opening chin-high fastball.

"Oh, by the way," he says, anything but casually, "I got a call from Bamford again."

"Did you talk to him?"

"No," he says, but so unconvincingly that Moody calls him on it. "Roddd . . . ?"

"Well," inhaling deeply now, "a little, maybe."

"Is that like being a little pregnant?" I ask, which causes both of us males in the room to take a quick glance at Moody's belly.

"But I didn't tell him anything," Rod insists, in the same voice a four-year-old would use in insisting that he had nothing to do with the vase smashed on the floor by his feet.

"Just let me ask you one thing, Rod," I say. "Then we'll drop the subject. Did you tell him you were talking with us, with Moody and me?"

"Well," he answers, "I couldn't lie."

Jesus, Rod, I want to scream, lying is what you do best—lying and cheating and stealing state secrets and doing dope and getting your pathetic butt cuckolded night after night in that sorry-ass camper parked off somewhere near the edge of the world. Instead, I draw a deep breath, count to five as I've trained myself to do in these circumstances (not always successfully), and say in as calm a voice as I can muster:

"Rod, don't complicate my life. Just don't. Okay?" Then I think to add, "Don't complicate Mrs. Moody's either."

And maybe it's the She-Moody part that does the trick, because I seem to see a look of resolve on Rod's face.

"I won't," he says, smiling apologetically both our ways. "I definitely won't." But of course how the hell do you trust a liar?

But time to move on—in fact, past time. If Bamford is still calling, ABC News is still interested, which means we've got to get the case against Rod Ramsay signed, sealed, and delivered before Rod once again finds himself starring in the nightly news.

"Rod," I say, getting back to where I intended to start this evening, "you were very helpful and up-front with us yesterday about Clyde and the computer chips. We really appreciate that, and I can tell you our boss appreciates it, too."

He smiles appreciatively.

"But we're still trying to help the Germans round out their understanding of Clyde—what motivated him, all that stuff. And now they're asking us if you could provide some insight on Conrad and money."

"Meaning?"

"Well, for example, gold. There's has been some indication, the Germans say, that Clyde was heavily into gold coins."

"With good cause," Rod says, settling into the subject and glad (as I knew he would be) to talk about anything other than himself. "Clyde never had *any problems* with money. In fact, we were at his house in Bosenheim one afternoon when he showed me this big box, and I mean *big*, stuffed with a huge collection of gold coins."

"How many?"

"Who knows," Rod says, "but he had gold coins from all around the world, especially South African Krugerrands. He kept them in that box the way most people keep loose change around for the parking meter."

"Did Clyde put any figure on the total value of the coins in that box?" I ask.

"No," Rod answers in a hurry, "but it had to be somewhere in the tens of thousands of dollars, and that wasn't his only box."

"It wasn't?"

"No, of course not. Listen, I don't mean to be rude, but you and Terry are government workers, probably living paycheck to paycheck." As if he isn't, I'm thinking, as he looks at us both with pity. "Clyde didn't think the way you do. He wanted currency that held its value through good times and bad and could be converted anywhere."

"Why?" Moody asks, in her best schoolgirl voice.

"He always thought about the future and where he might end up, and he was careful to bury the money just in case."

"In case of what?" I ask, trying to hold back my desperation to know. "Why would he do that? Bury the money? I mean, who does that?"

"Because," Rod answers gleefully, "he was hiding the fact that he was making money on the side. Clyde *always* planned carefully."

The side money we already knew about, of course, but Conrad's black market deals weren't bringing in so much side money that he had to bury Krugerrands in the backyard. This revelation is definitely moving us to a higher plane. I can see Moody itching to plead a pregnant woman's pinched bladder and rush off to the bathroom to scrawl notes, but I'm not quite ready to let her go yet, and I don't think Rod is either.

"Tell me, Rod," I say, not so much switching the subject as bending it. "All this stuff about burying gold coins—Clyde was no dummy, obviously."

"Spot on, Agent Navarro," with a ha-ha look toward Moody.

"In fact, it's pretty obvious," I say, "that Clyde was preparing for the future. [Emphatic nod yes.] He was lining other people up as well, wasn't he? People to help him. Maybe people to carry on his business [air quotes] in case he had to dig up all those gold coins and skedaddle out of the country, right? [Double nod yes-yes.] But it couldn't be just anyone, could it?"

Moody, for Ramsay and right on cue: "Well, of course it couldn't!" to which Rod again nods yes.

Me: "It had to be someone he trusted, someone who was really smart, someone who wasn't scared to push the envelope, someone as smart as Clyde himself."

Rod: "That would make perfect sense, wouldn't it?"—with emphasis on the word "perfect."

Me: "Sure, and pretty much everybody I've ever heard you talk about who was part of Clyde's team—the player-players, I think you once called them [more yes nods]—was shit-for-brains this and shit-for-brains that, Okies and West Virginia trash who had just enough brains to peddle cigarette PX coupons but hardly enough to wipe their own asses. Would that be more or less correct?"

"It wouldn't be incorrect," Rod allows, "to assume that Clyde and I existed on a different intellectual plane than the others who surrounded us."

"Not just existed but *played* on a higher intellectual plane," I reply, to a Ramsay now beaming from ear to ear. Moody is silent, but I can see from the corner of my eye that she's caught where I'm headed with this.

"Let me put it this way," Rod says, his arms spreading further, his fingers widening with confidence as he grips the back of the couch. "Clyde and I had no equals."

"Of course not. Now, again, correct me if I'm wrong," I go on, "but I'm betting that what Clyde was looking for was someone who was not only intelligent and clever but also . . . may I call that person 'entrepreneurial,' too?"

"You may."

"Someone who had the vision and the smarts and cojones to carry on the business in Clyde's absence if it came to that."

This elicits a modest shrug of the shoulders that seems to me to be saying considerably more.

"And, Rod, I got to tell you," I go on, rolling my chair directly in front of him and staring him straight in the eyes, "I see only one person in the Eighth Infantry Mechanized HQ that fulfills that role, and do you think he's in this room?"

Rod's eyes aren't meeting mine, but I see that sheepish grin creeping up his face as Moody leans in from her easy chair.

"So to sum up, Rod, I think that the person I've just been talking about is really . . . *you.*"

Rod is squirming in his seat now, but I can almost see the war going on in his mind—on the one hand the natural defensive instinct to deny what I've just said, on the other the natural desire to be recognized as a clever, intelligent entrepreneur and the worthy partner of, and if necessary successor to, the man he seems to most admire in the whole world, Clyde Conrad. In the end, as I hoped and was almost certain he would, Rod opts to feed the narcissistic beast raging inside.

"Well deduced, Agent Navarro," he says, pulling himself up erect on the couch and finally meeting my eyes. "I was in fact Clyde's right-hand man—his 'other half,' as he once called me."

"I should hope so!" Moody chimes in just as he finishes up. "Clyde Conrad would have been a fool to have picked anyone else."

And as much as I want to stand up and slug Rod for that "well deduced . . . 'other half' " pretentious crap, I also want to hug Moody for realizing we're only at the starting line and striking just the right note to keep our momentum going forward. Instead of doing either, I push my chair back to give Rod some psychological breathing room—a small subconscious reward for his admission—then invite him to take a bathroom break.

"It's that way," I say, pointing with my open hand exactly as I did the day before. I'm the gatekeeper to everything—dinner, cold drinks, even the toilet. For his part, Rod doesn't even question whether he has to go or not. He's on his feet and headed to the bathroom almost before I finish making the offer.

ROD AND I ARE talking—what else?—women when Moody emerges from her own turn in the bathroom and settles back into her easy chair.

"Cold drink?" I ask her, raising my own Coke can her way.

"No thanks," but without suggesting that I include Rod in the offering, as she would have yesterday. For his part, Rod is following the motion of my can with considerable interest. *Earn it, you son of a bitch*, I say to myself as I kick off the second part of our interview with a soft floater to the twenty-yard line.

"Rod, now that we've established that you are *the* [BIG emphasis] expert on Clyde Conrad, tell me, what was he best at?"

"Bullshitting and fooling others," Rod answers, back in his expert mode, "making himself indispensable so that no one would ask questions. Clyde understood human psychology and knew every trick in the book."

Moody: "Like?"

"Like the officers came and went every eighteen months. They were still trying to figure out the game, while Clyde had been there for more than a decade and knew how to game the system. He was always up to something, always scheming, and always in it for himself [said admiringly] but always looking good to the front office."

Me: "Front office? You make it sound like an insurance company."

"Okay, *brass*. Is that better, Agent Navarro?" Another moment when I want to throttle him. "The generals and full birds thought Clyde walked on water. No military exercise could take place without his expertise. He knew the lay of the land. He knew the war plans.

He personally knew each strategic and tactical location, and he knew the towns like the back of his hand. The generals had read about these places or seen them on maps—maps, by the way, that Clyde and I prepared. We actually walked these places and visited them on our terrain treks. Remember, I told you and Lynn about those?"

"I do," I say, aware that I was being put to a test.

"The generals drove around in their black-tinted Fords. Clyde and I walked the roads, the bicycle paths, and the fields. We could tell the generals how wide the roads were, if they were suitable for a main battle tank or if a field was too waterlogged in the spring— invaluable information that most senior officers had no clue about."

"So that was it?" I said, with a touch of disappointment in my voice. "You just walked the roads, in a sense, so the brass wouldn't have to soil their well-polished shoes?"

"No," Rod said. "It was more than that. Lots more."

"You want to enlighten us?"

"We knew more than the roads and all the choke points where troops would get bogged down. Clyde knew all the hotel owners and all the inns, and because he could speak German fluently, he always made sure that officers got the best rooms during training exercises."

"And the quid pro quo?"

"In return, Clyde always got great write-ups from all those same officers who counted on him, his expertise, and his command of the German language. It was a closed approval loop, and he was teaching me how to construct the same thing if"—he paused here, not quite certain where to head next—"if for some reason he could no longer be around or he retired."

"I see," I say, ignoring for a moment the bait he waved under our nose. "So that's the main thing you talked about on these terrain walks?"

"No," he answers. "We talked about lots of things—the lay of the land, the buildings, places to hide, where fuel could be obtained, the choke points, where antennas could be placed, where field artillery would be laid out, where helicopters could land, where we would place the field hospitals."

Moody, more gently: "Anything else?"

Rod, smiling slightly: "Sure. Girls, wines, best cities to visit, what would happen if war really did break out, his family, ways to make money."

"Money"—that's the word I'm waiting for. Moody, too, I realize—after all, her question has led him there.

"Rod," I jump in, "did Clyde ever help you out with money?"

"Sure, he'd buy me dinner, lunch, sometimes maybe a pack of cigarettes or a beer, maybe a bottle of Riesling if he was feeling really generous."

"Anything else?" The same question again from Moody, but this time with a bigger pot sitting on the table.

Rod seems a little hesitant. He stops talking, and his blink rate, which I previously pegged at about twelve times a minute, suddenly triples. Not only that: He's compressing his lips, a sure sign of heavy decision-making, and tugging on his collar, more of the ventilating behavior I saw outside that Tampa home where he was house-sitting when Al Eways and I first called on him.

"Rod," I say after a long pause, "you look like you have something you want to tell us."

Moody, meanwhile, is leaning in once more, with her head canted sideways and a smile on her face that would melt Hitler's heart.

"Rod?" she asks, again stretching out the "o" the way a mother would when asking a child.

Ramsay remains silent for what seems an eternity, so I back slightly off in my chair and look down at his feet to remove any pressure my face might be causing.

"Can I ask a hypothetical?"

"God, no!" I say. "Let's not do that again."

That, at least, is enough to jerk his head up and reestablish eye contact, so I press on with my point.

My Cuban passport photo, taken a few months before I arrived in Miami in 1962. Even at this young age, I was grateful for everything America represented and did for my family. I dedicated myself to repaying this great country that had taken us in as refugees.
Courtesy of the author

THE WHITE HOUSE
WASHINGTON

January 3, 1972

Dear Mr. Navarro:

Recently I had an opportunity to read an account of your alert thinking in apprehending a suspected shoplifter in the store where you were employed. I understand that you were hospitalized as a result of wounds you received when attempting to stop the fleeing suspect.

Your courage and effective assistance in an emergency situation merit the praise and respect of all our fellow Americans. I want you to know of my admiration for your courageous action, and this note comes to you with my warmest good wishes for the years ahead.

Sincerely,

Richard Nixon

Mr. Joe Navarro

A letter from President Nixon, commending me for my help in stopping a robbery. Though the injuries I sustained dashed my dreams of a college football career, eventually other doors opened to me.
Courtesy of the author

A photo from around the same time as the Ramsay case—my SWAT team duties also competed for my limited time
Courtesy of the author

Shaking hands with Vice President Bush in Puerto Rico. He'd come to thank our SWAT team for the takedown of the Machetero terrorist group.
Courtesy of the author

Lynn Tremaine, my first partner in unraveling the mystery that was traitor Rod Ramsay. Although she was relatively new to the job, Lynn showed great instincts for gaining Ramsay's trust.
Courtesy of the author

The photo I kept on my desk of my daughter Stephanie and me
Courtesy of the author

From left to right: Rich Licht, Susan Langford, me, and Terry Moody. Rich, Susan, and especially Terry offered critical help in bringing Ramsay to justice.
Courtesy of the author

Terry Moody and me. Her brilliant tradecraft and striking good looks made her the ideal partner as we sought to get Ramsay to lower his guard and spill his secrets.
Courtesy of the author

From left to right: Marc Reeser, Ihor O. E. Kotlarchuk, me, and Jane Hein—more proof that it takes a team, especially in the business of counterespionage   *Courtesy of the author*

A close up of Zoltan Szabo while he was still in the US Army. Szabo was the first to betray his country, followed by Conrad, then Ramsay—three generations of traitors. *Courtesy of the author*

Roderick James Ramsay's passport photo *Courtesy of the author*

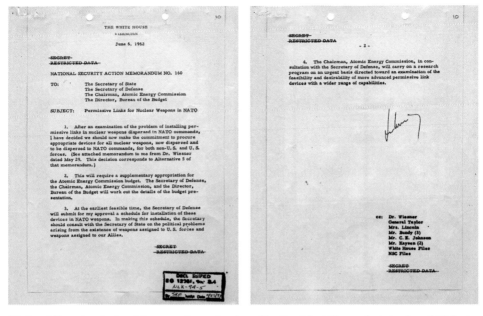

National Security Action Memorandum 160, signed by President Kennedy, introduced PALs to all US nuclear weapons under NATO command. In the wrong hands, these "permissive action links" could be devastating to America's nuclear strategy, and it was Ramsay's hands they fell into. *Courtesy of the John F. Kennedy Presidential Library and Museum*

Ramsay standing by his cab at the Orlando International Airport, taken from FBI surveillance footage *Courtesy of the author*

A photo of the "secret apartment" in Bad Kreuznach, Josef Schneider Plaza #4. It was here that Ramsay and his confederate Clyde Lee Conrad sorted through their voluminous and unprecedented haul of stolen secrets and prepared them for transmittal to the Soviet Bloc. *Courtesy of the author*

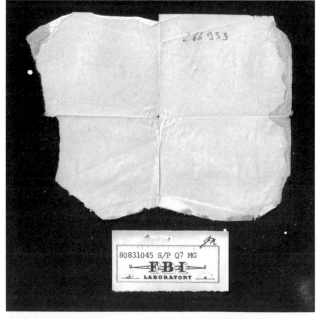

A cowbell used as a recognition signal by the co-conspirators *Courtesy of the author*

The "hello" number for Hungarian Intelligence was written on a piece of water-soluble paper. The discovery of its significance was the first important sign that my suspicions regarding Ramsay were correct. *Courtesy of the author*

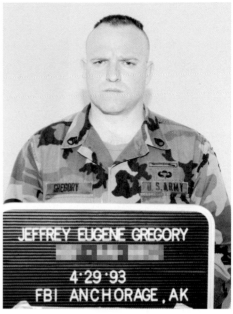

The arrest photo of Jeffrey Stephen Rondeau
Courtesy of the author

The arrest photo of Jeffery Eugene Gregory
Courtesy of the author

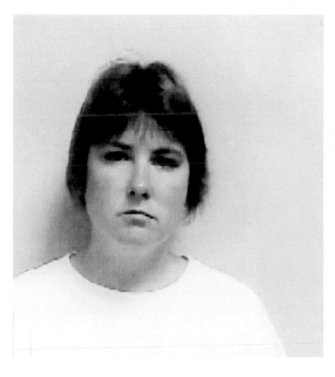

The arrest photo of Kelley
Therese Church, née Warren
Courtesy of the author

SANDOR KERCSIK

IMRE KERCSIK

Sandor and Imre Kercsik, Hungarian-born Swedish physicians, who served as couriers for the spy ring *Courtesy of the author*

Clyde Lee Conrad sitting just a few feet away from me at his trial in Koblenz
Courtesy of the author

Greg Kehoe, the prosecutor whose fierce determination to bring Ramsay to trial cowed a stuck-in-the-mud Washington bureaucracy and redeemed the two years I'd spent exhaustively coaxing from Ramsay chilling disclosures of wrongdoing
Courtesy of Gregory W. Kehoe, Esq.

"Rod, we've been talking for a while now, and some things just don't make sense. We know that Conrad was up to no good. Hell, he's been arrested by the Germans and is facing prosecution. You know that. You don't know this, but up in Sweden the Kercsik brothers have also been arrested, and they're singing like a Nordic choir at summer solstice." (Ramsay's Adam's apple jumps up like a bagel in a toaster at this news bulletin.) "And that piece of paper you gave me last fall, the one with the phone number on it—Clyde didn't buy that at a novelty store, did he? Come on, no more games, no more hypotheticals. Just be honest with us."

I say all this matter-of-factly, without a trace of anger in my voice but without pleading either. This is my show. I'm in charge, and I want Rod to damn well know that. We've been at this more than four hours now, I suddenly realize, and there's no place on Earth right now that I'd rather be. I'm watching Rod's feet to see if they turn toward the door. That's what jurors do when they hate a prosecutor. Rod's feet, thank God, are still facing me, but now he's pressing his arms close to his sides and his thumbs are inching farther under his cupped fingers—two important signs that his confidence is ebbing.

Finally, Rod unpurses his lips. There's sweat on his philtrum, the little indentation between his upper lip and his nose, as he reaches over to shake a cigarette out of his pack, then slides it back in.

"I'm afraid," he says, "that I haven't been totally honest with you."

"About what, Rod?" Moody asks. I'm so glad she says it and not me.

"About everything. I helped Clyde Conrad take documents from the G-3."

Holy shit, we're both thinking, this is it. Now the real fun begins.

"How did that come about?" Moody asks, without missing a beat, in that warm, comforting, soft voice that makes me want to confess my own sins.

"Conrad and I—"

"Wait," I say, sliding away from the coffee table. "Aren't you thirsty? Wouldn't a cold drink taste good now? Why don't you help yourself?"

"CONRAD AND I TALKED every day," Rod begins as soon as we're all back in our seats. A cigarette is burning in the ashtray beside him. He drained his Sprite in one long tilt. "He was always testing me in one way or another. Maybe he didn't completely trust me because I liked marijuana so much. He thought drugs were stupid." As he says this, Rod is furrowing his forehead in a way I haven't seen before. His eyes are squinting slightly—both signs that more admissions might be in the offing.

"They are," I say, with my fatherly voice, but that seems to slide right past him.

"One day we're on a terrain walk and he asks me, 'What is the most valuable thing in the world?'"

"What did you say?" I ask, wondering what my answer would be.

"What would you say?"

"Titanium, maybe."

Rod shakes his head at that, as if he's talking to a dumb third-grader.

"And you?" turning to Moody.

"Family."

"I thought you'd say something like that"—this at least with a kindly smile.

"How about you, Rod?" I ask, trying to get us back on track. "What did you say?"

"Well, my first thought was gold because he clearly valued it so highly, but then I thought he might be laying some kind of trap for me so I started thinking of diamonds or some kind of rare, exotic metal—something way beyond titanium," he adds, just in case I might feel my answer wasn't completely idiotic. "But in the end I said DNA."

"DNA?"

"Deoxyribonucleic acid, Joe. It's a molecule—"

"I know what DNA is, for crissake."

"And was that the correct answer, Rod?" Moody asks in voice that says Now, now, boys.

"Information. Clyde said information is the most valuable thing in the world. He then asked me if I was interested in making money by selling information. I said I was intrigued. At first I thought he was talking about commercial information—you know, like giving hotels a heads-up on when exercises were planned and lots of generals would be looking for cushy places to stay and bars packed with American whiskeys. That kind of thing. Then he explained it to me."

Me: "Go on."

Rod: "Well, take a base telephone book. What do you get from a telephone book?"

Moody: "Numbers?"

Rod, indulgently: "A lot more than that, Terry. You see who's in charge, who's transferred in, who's transferred out, what unit someone works for."

Me, playing dumb: "Wait a minute. We have an FBI phone book, but it just lists people by name. There's none of that other stuff."

"That's the FBI, Joe," Rod says in his grating, ever-so-patient voice. "In the military, the base phone book has you by what section you're in and so forth. That's very valuable."

"Okay," I say, "I can see that. What else is valuable?"

"When we're having exercises," Rod says. "That's very valuable, too. Some exercises are announced; others aren't. But even when an exercise is announced ahead of time, they almost never say such-and-such a force strength is going to be at such-and-such a place at 0320 hours."

"C'mon," I say. "They have freaking satellites. You don't need to know all that ground stuff now. You can sit in Moscow and watch exercises unfold in real time."

"Oh, Joe, Joe, Joe," Rod says as he lights a fresh cigarette, "satellites can tell you the trucks are leaving, but they can't tell you what?"

"Oh, Rod, Rod, Rod, for crissake, what?"

"Intentions," Rod says. "That's the valuable information."

Again, it's Moody's turn to step in between us.

"Well, what can they actually see from a satellite?" she asks Rod.

"We know they've got satellites that will bring you down to three meters off the ground—say, from here to the bedroom door," he says, pointing past me into the dark at the back of the suite. "And we know they have stuff that can actually see closer than that. The point, though, is that even if they see a truck going down the road and read its license plate, and can tell whether the driver is smoking a Gauloise or a Camel, they still can't figure out where the truck is going to stop, or why."

"Okay, I'm impressed, Rod," I concede, only half pretending. "I never thought of a base phone book as a commodity."

"Clyde was very smart."

"I can see that, but it seems to me that somewhere here a line was jumped from unclassified to classified information. I mean troop exercise plans and phone directories only get you so far, right?"

"Exactly, Joe," Rod says, still in his patient lecturing-to-an-idiot voice. "If unclassified information has value, it stands to reason that classified information would have greater value . . ."

"Even I can understand that, Rod. And top-secret . . ."

"Would have greater value still. It's like clothing," he says, turning to Moody with what he hopes will be a useful analogy. "You know, off-the-rack—cheap. Custom-fit—more expensive."

"Dior—most expensive?"

"Exactly!"

"And, Rod," I jump in, "Conrad wasn't the type to sell things off the rack when exclusive is so much better."

"No, that was not Clyde."

"I suspect that wouldn't be good enough for anyone working with Clyde either."

"Like I said," Rod goes on, ignoring my implication, "Clyde was always testing me."

"Example."

"One time, out of the blue, he said, 'I'm going to Austria in a few days to sell some information. I want you to come with me. All you have to do is carry the money back.' I said I would."

"Did you?"

"I didn't have a lot of choice, did I? Clyde told me to hang out at a restaurant near the Hauptbanhof in Vienna, while he met with someone in a booth near the back. I watched him hand the man a manila envelope that he'd been carrying under his arm. Then the man handed him a similar envelope and walked out of the restaurant. After that, Clyde came over to my table, handed me the envelope, and told me I'd be carrying it as we traveled by train back to Germany."

"What was in it?" Moody asks.

"Cash, about twenty thousand dollars in US dollars."

"Did you see it?" I chime in, for legal reasons as much as out of curiosity.

"Of course, Clyde made sure I saw it. He wanted me to feel the money and smell it. That was the most cash I'd ever seen."

"What was in the envelope Conrad gave the other man?" Moody asks.

"Wait a minute," I say. "Rod, help us imagine the scene. Put us in the restaurant you're talking about. What did it look like inside? You've got such a great memory."

Moody, I can tell, is wondering how in the hell I got started on this tangent when we were making such progress, but the point is important, and I make a mental note to tell her about it on the way back to Tampa. We'll need more than Rod's word that he was in that restaurant. If he can give us some convincing interior landmarks, our job is going to be a lot easier, and as I suspected he would, he comes through in spades.

"It was the Gasthaus Elsass; there was a mirror across the back of the room," he says, with his eyes half-shut. "I actually watched Clyde and the man exchange the envelopes in the mirror. The mirror was surrounded by a kind of gilded filigree, and what looked like a family crest of some kind was hanging above it—crossed spears, I think, and an elk—there was a lot of dark wood paneling."

"That's great, good details," I tell him. "You sure about the name?"

Rod looks at me with that look I have seen before, the one that says "My memory never fails." So I move on.

"Now, about Agent Moody's question—the documents Clyde passed?"

"He'd taken them from G-3, he said, but they were of little importance."

"Did you actually see them?"

"No, but Clyde made me carry them on the train till we got to Vienna—they stayed sealed the whole time."

"I don't get it," I say, even though I think I get it very well. "What's the purpose of you carrying the money and the documents?"

"Like I said, he was always testing me. Just to see how I'd handle crossing the border with hot items. I was nervous but not too much. When we got back to Bad Kreuznach, he gave me a couple of hundred dollars and thanked me. The whole experience was a high, like a drug. I was hooked."

"Did he tell you who gave him the money?"

"At some point he said, 'My Hungarian friends.'"

"Were you ever worried that you wouldn't be able to pass one of Conrad's tests?" Moody asks, with what sounds like genuine concern.

"The second test," Rod says. "The second test was a real son of a bitch."

"Why?" Moody asks, knowing when to lead as well as when to follow.

"It was after hours," Rod says. "Clyde took me into the G-3 vault, where all the documents are stored."

"After hours?" I interrupt. "Who's around?"

"Some guards near the front door. That's all. We often had to prepare plans for higher-ups on short notice. They were used to us being in there at all hours."

"So, you're inside . . ."

"We're inside, and Clyde points to some documents and says, 'I want you to clip those.' So I go, 'Okay, but what do I do then?' And he shows me how to roll the documents around my arm, put a couple rubber bands around them, then pull my sleeve back down and button it up again. 'I'll be back for you in five minutes,' he tells me, and he lets himself out the vault door."

"And?" I'm keeping my voice as bland as I can, but I can feel my pulse rate climbing toward triple digits. We'll almost certainly never get Clyde Conrad on the witness stand in a US court, but now we're hearing his voice through Ramsay—and every bit of what Rod tells us Clyde said will be admissible.

"And he must have talked the guards into taking a piss break, because four minutes later he starts pounding on the vault door as hard as he can and shouting in German, in a voice I don't even recognize."

"I don't understand," Moody says. "Why would he do that?"

"To test me. To see how I'd react."

"And how did you?" I ask.

"Well, at first I almost shit my pants, but I got through it. I passed. Afterward, we went to the bowling alley there on the base, and I slid the documents down my sleeve and gave them to Clyde, and he said, 'Good. These are really valuable. Now we can sell them.' All we had to do was make copies and get them ready for the brothers."

"The brothers?"

"You know, the guys in Sweden. The Kercsiks. We would turn the documents over to them. Then, they hid them inside medical journals—*Lancet,* the *Journal of the American Medical Association,* that kind of thing—so if someone checked their medical bags as they were crossing into Austria or Hungary, it would look just like the sort of stuff doctors are supposed to carry. According to Conrad, it was the perfect cover. Everyone respects medical doctors."

At this point I want to jump up and dance a jig. Intentionally or not, Rod has moved from "he" and "I" to "we." Collusion is getting easier to prove by the minute, but collusion to what end? That's the question I am still waiting to get answered. It is nearing midnight by now. One last push, I tell myself, watching Moody stifle a yawn. By this point, we've both been on duty nearly eighteen hours.

"Rod," I say, "not to puncture any balloons, but how do you know that Clyde wasn't just bullshitting you about how valuable the documents were? After all, you just clipped them, right? You didn't have time to actually read them."

"I had time enough to see what they were."

"How could you have? You said yourself you almost shit your pants you were so scared."

"That was at the end, when Clyde started pounding on the door."

"Okay, what were they, then?"

At that point Rod proceeds to rattle off two operational plan numbers—33001 and the OPLAN 33001 annexes—that couldn't have been more meaningless for Moody or me.

"Rod," I say, throwing up my hands in surrender, "help us here. Agent Moody might have made it to Girl Scouts . . ."

"I stopped at Brownies," she says. "Too much pressure."

"Okay, Agent Moody never even got her baking merit badge, and I served my country chasing terrorists all over the coast of Puerto Rico. What the hell do all those numbers you just spouted off mean?"

"Well, the first," he says, "was an update of the NATO go-to-war plan."

"The go-to-what?"

"War, Joe. You know, bang-bang. Where this division goes and that one goes when the bad guys with red stars on their tanks come rumbling through the Fulda Gap. You don't think that's important?"

"Well," I say, once again suppressing a "holy shit" gawk, "it sounds like it *could* be important, depending. How about you, Agent Moody?"

"I agree. *Could.* The proof is in the pudding," whatever the hell that means, and by the look that passes fleetingly across She-Moody's face, I think she's wondering exactly what in the hell she meant, too. I'm just wondering if we're both going to remember the nomenclature Rod just rattled off when it's time to reconcile our notes.

"How about if the pudding were classified?" he asks, and suddenly I realize how much easier it is for him to talk about a pudding than an op plan. "How about if parts of the pudding were classified top-secret? How about—"

I interrupt him here. "How about if this pudding could screw the United States and our allies to the wall?"

"Yes," Rod agrees, "how about that? If our enemies know our war plans, they have first-strike capacity, not us."

And I'm thinking: Thank God for cooking metaphors, however attenuated, because Rod Ramsay has just satisfied the part of the espionage statute that requires foreknowledge of grievous harm to America. But why stop there?

"But here's the other thing, Rod."

"Yes?"

"You say all this, but—and I don't mean to pour sour milk on the pudding . . ."

This draws a wince from Moody and sparks an indulgent chuckle all around.

"Okay, I'm not Julia Child. But the point is that you sort of bull-shitted about the advanced computer chips, and on national television, and now we're being asked to take your word about these documents being, you know, the Armageddon Papers."

"Joe," he says, that same damn "Joe." He's going to pay a price for that eventually. "If these documents were, as I think you indicated, the sour milk on the pudding, why would the Kercsik brothers have returned from Hungary with fifty thousand American for Clyde and me?"

"That could be more Conrad bullshit."

"Except," Rod says, "I saw that money, too. And I was there when the Kercsiks told Clyde how excited the Hungarians were to have such excellent intelligence."

"Let me ask you this, so I can understand this, because as you know I went to school in a small yellow bus, not a big one like you. If we had the equivalent to these documents from the Soviets, OPLAN 33001 and the 33001 annexes [intentionally repeating the official names so that my mind doesn't forget them and Moody hears them one more time for when we write our notes], what advantage would we have?"

"Total advantage. You would know everything needed to win the war."

"You mean the battle?"

"No, I mean the war."

We all pause for a second at that line.

"Rod," I say, looking at my Seiko watch, by now as giddy with fatigue as triumph, "we've covered one heck of a lot this evening, but we have a long drive back, you have to work tomorrow, and Mrs. Moody, well, she has to rest."

"I'm sorry," he says, looking at Moody's belly. "But you're absolutely right. She needs her rest so that little one will be born strong."

"We'd like to meet again tomorrow, or technically later today [ha-ha all around], if we can?"

"Of course, no problem."

In fact, it's going to take all day to write up what transpired this evening, and Moody and I both have other things already scheduled—I'll call Rod in the morning to cancel—but I needed to see his reaction and willingness to come back of his own will, and here, too, he hasn't disappointed.

"In any event," I say, hedging the obligation. "Let's see how Moody is doing after her beauty sleep."

"I understand completely," Rod says magnanimously, "just let me know."

"I will. But if for some reason we can't make it, I want you to eat well. That's an order! No more candy for supper." The truth is, I mean it. Moody chimes in with a wagging finger—she means it, too.

"I know, I know," Rod says. He sounds and looks like a chastened teenager as he leaves the room, and I'm thinking he's probably just as reliable as one, too.

MOODY AND I ARE both exhausted—how could we be otherwise?—but as we sit there in the hotel room writing notes furiously, we're both smiling like kids headed to Disney World (which happens to be only four miles away), and why not? We have a valid confession now, and details to boot.

In my haste to write things down, I forget to send surveillance the beeper code (11, for two legs walking) that Ramsay is on his way to his car. No sweat, though. Surveillance has planted a backup—an empty can behind Rod's rear tire. The crunch is enough to wake our agent out of a semi-sleep. When he calls in on the secure radio, Rod isn't heading directly for his camper park, but that could be for a host of reasons. "Stay with him," I instruct, as Moody and I head off on our own eighty-minute drive back to the office, where Moody has left her Bureau car.

Before we even get to I-4, Moody is fast asleep in the passenger seat. Beside her, behind the wheel, I'm basically on autopilot as my brain churns through its usual long algorithm of whats and what-ifs: What's next? What needs to be done? Where are we going to be blindsided: HQ, WFO, Bamford, the Germans, the Swedes, Ramsay's mother, a defense attorney, Rod himself, someone yet unidentified? And the biggest what-if of all: What if I've already screwed us to high heaven with that maybe, sorta, etc., prosecutorial waiver?

Sure, this is wonderful, I tell myself. We have a confession. But you can't convict on that alone, not in espionage, and you can't even bring the case to trial without corroborating every single thing Rod says . . .

Enough, I think, chiding myself. Eyes on the road. But I wonder if Moody, now in a deep sleep with a smile on her face—something I've never seen anyone do before—understands how much more complex this is going to get, how stressful, how time-consuming and draining.

Enjoy your rest, Moody, I say to myself, as I puzzle over that smile. *You done good.*

I wish I could sleep so bad it hurts.

12

THIS CHANGES
EVERYTHING?

Backstory: She-Moody and I leave Orlando a little after one-thirty in the morning, arrive at the Tampa FBI office (where I wake up Terry and walk her to her car) a shade after two-thirty, and then I head for home. My daughter is sleeping, of course, but as I cradle her face in my hands, she opens her eyes just for an instant. Will she think it a dream in the morning? I have no idea what time I fall asleep, but the alarm gets me up at 5:55 a.m. I leave a note propped up on the breakfast table for Luciana and Stephanie that reads, "I Love You," but I've done this so many times, they have to take it on faith.

Strangely enough, as I head toward the office, I find myself thinking about astronauts and moon rocks. Just about the first thing Neil Armstrong did when he set foot on the moon was to reach down in his Michelin Man spacesuit, pick up a rock, and stow it in his utility pocket. Why? Because that rock was his insurance. If everything else went to hell in a handbasket as soon as they started walking around the lunar surface and he and Buzz Aldrin had to hop back in their Eagle lander and blast off for Michael Collins and Apollo 11, they would still have that rock to show for the 239,000 miles they'd traveled and the infinite dangers of their journey.

That's what Rod's confession was last night—our moon rock, enough to go to trial on, enough to satisfy the statute on at least one count of espionage, enough to put Rod Ramsay in the prison cell he so deserved to occupy. If, of course, I hadn't "fucked the whole business to high heaven," as Koerner had put it, with an implied prosecutorial waiver.

When I call Jane Hein, my trusted friend and now case supervisor at FBI headquarters, on the secure phone at 8:00 sharp, I decide to concentrate on the good news only. She'll have already had her morning run. I know how religious she is about it because years ago back in the Big Apple we used to run together when the city was just waking up. We stayed side by side for the first half mile or so, but after that all I saw was Jane's butt and elbows—that woman can cover ground.

"Jane, are you sitting?" I ask, in my best early-morning voice.

"Why?"

"Are . . . you . . . sitting?" I repeat, spacing my words out, making sure I have her full attention.

"I am, Joe. Break it to me gently. What happened now? How bad is it?"

"O ye of little faith," I say.

"Is this going to cost me my retirement?" she asks, sipping on her morning tea.

"You sure you're sitting?"

"Yes, dammit, let's hear it!"

"Ramsay confessed last night."

"What?" Jane wants to make sure she heard right.

"Ramsay confessed last night, in front of Moody and me."

"Holy shit, are you serious?"

"Serious as a heart attack, Jane. He confessed."

"To what, exactly?"

"To taking documents from the G-3 vault. To being Clyde Conrad's 'right-hand man' in espionage. To knowingly transporting classified documents to Vienna for the purpose of selling them to agents of a foreign power. To knowingly transporting the proceeds of said transaction—twenty thousand dollars by his estimate—back to Germany. To helping steal the go-to-war plans for the Eighth ID."

"The go-to-war plans, for crissake?"

"You heard it right. Go. To. War. And along with Conrad, using the Kercsik brothers to transport those plans to the Hungarians, knowing they could cause grievous harm to the United States of America."

"How much?"

"How much what?"

"How much did the Hungarians pay?"

"Fifty thousand dollars, according to Ramsay."

"Cheap. They got a bargain."

"That's what I was thinking."

"So, do we roll Ramsay up now, or does he have more to say?"

"More, I'm sure of it. Maybe lots more."

I can hear Jane scrawling notes. Finally, she takes a deep breath.

"I want the paperwork, Joe, all of it."

"It's on the way," I say, only slightly lying. "I've also got a request in there for our legal attaché in Vienna. Ramsay described the interior of a restaurant where he watched Conrad hand stolen documents off to another man and get back an envelope stuffed with money. I need someone to vet the description and . . ."

"And you don't want this request to go through the Washington Field Office. Would that be correct?"

"You can read me like a book, Jane."

"Don't worry," she says. Then just before hanging up she adds, "Joe, this changes everything."

Does it? I hope to hell so.

AS I SIT AT my desk, I'm stewing about the ability of a good defense attorney to argue that, by engaging so freely in hypotheticals, I'd intentionally confused Rod into thinking he'd never do time for his actions.

What bothers me even more, though, is that we're no longer dealing with a semi-bullshit charge. Rod Ramsay was never going to do heavy time for a contemplated end run around the computer chip embargo. Now, though, he's confessed to something far, far more serious, and that same good defense attorney might well argue that Rod believed the prosecutorial waiver he assumed applied to the computer chips extended to anything else he might subsequently tell Moody and me. If so, all that giddy exhilaration Moody and I felt early this morning driving back to Tampa is going to turn sour in a big hurry.

A thought I can't banish from my brain is that Rod intentionally led me into this legal maelstrom. I know it sounds a little paranoid, but as I mentally replay the interview from two nights ago, I keep seeing Rod baiting the conversation with hypothetical this, hypothetical that, teasing me along with nebulous words and elastic meanings until I fell right into the rabbit hole he wanted me to stumble into. *Is he that smart?* I keep asking myself. And the answer that keeps coming back is *Yes.* Which is this why he talked so freely to Moody and me last night—because he knew that even if he confessed to us that he'd kidnapped the Lindbergh baby and committed mass murder, he already had a "Get Out of Jail Free" card sitting in his pocket.

Either that or we have outsmarted him. I can't decide.

JAY, TO HIS EVERLASTING credit, celebrates the good news when Moody and I enter his office a little before nine ("Confession? That's great!"), not bothering to point out what all of us full well realize: that this great confession might not count for diddly-squat. I'm not much of one for hiding my feelings—he can tell how this is gnawing at me. And he knows that in addition to the tour through legal hell that will take up most of my morning and afternoon, I'm subbing for one of our pilots and flying surveillance tonight.

In fact, the only direct mention Jay makes of my quandary is to remind me to start with the division legal counsel and be sure to read him in on the case, which is exactly what I'm doing forty-five minutes later.

A word of explanation: Each division of the FBI has a full-time attorney who provides the Tier-One legal advice necessary so agents can stay up-to-date with new cases and perform their work properly. But the fact that these counsels have a law degree doesn't exempt them from normal security precautions. When cases are particularly sensitive and involve highly classified materials—as the Rod Ramsay case now does—the legal counsels have to be "read in," or reminded that the issues involved are not to be further discussed.

I've just finished sketching the issues for our division legal counsel, and reminding him that silence is not only golden but mandatory, when he reiterates exactly what has been eating at me for the last thirty-six hours: This case needs to stand up to both general judicial scrutiny and to a spirited attack from a competent defense attorney, and sad to say, it looks as if there's adequate room here for the defense to argue that my little icebreaker got so out of control and convoluted that Ramsay could reasonably have been expected to confuse what was real and what hypothetical.

Solid advice, I'm sure, but not really what I want to hear, so I move on to Tier Two, the US Justice Department's Internal Security Section. Normally, these are peer-to-peer calls. I relay a request to the special agent in charge of our field office, and he does the calling on my behalf. This way the ears of the Internal Security lawyers aren't sullied by having to listen to a peon field agent, especially one like me who's butted heads with them plenty of times already. But our special agent in charge cares about his career, and relaying any kind of question or request from me is bound to at least ding it. Besides, time is short, and even on a red alert, Internal Security attorneys work at the rough speed of honey dripping out of a bottle.

So I find a secure line, call, and get just about what I expect—a wavering, on-the-one-hand/on-the-other response that muddles more than clarifies. The good news, I guess, is that, except for some concern over Moody and me not having yet read Rod his Miranda rights, the ISS attorneys don't seem to think my little hypotheticals game with Ramsay is all that big a deal, but I chalk that up to their not having any great stake in the matter. They're not going to be prosecuting this—they're advisors, and in DC advice is cheap.

Happily, the Third Tier of legal advice I seek that day is Greg Kehoe, and Greg, believe me, is the real thing. Greg was already famous among people like me for taking down Miami drug dealers before he became the first assistant at the United States Attorney's Office in the Middle District of Florida. More recently, he's been putting together a drug-trafficking case against Manuel Noriega. The feds will still need to find a way to get the Panamanian dictator to the States for trial, but if I were Noriega, I sure as hell wouldn't sleep comfortably with Greg on my tail.

I've worked with Greg on several cases by now, and I like his style. I admire his legal acumen almost to the point of envy, and I especially admire his philosophy, which boils down to "Let's put bad people away right now." No wonder people in Washington know him. The sit-on-their-asses-and-don't-rock-the-boat crowd at the Justice Department probably see Greg as a grave threat, but I've heard he's a favorite of Bob Mueller, the new assistant to Attorney General Dick Thornburgh, and for good cause. Greg puts points on the board. He kicks ass and takes names later—he's the one litigator you don't want to go against. Since I know Greg is going to get the Ramsay case if we can get past the legal hurdles I've created, I suck up my pride, walk downstairs to the US Attorney's Office, and throw myself on his mercy.

"Do you have a SCIF where we can talk?" I ask, a Sensitive Compartmented Information Facility—i.e., a secure room for discussing top-secret matters.

"Sure," he answers, and leads me into the biggest SCIF I've ever seen.

I don't even have to ask what a secure room this size is doing in little old Tampa. Greg can read the question in my face.

"Just finished it," he says in his heavy Rockaway-Queens New York accent. "We're going to debrief Noriega here once we lay hands on that piña-faced dictator." And from the expectant tone of his voice, I'm guessing that's going to be before year's end. (*Piña*, by the way, is Spanish for "pineapple"—a reference to Noriega's pockmarked face.)

"What's up?"

And so for the next twenty-five minutes I sketch out the case against Rod Ramsay while white noise hums gently around us and the lead walls protect us from signal penetrations of any sort—incoming or outgoing. (I've been in SCIFs where the floors basically float in air, true rooms-within-rooms. This one doesn't possess that particular feature, but Noriega's spies aren't likely to be as sophisticated as the KGB.) As I knew he would, Greg glowers menacingly when I get to the enforced-from-above year-long hiatus in interviewing Ramsay. "What the fuck . . ." is all he says—street-loud, like he's shouting to be heard above the traffic—but we've both done enough battle with the ass-coverers and raging egos on the Potomac that nothing more needs saying.

The good part of all this is that I can see Greg's interest growing with every new revelation. By the time I get to the documents "clipped" out of the G-3 vault, he's on the edge of his seat. When I tell him about selling the go-to-war plans to the Soviets via the Hungarians, he starts pacing the SCIF in anticipation of the trial that lies ahead.

"More?" he asks, hungry for it.

"More," I say, with near certainty. "But there's a problem."

"Well, finally," he replies, settling back into his chair.

"Finally?"

"Finally, Joe, we get to why you've come down two flights of stairs to meet with me on this lovely Tuesday midday when you could be out kayaking in Tampa Bay."

The kayaking part reminds me of how much I like Greg—and of the fact that we've kayaked together for hours at a time. That, in turn, makes what I'm about to say even harder.

"Very astute, Counselor," I say nervously, even though we're good friends.

"Talk to me, Joey," in a voice that beneath Greg's gruff bark says, "I got your back; you know I'm a stand-up guy." And I do.

"The deal is that I might have left Ramsay with the impression that I'd granted him prosecutorial immunity."

"Which, of course, you have no standing to do."

"Correct," I say, squeezing the knot on my tie, tipping my own distress.

"And how did this fairy tale get uncorked, Navarro? I'm guessing this is a doozy."

"The short answer: I opened my mouth."

"Joey, Joey, Joey, how many times have I told you—you never have to explain what you don't say?"

"Thanks, Greg, that's good. In fact, this is just what I need, a fucking lecture on the obvious."

I choose to ignore Greg's menacing De Niro "just saying" look.

"Another thing. Agent Moody and I have yet to read Ramsay his Miranda rights. Internal Security thinks that could be a problem, too."

"Is Ramsay under arrest?"

"No."

"You intend to arrest him?"

"Maybe one day, but that decision as you know is not mine."

"I can live with that. There's no requirement to give Miranda warnings unless he is under arrest or about to be arrested."

"Neither has transpired."

"So what, then, is the fucking issue?"

I go through the whole sequence of events: Rod asking questions in hypotheticals and me answering back the same way. Greg, meanwhile, listens with piercing blue eyes that, I'm betting, could melt steel.

"Joey, Joey," he says when I finish. "I gotta tell ya, I love you, but you fucked up. Is there another word for it? Maybe, but I can't think of it right now. It's a fuckup. Why? Because defense counsel is going to bring this up at a suppression hearing, or he is going to stick it up your ass at trial. *Capisce?*"

"I know, Greg, I know," I say, feeling very cold. In fact, my hands are freezing as if I've been exiled to Superman's icy Fortress of Solitude. Part of me wants to flee and run, but where? There's no getting away, and Greg has more to say.

"I don't want some schoolteacher on the jury feeling sorry for this guy, thinking we led him astray. If you don't clear this up, you're going to dig a deeper and deeper hole, and then you're going to really get jammed up. And from what you're telling me, this is the only prosecution we're going to have in the United States, so you've got to make this right."

Easier said than done, I think, sinking ever lower in my chair.

"Eventually this case is going to come to me, and I want it to be pristine. I want to nail this guy to the fucking cross, you understand, but I don't want to deal with issues having to do with admissibility. And . . ."

"And?" There's an ominous ring to it.

"And I don't want to hear the defense even utter the word 'Miranda' the entire fuckin' trial!"

Nothing like getting kicked in the gut, especially by a guy you think so highly of. Nothing like deserving it, either.

"Look, Joe," Greg says as we're heading for the door and back into nonsecure land. "How many agents in this division?"

"A little over a hundred," I say, wondering what this is about.

"And how come I see only you and about twelve other agents in our office every month?"

"I don't know," I answer, still not sure where he's headed.

"Out of one hundred–plus agents, I only see the same ones over and over because you guys are the racehorses—the guys the Bureau runs into the ground. You're the guys who bring me the cases to prosecute. The others don't do squat. Why they get paid, I don't know."

I'm still wondering where Greg is ultimately going when he delivers the punch line.

"The others—they're the turds of this world, Joey, the floaters. They don't do anything. I have them here in the US Attorney's Office, too. They get a paycheck but they don't do shit, and when you don't do shit, you don't make mistakes. I don't give a fuck about the mistake. Big cases come with big problems. I know you—you will fix it because you're one of those thoroughbreds. All you know is what is in front, not behind. Fix it before you do anything else, and we'll be fine. I got your back."

I'd gone in there with my tail low and chin down, but Greg's pep talk lifted my spirits instantly. His challenge to "fix it" was as good as the opening bell at the Kentucky Derby.

WHICH IS WHY TWENTY-NINE hours later, She-Moody and I are back in Greater Orlando, waiting for Rod in a steakhouse close enough to Disney World to overcharge for dinner and still pack 'em in.

I'm tired. Last night's surveillance didn't produce a damn thing—the cigarette boat packed with cocaine that we were hoping would pull into Bradenton, just south of Tampa Bay, either never existed or headed for some other drop-off port or offshore rendezvous instead. But five hours in the sky is still five hours no matter what you net. Also—big surprise!—I'm a worrier: Sleep isn't easy when something like this is staring me in the face, especially when I know everyone from the Germans to the Swedes to DOJ, HQ, and WFO is going to be reading our latest FD-302s and wondering just what in hell I was thinking. Plus, I had a ton of other things to catch up with today.

Moody might be even more tired. She's been detailed to me, but she hasn't been un-detailed from other assignments. Plus, her husband is gone on training, she already has one kid, and a bun in the oven, and her nanny arrangement has been unraveled by what might be the Asian flu. If I were in Moody's shoes, I probably would have told me to get lost when I begged her to join me in Orlando, but she knows the stakes, and maybe she feels a little complicit for not jumping in when I was hypothetically accommodating (playing?) Rod's game.

In the end, we struck a compromise: She agreed to drive herself up to Orlando and join us for dinner and an hour's session back at the Embassy Suites during which I would try to right my previous wrongs. After that she would head for home, and I would stay behind and see if I could push the line of scrimmage ever closer to the goal line.

Now, as Rod shows up by the maître d' stand, I'm plagued by angst-ridden thoughts. Our always-eager-for-a-meal traitor waves cheerfully our way, and hotfoots it through the teeming crowd. One of us, at least, is in a tip-top mood, despite having confessed to us to crimes against his country less than forty-eight hours earlier, and almost in spite of ourselves, Rod's good spirits soon affect the whole table.

He describes his day for us, tells us what it's like to spend literally hours waiting at Orlando International for paying customers. His favorite time-killer, he says, is to read books—two of them today alone, if he is to be believed, sitting in the cab queue and tearing pages out as he finishes.

Vaguely, I remember Rod telling us that this was a trick he learned from Clyde. While enthusiastic readers often speak of "tearing through" books, Rod means it literally.

That, at least, clears up one confusing report from a surveillance agent who spent an hour at the airport, watching Rod edge forward in the cab queue: "Subject appeared to be destroying books as he waited." That was the same agent who'd tracked Rod when he left the Embassy Suites two nights ago, after our marathon interview session. Turns out, after he left us, Rod made a beeline straight to a flea-trap motel on South Orange Blossom Trail. Maybe that's why he's so jaunty tonight. He sure as hell doesn't seem to be getting any loving from his camper mate.

Rod is still full of bonhomie when the waiter finally wanders over to take our order. At Moody's urging, I opt for the steak again, a New York strip this time, blood-rare with *pomme frites* ("French fries," Rod helpfully explains) and a garden salad with blue-cheese dressing, instead of the sautéed spinach. Next, Moody selects the mahi-mahi, and when the waiter turns to Rod, he orders exactly what I did—if I'm not mistaken, in exactly the same words and with the same snarky look at Moody to let her know we're not taking any salad-dressing shit tonight.

Odd, I'm thinking, *he always asks for his steak medium-rare*. But there's no time to dwell on the mimicry because Rod has suddenly become an erudite oenophile.

"Mahi-mahi? You'll need some Riesling with that, Terry!" he insists, then engages the waiter in a five-minute discussion of grapes, vintages, regions, blah, blah, blah, from the upper Rhine to the Alsace. When Rod turns to me and asks, "Two glasses or three?" I finally have to put a halt to the whole business. If the prosecutorial waiver stuff doesn't kill us in court, then plying Rod with alcohol before somehow getting him to waive his Miranda rights surely will.

And of course somewhere in the back of my mind, I can't help wondering if this, too, is another trap Rod is setting for us, knowing full well the damage that a cheerful bottle of Riesling would do to the case against him. If that's what he's up to, though, he takes this little setback in stride. We sail through our entrées buoyed by Rod's tales of imperial Russia. Dessert finds us traveling back in time with him along the ancient Silk Road (a spy's wet dream, by the way). By coffee—Rod has his black, like mine, instead of with cream as per usual—he has moved on to the global dangers posed by electromagnetic pulses from the sun, the subject of one of the books he shredded today.

Normally, I'd challenge him on the facts occasionally or see what other byways I might take him down—partly for the sport of it but also to remind him of who is ultimately running this show. But I've got a more important agenda this evening, and Rod's good spirits are still much in evidence by the time we get back to the Embassy Suites and settle into our original haunt, 316, with Rod once again sitting by the door.

I begin the evening's festivities by reminding Rod that Agent Moody is a short-timer tonight.

"We were fortunate she could even carve out this little piece of time to be with us," I say.

He dismisses the very thought of inconveniencing her with a wave that would do the pope justice.

"Mothers must be mothers," he adds in what I've come to recognize as his magnanimous voice, so I figure why not pile it on?

"Let me say it again," I begin. "I—we—Terry and I are very appreciative that you were able to clear up the microchips issue for us the other night. The last thing I need right now is an illicit technology transfer case on my plate, and so I personally am very thankful for that and glad that nothing happened."

Again that dismissive wave that says, "Really, how could I have done otherwise?"

Moody, I can see, is wondering where I'm headed next. If I knew for sure, I would try to signal her somehow, but I've gotten to the point where all I have to go on is instinct honed by thousands of interviews and a gut feel for the person directly across from me. I take a deep breath, open myself up nonverbally as wide as I can—big exhale; a tilt of the head so Rod and I aren't talking face-to-face, eyeball to eyeball; a kind of downward glance that says I'm vulnerable—and then, what the hell, I jump off the cliff and begin what Terry and I really came for.

"Rod, when we talked about the computer chips, we talked, of course, about hypotheticals. ["Of course," he mouths, silently.] But we need to be clear about something. Neither I nor Agent Moody can make a decision as to who can be prosecuted, why, or when. You asked a hypothetical, and I answered the same way, as a hypothetical, not as a binding legal opinion. Was that clear to you?"

"Could I have a Coke?" Rod asks, nodding toward the ever-present mini-cooler on the coffee table.

"Of course," I say. "Let me get it for you." This isn't the time for dominance games, and Rod clearly understands that.

"I know we were talking about hypotheticals," he allows, once he's fired up a cigarette to accompany his soft drink. "I know you don't decide who gets prosecuted. I get it."

"That's good, because, Rod, I don't have to tell you this, you're a smart guy, but a prosecutor can come along and indict a tuna sandwich or prosecute a Rod Ramsay or even a Joe Navarro if he really wants to."

"Sure," Rod says, "I got that."

"Good, good," I tell him. "I'm really glad we cleared that up."

Relief Number One. I celebrate silently while Moody jumps in with some follow-up questions we rehearsed, on Rod's Vienna stint as Conrad's money-and-documents mule. She's in the middle of one of them when I jump back in with both feet, hoping for a soft landing.

"Rod, there's something else I want to thank you for."

He looks at me quizzically, one eyebrow arched in a way I recognize as my own "what's this about?" look.

"Your candor two nights ago."

"My candor?"

Moody, I notice, is looking at me with her own quizzical look, more of the "what the hell are you doing now?" variety.

"Yes, your forthrightness about your relationship with Clyde, the tests he put you through, how you helped him, all that."

"Ah, well," he says, "you know, what happened happened."

"I appreciate that," I say. "Maybe all of history could be summed up as 'what happened happened.'"

That at least gets an approving nod, so on I charge.

"Here's the thing, though. My supervisor . . ."

"Koerner?"

"Yes, Koerner. He is concerned that Mrs. Moody and I are taking up too much of your time and that we're bothering you, and I want to get your opinion on that because he gets upset with me."

"No, no," Rod says, "it's no problem, I really appreciate you guys coming over," and for whatever odd reasons, I think he truly means it. "It's no bother at all."

"Good," I say, "I'm very glad to hear that because I want to get Koerner off my back. He's always overanalyzing things, and he thinks I am intruding into your life. I just want you to know from the bottom of my heart that if at any time you feel that you don't want to talk to me or Mrs. Moody, then you don't have to. You talk with us because you feel like it, because it's fine with you, for whatever reason, but the key thing is, you have a choice in the matter."

"Joe," he answers, "Terry [turning her way], I know I can stop at any time."

"Good," Moody answers, "because the last thing we want is for people to think you're being forced."

Rod laughs as if the very possibility of his being forced to say anything is inconceivable.

"Rod," I go on, wanting to make sure we nail this once and for all, "you watch TV, right? [Yes, he nods.] And I'm sure you have seen plenty of police shows."

"Sure," he answers. "Of course."

"Well, then you know what police officers say to arrestees: 'You have a right to remain silent . . .'"

"And 'Anything you say can be used against you,'" Rod pitches in helpfully, in a voice a lot like Captain Frank Furillo from *Hill Street Blues*.

"Correct. And they also say 'If you cannot afford an attorney, one can be appointed for you.'"

"Yes, I know that."

"Well, I just want you to know that those things apply to everyone, not just people in cop shows. You've never been in trouble with the law before, at least that you've told me, and it's important for me that you know that even if a person isn't arrested, they have those rights. When you leave here tonight to go home, I want you to be absolutely assured that if you decide you don't want to talk to Moody and me, we won't ask you any more questions. Do you understand that?"

Rod looks at Moody and says, "Yes, I do." She smiles back.

"Well, that's great," I say, "because Koerner really had it in for me this morning."

"You want me to call Koerner and tell him it's okay?" Rod offers.

"No need. So long as you understand this is all voluntary and you have the right to an attorney."

"I do, Joe. Mrs. Moody," he adds, turning to Terry, "look, don't worry."

"I won't, Rod," she says, "but I don't want you to feel trapped any more than Agent Navarro does."

"I even know a good attorney if you need one," I say, picking up Terry's cue and very thankful for it.

"My mother knows several good attorneys," Rod says after a short pause, "and she hasn't been exactly shy about giving me their names and telephone numbers. So I'm okay, I thank you both, and you can tell Jay Koerner to chill." And with that, Ramsay's look affirms there's no need to go on.

"Okay, then?" I say, to double-check.

"Understood," he says, and when I reach over to shake his hand, he gives me a firm grip in return.

"Well," I say, "you've taken a great burden off my mind."

"Oh," he says, and all of a sudden, he's back to solar electromagnetic pulses and potential global catastrophes—i.e., exactly where we'd left off at the restaurant. I wait until Rod pauses to light his cigarette to look Moody's way, and when I do, I can see that she's finally realized what has just happened.

I've given Ramsay his Miranda warnings, and he's agreed to cooperate. It's that simple. True, the rights have been presented a little differently, but the Supreme Court never said that the Miranda warnings had to be the "virtual incantation" heard so often on TV. All that matters is that Rod has verified he understands his rights and that Agent Terry Moody was there as my witness. And the smile now spreading across She-Moody's face tells me she's as relieved as I am to finally get this behind us.

Son of a bitch, I'm thinking, as Rod drones on. He's somewhere between the Earth's magnetic field and a fried global power grid when I gently remind him that Mrs. Moody needs to be saying goodbye. Gallant that he is (for the moment), Rod rises and shakes Terry's hand, wishing her a safe and pleasant journey. Then he turns to me with a more serious look on his face.

"Why don't you and I talk a little longer," he says. And thinking that this could be heralding even more revelations, I readily agree. Turns out, I'm wrong.

SHE-MOODY IS PROBABLY STILL waiting for the elevator when Rod settles back into his corner of the couch, lights yet another cigarette, hunches slightly forward (exactly as I'm hunched slightly forward in my swivel chair, I can't help but notice), and lets me have it hard.

"I want to know if you're lying."

"What are you talking about?" I ask, desperately parsing this little salvo as I ponder what might make him question me.

"The guy from ABC news, Bamford—he says my arrest is imminent. Are you lying to me, Agent Joe Navarro?"

This time Rod is not playing, and I can see why he waited till Moody was gone. We're hombre to hombre now, but I still have to be careful. This is going to be a no-extra-witness, his-word-against-mine moment.

"Rod," I say, looking straight into his eyes, "no one has authorized your arrest. Not that I am aware of, anyway, and I'm the only agent on this case, except for Mrs. Moody. You have my word on that."

Rod is scanning my face, trying to see if I'm lying, but I'm not. Every word I just spoke was true, even if not the whole truth.

"Christ almighty, Rod," I go on, trying to press what I sense is an advantage, "stop talking to ABC News! They're in the business of reporting news, and you're helping them make it. I thought you played them well that first time you talked to them. [He nods in agreement.] But now I've got a fresh news bulletin for you: They won't leave you alone until you tell them to fuck off."

I don't know why, but the "fuck off" kicker seems to drive everything else home to Rod.

"I just wanted to check with you," he says, almost apologetically.

"Rod, I'd be the first to tell you if you're under arrest. Now let's get the hell out of here. Frankly, I'm tired and have a headache coming on, and you have plenty of other things to worry about, like your so-called girlfriend."

"Don't remind me."

"You game for another sit-down with Moody tomorrow?" I ask.

"Sure," he says, his face brightening to nearly the magnitude it was over dinner. "Same time?"

"Yes, and bring your appetite."

"One more thing," Rod says as the elevator is opening in the lobby. "I'm sorry I questioned your word."

"Rod, come on, that's your right to do, anytime," I tell him, and with that he gives me a bro-hug, an *abrazo*, and in an instant he's gone.

I wait until he's out the door to punch 11 on my pager for surveillance: suspect walking.

NINETY-ODD MINUTES LATER, AND thanks to an apparently colossal wreck on I-4 that forces me to find an alternative route home, I'm on Highway 60 near the strawberry capital of the world,

Plant City, when a huge sleep deficit finally catches up with me and I go from awake and alert to asleep with no transition that I can remember. With my brain on shut-down, I careen off the highway, thank God to my right and not across lanes, and when I wake up seconds later, I'm sixty yards into a plowed field, with the windshield caked with mud.

13

COGNITIVE DISSONANCE

November 9, 1989

I'm lucky. It rains cats and dogs while I'm at home getting a brief, fitful sleep, and when I awake, the Bu-Steed has been washed almost clean in the driveway. All I have to do is dig some grass out of the grill and give the underside a good hosing down, and I can't see a reason in the world to report this, or even mention it to anyone.

I'm lucky in another way, too: nothing broken, not in me, not on the car, just a little knot where my dozing head hit the steering wheel, barely visible, and a sore shoulder, probably from the strap that kept my head from smashing into the windshield instead. No dead bodies scattered around the smoking remains of a head-on crash caused by one Joe Navarro, soon-to-be-former FBI agent. I shook like a man with palsy all the way home from that farmer's field last night, just thinking about what could have been. My God—what could have been!

I'd ponder the issue some more, but my first duty now is to get the paperwork done because nothing exists in the Bureau until the paperwork is in, and nothing requires more of it than espionage. With criminal cases, FD-302s are straightforward. They catalog what is observed or what is obtained from an interview—pretty much the bare essentials of what is necessary to prove the crime, maybe two or three pages at the most. But espionage is a totally different world because here everything matters—not just what was said and observed, but how it was said, when, in what order. In fact, the nuances of counterintelligence are surreal at times.

No other crime brings together so many factors: tradecraft, nation-state participants, specific diplomats or intelligence officers, areas of operation, means of communication, modes of concealment and transportation, politics, allegiances, intra-ethnic empathy, time of day, day of week, even history. Beyond the crime itself, there's also ancillary information that will lead us to how the enemy conducts espionage: where, how, and what they're interested in or not; how they target spies; where they meet; where they operate or won't; how much they pay, what value they attach to certain information; who their best operatives are; and on and on. Criminal agents like to accuse those of us in CI of writing *War and Peace* every time we fill out an FD-302, but while there's no question our FD-302s are long by comparison—this morning's report on last night's meeting with Rod will probably run to twelve pages—we need to be thorough because we're held to a higher evidentiary standard. Besides, not all paperwork is boring.

Today's FD-302, for example, is a sheer delight to pen. Suspect Ramsay acknowledged that he'd talked of his own free will and with no understanding that a prosecutorial waiver had been granted or even suggested. Suspect Ramsay further was made aware of his Miranda rights and specifically waived them. Agent (Mrs.) Terry Moody was present throughout this portion of the interview and will serve as witness to the above. I've got a bunch of detail to fill in, but the legal minefield of my last few days is—*poof!*—gone. I can almost see the long faces lined up at the Washington Field Office when this one comes over the teletype. What? Navarro's not the knucklehead we thought he was? Damn!

As I draft the FD-302, I'm also keeping Greg Kehoe in mind. He's no doubt going to be very happy to see this. I've fully met his challenge to clean up the mess I created. We can both rest easy about that. I've also got Rod's defense attorney in mind, whoever that ends up being. I want his lawyer to sense the completeness of these interviews—to feel the full weight of Rod's words—leaving no doubt that this is a case based on so much inculpatory information that there is only one choice: a guilty plea.

I'm just moving on to Rod's and my few closing minutes on the elevator—his (frankly) touching apology, our *abrazo*—when the phone on my desk rings, and thinking it's She-Moody checking in from home before heading downtown, I pick it up with almost a lilt in my voice.

"Terry!"

"No, Rod." He sounds terrible—his voice is quivering.

"Rod?"

"Joe," he says. "You gotta help me. I got the clap."

THE FBI ACADEMY IN Quantico, Virginia, teaches a dazzling array of subjects and offers expert instruction in every one: how to take down a gunman, determine the time of death of a body, conduct surveillance—even the best ways to lift fingerprints from twenty different surfaces, including skin. But I can safely say that the Academy never has offered—and probably never will offer—training in what to do when your prime suspect in an espionage case calls early in the day to announce that he has VD.

The first thing that jumps to my mind is, *How in the hell am I going to write this up? How will I title the report? What will I put in and omit?* That's just the reality of life in a huge government bureaucracy. For now, I have to cope with what every CI agent learns in dealing with valuable sources of information: the human factor, the reality that humans are flawed. Even if you're fundamentally repulsed by the person at the other end of the phone, you guide them or help them because that's what good agents do. I've been recruiting sources for a decade, and half my time is spent playing therapist, no matter how squared away they seem, because everyone has issues. But this is a new one—a urinary tract infection that could temporarily or even permanently derail a vital investigation.

Thus, off comes my FBI agent hat and in its place I don my father hat, or at least, something that vaguely resembles it.

"Jesus, Rod, how long have you had this?"

"Well, it started out as an itch a few days ago, and now every time I pee I'm in so much fucking pain."

"That sounds about right," I say, thinking back on my EMT training. "So which door handle are you going to blame this on?"

"Very funny," he says. "What can I tell you, I was lonely. I was on South Orange Blossom Trail, and, you know, there are some motels there . . ."

Yeah, I'm thinking, our surveillance was right behind you when you turned in to one, you dumb shit—and this was what? No more than forty minutes after you assured us you were going to eat better and call your mom more often. But I don't say any of that because (a) it wouldn't do any good and (b) I'd be tipping Rod to the fact that we had a tail on him. Instead, I continue with my best imitation of a mildly reproving but concerned father.

"Rod," I say, "you *have* heard of AIDS, right?"

"Of course."

"And you do know that the number of AIDS cases has reached epidemic proportions, in this country and all around the world?" Even as the words leave my mouth, I realize I'm speaking to him as if he were my son.

"Joe, I do follow the news. Rather carefully."

"Well, that's good, meathead," I say. "Then you also know that, contrary to early reports, AIDS is not spread solely by sexual acts involving homosexual males?"

"Don't get into epidemiology with *me*!" Rod warns, suddenly as confident as a PhD section head at the Centers for Disease Control. "I know the goddamn vectors."

"Well, brainiac, then obviously you weren't thinking, were you?" I respond in a tone considerably less fatherly.

"No," he concedes.

"Let me amend that. You *were* thinking, but not with your higher brain—this is what happens when the blood flow is dominated by the little general in your pants." This gets a rueful laugh, at any rate, but I can tell Rod is struggling and worried.

"Okay, okay, all kidding aside, how bad is it?" I ask, noticing that I'm now whispering into the phone as if talking to my wife about a problem at home. I can almost hear the people passing by my office saying to themselves, *What in the hell have you done now, Agent Navarro?*

"Oh man, Joe," he answers with such quivering intensity that I'm now aching in my own lower parts. "It's really bad. It's burning when I piss. I can't sleep." I've never heard him sound this bad.

"What else?"

And suddenly instead of filling out the joyous final paragraphs of my triumphant FD-302, I'm taking copious notes on Rod's sore penis, his swollen testicles, the yellow/green discharge that just this morning showed up in his underwear and crusts together when it dries.

"Yep. Sounds like gonorrhea," I summarize when he's through. "Way to go."

"Thanks a lot."

"Hey, you're the one who can't keep his dick in his pants, and obviously wearing a little raincoat is too much of a hassle," I say, still trying to knock some sense into him.

"I'd laugh but it hurts."

"Hurts where?"

"I don't know. My stomach, my gut, all around there."

"Okay, this is not good," I say. "This means the infection has worked its way into your bladder, and it may have spread to your kidneys." Rod is silent when I finish, but I can hear his breathing—those long, cathartic exhales that acknowledge he's in way over his head.

"What should I do?"

"You're going to wait by this phone while I make some calls. You're going to drink water like there's no tomorrow, and you're going to take aspirin every four hours."

"Why?"

"Because I fucking say so, that's why." I spit out that last line as I'm all but slamming down the phone. I don't have time to explain that his urinary tract will benefit from the extra flushing and that we want renal flow going out. The FBI, the National Security Council, the NSA, our friends at Langley, the Germans, and NATO all need to know what Rod can reveal to them, but for now I have to play nursemaid to Mr. Happy Dick, who at best has gonorrhea and at worst may have contracted AIDS. As I start flipping through my Rolodex, I'm reminded of why we agents always say "*semper* Gumby." Like the clay-animation figure, we have to be always flexible.

I START WITH THE doc who has the biggest ad in the yellow pages, on the assumption that any physician trolling so openly for patients is likely to have a low ethical threshold, but since the doc won't even talk with me until I've signed up and prepaid for a three-part "whole body" exam, including blood test, I never get past the front-desk receptionist.

That leads me to one of the doctors I train with every few months to maintain my EMT status, but he isn't exactly buying my storyline.

Me: "Listen, Fred, I've got this friend . . ."

Him: "Friend?"

Me: "Yeah, this friend who thinks he has the clap."

Him: "So your *friend* [huge air quotes, or so I imagine] is suffering from painful urination?"

Me: "Really painful . . . he says."

Him: "Painful micturition," reminding me of the proper term in describing this medical condition.

Me, rolling my eyes: "Yes, thank you, Fred, but today is not a good day for pedantry."

Him: "Swollen testes?"

Me: "Exactly."

Him: "Discharge?"

Me: "Yellow/green."

"Joe," Fred says, "can we just cut to the chase? How long have you had this? And why are we doing this on the phone?"

More back-and-forth ensues, none of which I sense is totally convincing Fred, but he knows I'm FBI, and in the end he's willing to grant the possibility that I'm not lying through my teeth.

"Tell you what," he says, "I'll call in the prescription, twenty-one days of tetracycline. It'll kill everything, but your friend will need to take the full cycle. Gonorrhea can lie low for a week, then come storming back if you don't kill it dead. Got it?"

I assure Fred I do and thank him from the bottom of my heart, but no sooner have I hung up than I start to have second thoughts about all this. For starters, if the tetracycline is dispensed in my name and I then pass it to Rod, I'll in effect be acting as a medical provider, and in Florida, practicing medicine without a license is a third-degree felony even if you carry a badge.

That gets me to a second and larger concern: whether Luciana and I are going to spend our declining years in relative comfort or in grinding poverty. No one gets rich working for the FBI, but if you put in twenty-five years, you're rewarded with three-quarters of your final salary annually for the rest of your life, no matter whether you subsequently win the lottery, launch a billion-dollar computer company, or just settle down to eighteen holes a day in the Florida sun.

Personally, I'm hoping for a good thirty or more years on the public dole after I step down—I owe my wife at least that much after all the missed dinners, school plays, holidays, and Stephanie birthday parties—but I won't be getting there if I take a bullet between the eyes, and even being charged with a third-degree felony almost certainly would be enough to murder my career, especially given the many well-placed enemies I've been making at HQ and beyond.

I'm envisioning myself being led away in handcuffs, indicted for dispensing medicines, and flipping burgers (once I'm out on parole) at some off-brand fast-food joint near Busch Gardens because no one else will hire me. Not fun for me or my family. I also recall from my pilot training the sometimes extreme dangers of decision-making when you're dead tired and the unreasonable suddenly seems perfectly rational. This is how pilots land on interstates instead of runways or climb when they should descend.

When I pick up the phone once more, the better me is making the call. I find a public-health clinic in Orlando, emphasize my Bureau special agent status, which in some circles still carries weight, and basically beg the director of the facility to begin treating Rod today while assuring him the federal government will be picking up the tab for any related expenses. Turns out, the fed is off the dime. Orange County will pick up the tab, and the director, a former navy medical officer, finds an opening at three in the afternoon.

Immediately, I call Rod, who has been waiting as ordered by the pay phone at the convenience store next to his campground, tell him to get his ass over to the clinic, and remind him that Moody and I will be meeting him at six-thirty at the Embassy Suites and heading from there to dinner.

"Try to clean up, Rod," I tell him, "and let's not mention this leaky faucet situation to anyone."

"You're not going to tell Moody, are you?"

"No, this is our secret."

"Good, but I don't think I can make it tonight."

"Why?"

"I didn't break even driving yesterday. In fact, I lost money. Right now, I'm in the hole about twenty-three dollars, with all of eighty-six cents on me. That's not enough money for gas to do both trips."

"Okay, Rod," I say after a few deep breaths, "here's the plan. You go to the clinic, you do *exactly* what the people there tell you to do, and I'll meet you back at your camper at six-thirty with dinner. We can eat and talk. I'll give Agent Moody the night off."

There's a long pause on the other end. When Rod finally speaks again, his voice sounds strained, as if he's been crying.

"Thanks, Joe," he says. "Thanks a lot. This clap is killing me," he adds as he hangs up.

"Killing *you*?" I say to the dial tone and my file cabinets. "Your clap is killing *me*."

That's when Shirley walks into my office, clipboard in hand.

"MR. NAVARRO!" SHIRLEY SAYS, as if she's been waiting all day to say that.

"What now?"

"Mr. Navarro!" she says again, maybe even more emphatically and tapping the clipboard with her right index finger—which, naturally, gets me thinking of exactly where that clipboard might be shoved.

"Yes, Shirley?"

"Do you realize that you haven't been to the firing range in *over six weeks*?"

"I've been a little busy . . . ," I start to say, thinking that I also haven't had a day off or played with my daughter or . . .

"Bureau regs say every *four* weeks. You're [studying her clipboard] two weeks past due. That's, like [a long pause for mental calculation], that's, like, *50 percent* over regulation!"

"Shirley . . ."

"Also . . ."

"Also what?"

"Also," Shirley says, casting a wary glance at the perfectly arranged but slightly towering file stacks on my desk, the tops of cabinets, and every other available flat space, "don't you think you should tidy up your office before?"

"Before what, for God's sake?"

"Before the Director visits on the thirteenth."

"Judge Sessions?"

Condescendingly: "He's been Director for over two years, Joe."

"I know that! He's coming here? To Tampa?"

Maybe even more condescendingly, if possible: "Well, there wouldn't be much point in tidying up your office if the Director were visiting in, say, Miami, would there?"

Aargh! This is the last thing we need, the Director with his entourage.

"We just found out this morning," Shirley says with a broad smile as she turns on her heels and plump ankles and heads off to brighten the afternoon at another office.

That, at least, explains part of the mystery. Koerner is gone today, off to the Academy at Quantico for some kind of executive training session. Who else would have cued me in to what might be a routine tour through the farm system? But I'm betting something bigger is going on here. From what I've heard, the Old Guard at HQ is not wild about Bill Sessions, his management style, or his wife, who seems to get in the way. Plus, there's been talk among Bureau pilots—a tight-knit sewing bee—that Mr. and Mrs. Sessions have been using Bureau aircraft with far too much frequency and beyond the scope of work. That's not my fight, but the more Judge Sessions (as he insists on being called) travels hither and yon, the more work for SWAT team members, who in addition to all their other duties have the added burden of being the Director's (and his wife's) bodyguards.

As for the ultimate purpose of the visit, I'm guessing that the news Conrad and Ramsay sold the NATO go-to-war plans to our enemies has blindsided Sessions completely—his Washington Field Office, after all, had already declared the case dead and the bodies buried. My hope, of course, is that the Director fully grasps the gravity of the case, but I've also heard via the same pilot grapevine that Sessions is more political than his predecessor, William Webster, and nothing scores points with the Hill and the media like a good spy case.

ROD IS SITTING IN the open door of his camper when I pull in a little before 6:30 p.m. That's good, I'm thinking—lover-girl and her lover-boy aren't here to further pollute the atmosphere. But when I get a look at Rod, I can see that he's about as low as a person can get. Temporarily, Perrera's helps pull him out of that. I've brought two large sacks of carry-out: *frijoles negros, arroz con pollo, carne con papas,* even two big cups of Cuban *garbanzo* soup—if this doesn't fatten him up nothing will. We're barely into the second bag, though, when his misery starts seeping through again. And before I know it, Rod isn't just crying, he's sobbing, almost choking on his own tears, and the camper, at least initially, seems to be at the heart of his distress.

"Let's go for a walk, Rod," I say, folding up the last food bag and placing it inside my car, where the rodents and/or returning lovers won't find and devour the contents before Rod gets a second crack at them.

"I don't understand," Rod says when he can finally get his emotions under control. "You know, I give her a place to live; I do everything—"

"And she's fucking another guy under your roof?"

"Joe . . ."

"Rod, can I tell you something?"

He nods.

"You've got to let this girl go. This isn't healthy. You've just got to move on."

"Sure," he says, seeming to agree, "but I can't just leave her with no place to live."

"Rod," I want to say, "you *can* leave her with no place to live and secretly pour cayenne pepper all over Romeo's prick, and no jury of peers in the land would convict you," but this isn't what Rod wants to hear, and his romantic and housing problems, I feel certain, are only entry gates to levels of fucked-upness that I haven't yet begun to imagine. I'm not sure if I want to open them, but honestly, I don't see how I can help him if I don't.

"It's not just the girl, is it, Rod? Not just the camper?"

He's looking at me now, with tears back in his eyes, a cigarette jammed between his thin lips. If Rod weighs 130 pounds, I'd be surprised. He's been wasting away in front of Moody's and my eyes ever since we resumed interviewing him. Without the dinners we've been buying him, he might just disappear into his own shadow. But maybe because of the clap, Rod's worse than ever today. He stinks—there's no other word for it. His breath is rancid with nicotine and neglect. This is the Campground of Wounded Souls, as I've come to think of it, but even here as we walk in the darkening evening, Rod stands out.

"What is it, Rod?" I ask. I've got my hand on his shoulder, turning him toward me. "What's wrong?" And that's when he loses it completely.

"Everything, Joe," he says, practically begging me to embrace him. "Everything under the sun."

And so, with Rod literally weeping on my shoulder, we begin the long unraveling of his utterly fucked-up life. The father he never really knew. The mother he knows he's let down time and time again. The bank he and some pals robbed when they were eighteen. There's also the failed drug test, not so funny in this telling when it's clear to me he desperately misses the army life. And of course the hours upon hours he spends waiting in line at Orlando International every day in a cab he can pay the rent on only if he gets more fares than time permits. ("Why don't you work the hotels, Rod," I suggest—"the people going to the airport, instead of coming from it? The distance is the same, but there's never more than a couple cabs waiting at the Embassy Suites." "But there're lots of people to talk with in the cab line," he counters.) Even ABC News, Rod says, has been screwing him, making him promises (of what, he doesn't say) then never delivering.

We're walking again, circling the campground, when a word comes to me: *inchoate*, that sense of beginning many things but never having a fully formed plan or seeing things through. That's the story of Rod's life, I'm thinking. He strives, but he never achieves. He robs a bank (or says he does—I'll be checking on this) but walks away with pocket money. He torpedoes his army career with cannabis. He moves a girlfriend into his camper without ever considering that she might end up screwing another guy on his bed. He rents a cab so he can wait in a long line and gab with other cabbies, undoubtedly impressing them with his vast erudition. We've got no way of confirming what Rod claims to have been paid for his espionage work—two hundred bucks serving as a documents mule, five hundred for stealing the go-to-war plans—but you can bet it's only a tiny fraction of what Clyde Conrad netted from the same activities.

God, I'm thinking as we close in on Rod's camper again, Conrad must have seen this guy as a godsend—a brilliant, needy, inchoate sucker, ready to sign up for the riskiest schemes.

NONE OF THIS IS interviewing the way I'm used to doing it—no chairs placed just so, no order of entry, no script in my head or anywhere else. I'm making this up on the fly, and so when we get back to Rod's camper, I wing it one more time, pulling out two $20 bills and handing them to him outside.

"Here," I say, "take it, but I don't want you to spend this on drugs. I don't want you to spend it on alcohol, and I don't want you to spend it on her," pointing toward the camper door with my chin.

"Of course not," Rod says. Then he gives me a hearty slap on the back, thanks me for the "super chow," and walks jauntily away in the direction of his camper rubbing the two crisp twenties together over his head so I have a good look at them. And that's when it dawns on me that maybe I've just been played for a five-star sucker—lured into driving two-plus hours round-trip so Rod can get a square meal and practice his melodrama. What's more, if I'm reading that slap on the back and upbeat exit, Rod wants me to know exactly what just happened.

That's the thing with Rod: Even if his sobs are for real, you never, ever know for sure what level of truth you're playing at.

I BEGIN THE RETURN drive to Tampa with a hideous cup of carry-out coffee from the campground convenience store, thinking that I'd rather have a stomachache in the morning than do another off-roading adventure on the way home tonight.

By the quarter-way mark, I'm convinced I have, in fact, been conned, scammed, sucker-punched, wheedled, and cajoled not just out of my time and forty bucks but out of my emotional and intellectual comfort zone. Rod wanted to unsettle me—set me up, make me feel for him, then spring the joke. That's what this whole thing was about. Ha ha. Who knows, maybe even the clap was part of it. God knows, I never checked his pecker personally, and never would, for that matter. But I did make that first call about securing drugs for him. And of course, looked at one way, I've also just bribed him for testimony.

By halfway, I've swung the other way. The whole fucked-upness of his life is far too real to be staged and far too deeply seated to be part of some plot to (a) ruin Joe Navarro's life and/or (b) assure that any case ultimately brought against Rod will be thrown out.

That leaves me free for the rest of trip home to concentrate on the paradoxical nature of what I'm doing. The fact, for example, that I'm both Rod's therapist and confessor—the one who must help him find some stability in his inchoate life, and the one who'll eventually write the affidavit in this case, be the lead witness testifying against him in court, and, hopefully, cause him to spend the rest of his life behind bars.

Cognitive dissonance? In spades.

There doesn't seem to be an out, though. At this point I'm the only one who can coax the rest of the story out of Rod. (Not even She-Moody, I'm guessing, can pry loose the secrets buried in him, though I wouldn't tell her that.)

As I approach the glowing lights of Greater Tampa, I punch in the local all-news station. *Flash!* While Rod and I have been pacing his Wounded Souls Campground in almost-exurban Orlando, 4,900 miles away in divided Berlin, Germans on both sides of the famous Wall are sledgehammering it to the ground.

Great, I think. So long, Marxism/Leninism/Stalinism, etc. But bears are never more dangerous than when they're wounded, and this reeling Soviet bear still has enough kilotons of nuclear explosives to level every major European and American city from Vienna to LA, and more than enough throw-power to reach the surface of the moon and beyond. What do the crazies left in the Kremlin really have on us? I'm wondering. And will they panic and start something with whatever they know? Inevitably, that line of thought leads me back to one person: Rod.

14

"SOMETHING'S GOT TO GIVE"

November 10, 1989

"If you're lost ... la, la, la."

Stephanie is singing at the breakfast table, an echo of the days when we were stationed in Puerto Rico. She and Luciana loved to watch Cyndi Lauper on VH1. They would sing these lyrics over and over again. I can hear traces of Luciana's Brazilian-accented Portuguese in Stephanie's voice. I see Luciana, too, in the way Stephanie taps her wrist with her index finger as she repeats the chorus: "time after time ..."

I have a memory of Stephanie singing this very song at some talent show—belting it out, fearless, giving it her all—but where and when? It couldn't have been more than a few years ago. She's only eight. But it seems almost like a memory from another lifetime.

I'm showered and dressed after another night of broken sleep. Over at the toaster, Luciana is holding up a sliced English muffin as if it were a question mark.

"Maybe with some yogurt and fruit?" she asks, hopeful that I might for once sit with them for breakfast and, judging by the sound of her voice, almost certain that I won't. Her eyes, I notice, aren't quite on mine, as if she's chosen another me, a few inches to my right, to talk with.

"Sorry, dear," I say, "not today. Places to go, people to see, like always."

I think I hear her say "What day, then?" as I give Stephanie a kiss on the top of her head, inhaling deeply to capture her scent— something to take with me into a beautiful morning, the air scrubbed clean by a late-season storm.

But I don't get away quite so cleanly. Luciana is tapping on my window as I slip the car into drive.

"This case," she says as I'm lowering my window, "whatever it is, it's like an *obsessão*, an . . ." She struggles for the proper English rendering.

"An obsession, *amada*. I know it seems that way, but it's not. It's duty, that's all. It's my job. This case was poorly handled. I need to make it right before bad people walk away."

"Ramsay," she says, "the name you mumble in your sleep . . ."

"You have to forget that name," I tell her. Our hands are joined at the window, our closest physical contact in months, it seems. "I never should have said it, even in a dream."

"I know," she says, still not quite looking square at me. *"Segredos."*

"No, no," I say, "not secrets, need-to-know."

"I hate not knowing, Joe. I hate what this case is doing to you."

I want to explain it all—how badly Rod Ramsay has damaged this country, how far behind we are, what's at stake. But that can't happen, and Luciana has lived through this before. Still, she's not alone. I also hate what this case is doing to me, personally and at home. Driving away, thinking of Stephanie and how little time we have together, my eyes well up with tears, so I force myself to think of something else.

THE ZACK STREET SANDWICH Shop must have been a nice place thirty years ago, I'm thinking, as I drop gently down on my usual stool at the far end of the counter, but time hasn't stood still.

I can feel one of the springs in the seat just itching to burst through the cracked red plastic cover. Half a year ago, I was sitting in one of the booths toward the back when that very thing happened. By the time I untangled my pants from the coiled metal, they were, in Bureau terms, non-salvageable. More than a few snickers trailed me as I walked back to the office covering my behind.

"Where's your better half?" Linda asks as she plops a watery coffee down in front of me. This morning, she's even more bristling than usual with piercings and ear studs and the oddest damn assortment of nature-themed tattoos I've ever seen. "You make her park the car today?"

For an instant I'm wondering if Luciana has ever been here. And if so, why?

"Oh," says Linda, slapping me on the hand, "here she comes," and as I turn, I see She-Moody winding toward me through the crowd.

Then I get it. "Moody? She's not my wife!"

"You could have fooled me," Linda says, utterly surprised. "You guys are tighter than pointed shoes."

"That's her husband over there—the redhead," I tell her, pointing to He-Moody already sitting in the back with a gaggle of criminal-division agents.

"Well, I'll be goddamned!" Linda says loudly. "I've never seen those two together—he's always with those other wet-behind-the-ear agents."

Somehow Moody has picked up instantly on the drift of this conversation, because the first thing she says as she sits on the stool next to me is "Believe me, Linda, I couldn't be married to this man—ever. No sane woman could."

"Nice, Moody," I say, but with no real resentment. I've long since abandoned any illusion of popularity.

Linda breaks the silence for us.

"Well, if you guys aren't married, you sure as hell sound like it. The usual?"

"With grits today," Moody says, patting her belly. "The Bump has been doing somersaults all morning. I need to feed the beast."

The reality, of course, is that Terry and I *do* spend a hell of a lot of time together—here, laying out the daily Rod strategy; back and forth between my office on the fifth floor and hers on the sixth, often whispering because we're talking about things that most of our fellow agents aren't cleared to hear; in the Bu-Steed, God knows, back and forth, back and forth, back and forth to Orlando; even (to get back to the romantic theme) in hotel rooms, although most of that time in the voluble company of a narcissistic traitor to his country.

Is Linda the only person who thinks we're hitched, or at least having an affair? Probably not. If you strip out the Rod part of the equation, all the telltale signs are there. You wouldn't have to be a genius to read them. I'm wondering if Luciana has considered the possibility, maybe even Rod.

"Do you think we're spending too much time together?" I ask, as Linda heads back our way with tea for Moody.

"Think so? I *know* so. How does your wife put up with your hours?"

"Not well," I say, remembering this morning's failure to even make full eye contact. "I don't blame her. This past year I haven't been a great husband or father. This morning Stephanie was singing her favorite song, and I realized I hadn't heard her sing in months—not just weeks, months! That sucks."

"When was the last time you and Luciana went on a date or to a movie?" Moody asks.

I'm searching my mind for any such moment when Moody answers her own question. "I bet it's been over a year. Joe, you *never* take time off. You're pulling double and triple duty."

"I know, I know."

"And you look like shit today, by the way."

"Thanks. People keep saying that."

"No, really, you look terrible."

She stops, looks down at the floor for maybe half a minute while I watch more of my office mates trickling in for the breakfast, and then looks back up and stares at me straight on.

"You're doing it, aren't you?"

"Doing what?"

"Studying me as I talk, checking out the arch of my eyebrows, whether I put my hand near my mouth. You're probably hoping I'll take up cigarettes so you can study my smoke contrails, for God's sake."

"My 'body-language shit'?"

"Not shit, Joe. Not shit at all. This stuff works. But me, Joe?"

"Habit."

"I'm your partner, Joe. You've got to trust someone. You've got to believe in someone."

Trust? Believe? Suddenly, they sound like words from some lost tongue of the ancients.

"I didn't tell you. I went off the road two nights ago, coming back from Orlando—I fell fast asleep behind the wheel."

"Joe!"

"Well, I blame you for wanting to go in separate cars. If you'd been with me, I would have been wide-eyed awake all the way home."

"Nice try. More likely we would have both been killed. What happened?"

"There'd been a wreck on I-4. I was on US 60 near Lakeland or Plant City—I can't even remember exactly where. The next thing I knew my face was bobbing up and down and my teeth were chattering like a dashboard ornament on a low rider as I plowed through a strawberry field."

"Are you okay? Did a doc check you out?"

"No, I'm not okay, but I survived, and more important, the Bu-Steed did, too. The rain had washed it almost clean by morning."

"You going to report it?"

"Ask me in a few days, and I'll tell you what my conscience says. The only damage was to my pride. The field had about sixty yards of Goodyear tire marks, but that was about it—no fence knocked down."

"How about that shoulder you keep rubbing? You don't look very comfortable."

"I sprained it maybe—the clavicle feels loose. I might have torn a ligament. The seat belt caught it pretty hard."

"Okay, that does it," Moody says as Linda sets our plates in front of us—bagel and cream cheese for me, the Hungry Girl special for Terry. "You're going to see a doctor this morning."

"Right," I tell her. "And who's going to find me the time to do that?"

"Joe, something's got to give, or you're going to end up in the ER one of these days, and it'll be for something a hell of a lot worse than a bad shoulder."

"Everything is starting to give, Moody," I tell her as she begins diving into her fried eggs and sausage.

"Like?"

"Don't play analyst. Things are tough at home. Luciana keeps telling me this is unfair—how I need to spend time with Stephanie, how she needs help around the house. She needs a husband, not a *convivado*."

"What the hell's a *convivado*?"

"It's Portuguese for houseguest."

"Ouch! You need to get your act together at home, Joe, seriously. What did Luciana say about your going off the road?"

"I haven't told her. How can I? She won't even make eye contact with me. We haven't eaten together in months. I'm almost afraid to by now. What are we going to talk about?"

"God, Navarro, you can be a real selfish prick."

"Thanks again, Moody. Another thing I really need to hear this morning."

"You need to hear this *especially* this morning." Moody has lowered her voice and is almost spitting her words out now between clenched teeth, but I can see the guy two stools down leaning his ear our way, caught up in our morning soap opera. "You could have died in that accident, goddamn it. A lot of good you would do then."

I just look at Moody. I know she's right, but I'm too tired and my shoulder is too sore, and unless I'm wrong, the wheels are starting to come off more things than my car.

"You can make changes, Joe. Rod can adjust his schedule. And you don't have to go see him every damn day. What was that trip about yesterday—another night of hand-holding?"

"I told you. I can't say. I promised Rod."

"You promised Rod? What is this? Honor among thieves? I'm your partner."

"It's something he's too embarrassed for you to find out."

"Oh, for crissake," Moody all but shouts out.

"All right, he's got VD, but you didn't hear it from me."

"It figures: boys and their aching penises. But we don't have to do the interviews in the evening every time. You can be home with Luciana—"

"No," I say. "I thought you understood this. There is less resistance from a suspect at the end of the day because of low blood sugar. Besides, daytime is his best shot for fares at the airport."

"Okay, but all the planning, Joe. What topics to bring up. Where we sit. What we wear. The order of the questions. The 'meaningful' pauses and props. Can't we just let it fly sometimes? We put in whole days doing this kind of stuff."

"Not whole days," I say.

"You're right—more like weeks, Navarro."

"But we can't leave things to chance. Every encounter is a new encounter with him. Haven't you noticed? No two interviews have been the same. There's always something we have to deal with, something we have to coax out of him. I've got a list a mile long of things in my head that we've got to cover, not just to satisfy the intelligence community but also for trial."

"How about the reports?" Terry goes on, ignoring my rising voice, and the way that guy two stools down has started leaning our way again. "They don't have to be this thorough, and they don't have to be on Koerner's desk by 11 a.m. every single damn day."

"You're wrong! Moody, you screw up a criminal report, and it's no big deal—nobody gives a shit. Oops, we'll catch them another day. But this is counterintel. This is espionage. You know where these reports go? Did I ever explain that?"

"Sure. Koerner. SAC. HQ."

"That's the beginning, Terry. The very beginning. They go to the CIA, the State Department, Army, and Justice. Can it get worse? Yes, of course, it's the Bureau. Now we have to send it to the NSA, and did I forget the National Security Council? Also the White House gets a brief, just in case they get an inquiry. This is why we send ten copies. This stuff counts. That's why we have it done by eleven o'clock each morning and why I'll keep having it done by eleven o'clock each morning until this case is done, if it's ever done, even if it kills me."

"Navarro." There's alarm in her voice now, as if maybe I've just sounded my own death knell. "You may be right on all counts—in fact, you're always right when it comes to work—but I know a thing or two about life, Mr. FBI man, and this lifestyle you're leading will destroy you."

"You don't understand. You know what I feel like?" I ask.

"No. Tell me."

"I keep thinking I'm in a football game where I don't know what the playing time for each quarter will be or where the goalposts are located. All I know for certain is that I have to keep running, nonstop, until the whistle blows. When will that happen? When are we going to pull the trigger and arrest Rod? That's all beyond my control, you understand, but at the same time it's all-consuming because we're dealing with existential threats, not another bank robbery. I'm being told to keep Rod talking by people who often have no faith in what he tells me or in the techniques I'm using. And just for a little kicker, every confession Rod makes adds to the certainty that he'll spend the rest of his life behind bars. That's okay—prison is what he deserves—but I'm the guy who has to lie to him and lie to his mother, day in and day out. And I'm also the guy who has to get this perfect because I'm the case agent, and I have to undo the nonfeasance of WFO. I might have been sucked into this case gradually, but I sure as hell can't get out of it now that it has become almost unmanageable. And . . ."

"Yeah, and?"

"And it's not just me doing this, Terry. It's you, too. All that time away from your husband. All that time away from your son. Who knows what will happen when your baby is born. I feel guilty about that, too."

I'm watching Terry sop up her yolk with a piece of toast speared on her fork when she carefully lays her utensils down, wipes her lips with her napkin, and swivels on her stool to face me head-on.

"What's my son's name?" she asks.

I can't say anything. There's a memory there somewhere, but I can't pull it back.

"How old is he?"

"I don't know," I say. "Little. Maybe ten."

"His name is Kyle. He's fourteen years old, Joe, growing like a weed. He's going to be up to my shoulders soon. You want to do the math?"

"Math?"

"Yeah, math. I'll help you. I'm thirty-three. Terry and I were married two years ago."

"So, maybe he's not He-Moody's child?"

"Good, you can subtract. I was nineteen when Kyle was born, not what I expected, but it happened just like your parents always warned you about. His father was drop-dead handsome, but he sure as hell didn't stick around. I put myself through college, Joe. I had no help. I worked and went to school with Kyle at my side. The point is this . . ."

"The point?"

"Yeah, Joe, the point. I'm not just telling you all this for the fun of it. Everyone else in our office already knows this, even Shirley, maybe most of all Shirley. We come to social events. We ask after each other's families. We tape photographs on our cubicle walls of our kids sitting in Santa's lap. If Kyle walked through that door right now, everyone at Mr. Moody's table back there—and yes, he is his father as far as I'm concerned—would know exactly who he was."

"And?"

"And for all the hours and hours and hours we've spent together, you don't really know anything about me or my family. You don't come to the social events. You don't stop at people's office door and ask how the kids' soccer games went over the weekend. You're a stranger to the office socials and the FBI Recreation Association. That photo of you and your daughter . . ."

"She was eighteen months old then. That was in Puerto Rico . . ."

"I know all that. My point is this, Joe. You keep it on your desk surrounded by files where almost no one can see it. You're so damned solitary and inaccessible."

Linda agrees. "You scare people," she says as she slaps our checks on the counter. Terry as usual has left a clean plate behind: two eggs, toast, grits, and sausage all down the hatch. Meanwhile, I've left half a bagel and cream cheese on my plate.

We're halfway to the cashier, edging our way between counter stools and tables, when Terry leans into me in another of those gestures that a bystander might well take for intimacy and whispers, "Remember when I said you didn't have to be an asshole?"

"Remember?" I whisper back. "How could I ever forget?"

"Well," she says, her mouth practically in my ear now, "you don't have to kill yourself, either. And you don't have to be so alone or aloof."

Don't I? I wish I could be so sure.

15

FIRST DATE

February 12, 1990

When it comes to espionage cases, Marc Reeser is quite simply the best analyst the FBI has ever produced. He also may be the most un-FBI-looking FBI employee I've ever worked with.

Face it, there's a certain cookie-cutter look to agents. Most of us are athletic, square-shouldered, and probably way too buttoned-down. Not Marc. He looks permanently disheveled—wrinkled clothing, shirts that always seem way too big, a tie that's never pulled tight. Marc did time in the military, but he never acquired military bearing, that's for sure. What he's really good at is what most agents (this one included) detest: poring over databases and studying lists for hours on end. He finds patterns in the phone numbers used by suspects, and thanks to his prodigious memory, he recognizes addresses in, say, Vienna that have been used by previous spies.

But here's the really nice thing about Marc: Despite being a brainiac, he's a regular Joe, an ice-hockey fanatic, and an incurable optimist. I found all that out back in early December, on the day I picked him up at Tampa International, less than a week after he'd been detailed to the Ramsay case. The first item he grabbed off the baggage carousel was a normal-sized suitcase crammed with whatever clothes and other accessories he figured he needed for however many months he was going to be detailed to me. Item Two was a huge, overstuffed duffel bag—almost as big as Marc himself, who's a compact five-eight or so.

"What's in that?" I asked.

"Skates, pads, and pucks."

Before he could explain further, Item Three came clattering out of the shoot: half a dozen hockey sticks bound together with duct tape.

As we struggled our way to the parking garage, I asked, "What the hell is all this shit? Are you going to play sand hockey on Clearwater Beach?"

"I checked it out. There's an ice rink near I-4 and I-75."

There is? That's not far from where I live.

"Besides," Marc said, handling all the bags with expert skill, "Tampa is going to get a team soon."

"Huh?"

"The Lightning, or whatever they end up calling it. Hockey's going to be bigger here than Cuban cigars, Joe."

"Hockey in Tampa? Right. Make way for the Stanley Cup!"

"O ye of little faith. In any case, I've been in touch with a local amateur team, and they've invited me to play."

"Really?"

"Yeah, tonight."

"Tonight? You just got here."

"I know, and we have to get moving."

"What about the case?"

"Who do you think reads everything you send up? The agents don't read it. Jane is the only one who follows everything. I'm the only guy at HQ who has followed this case from Day One. I don't know as much about Ramsay as you do, but I know more about the overall case than anyone else. Besides, you're stuck with me, and tonight I play hockey."

Bottom line: Marc is his own man. And in the two-plus months he's been with us in Tampa, he's become damn near indispensable. His military experience—mostly as an MP—means he can help me out with a lot of basic stuff I don't understand about the army. More important, he knows all the names in the case, all the players, all the dates, and all the key facts. In the Bureau, analysts are seen as support staff. But to me, Marc is more valuable than an agent. I treat him as such, and so does Koerner.

EVER SINCE EARLY JANUARY, Marc and I—and Terry if she's not otherwise obligated—have been meeting daily a little before noon to plot where we're headed next. Today's no different. Marc starts out by handing me a chart. I look at it, but I'm too preoccupied with other matters to focus on what's written there.

"Do you see what's missing?" Marc asks, forcing the paper closer to my face.

"Yes, the eyesight I once had and a working mind. For God's sake, just explain it to me. I don't have time to guess."

"These are the documents Rod has told us about," he says, running his finger down one column. "These are the ones that we have confirmed, these are the ones that the army knew about, and these are the ones the Swedes think they saw."

"Okay, what am I missing?"

"The list looks fairly robust, doesn't it?"

"Agreed. A lot of work went into this."

"Well, it's not."

"It's not?" I say, taking it from his hand.

"True, Joe, you've gotten a lot out of Ramsay. More than enough to prosecute and put him away for sure."

"But?"

"I can tell there are documents missing."

"How?"

"I checked with a similar base in Germany through our friends at the army and I talked to a few other people."

"And?"

"For G-3 Plans to function at the Eighth ID, there had to be more documents—many more, and far more sensitive documents, things Rod hasn't even hinted at."

"Shit."

"Like I said, we have a lot, but the only person who can give us the full inventory is Ramsay himself. Right now we don't have an accounting; we can only speculate."

Before he's finished, I'm on my feet and headed for the door.

"Where you going?"

"Where do you think? I'm going to call Rod and see if he'll go on a little date with me."

"I thought that wasn't until tomorrow."

"No, thanks to you, it's going to be today."

"Joe, don't go there half-cocked."

"I'm not. I just don't like to think there's more out there I don't know about."

"What about Moody? She's on her way here."

"Tell her to take the rest of the day off—she can use it."

ROD, IT TURNS OUT, tells me he needs to work extra hours. He's just about flat broke and way behind on his cab rental payments. His boss has told him he has to drive tonight or find another job. It's the old story—I thought clearing up the clap and getting Typhoid Mary out of Rod's camper might steer him onto a better path. But if you gave Rod a million bucks a year and a free suite at the Plaza, he'd still find a way to screw everything up.

"Tell you what," I say, "pick me up at the usual place—Embassy Suites at six-thirty in your cab and don't be late."

"You're not listening, Joe. I have to drive tonight. I gotta work, make some money."

"I *am* listening, Rod," I say, "better than you give me credit for. I'm hiring your cab for three hours tonight just like those Japanese tourists you get every once in a blue moon. I'll bring us dinner, and while we eat, I'll be on the meter."

"Perrera's? That's so good."

"Perrera's it is."

"*Ropa vieja* and plantains, the twice-fried?"

"Yes, for crissake. *Ropa vieja* and plantains, and would you like to supersize that with a side of *frijoles negros*, sir?"

"*Por supuesto*," Rod answers with a near perfect accent, "and ice tea, *sin azúcar*."

"Got it," I say, feeling a good deal like that burger flipper out near Busch Gardens I've always feared becoming. "And, Rod . . ."

"Yes?"

"Clean out the damn cab before you pick me up. I don't want to eat dinner knee-deep in pages torn out of *Foucault's Pendulum*."

REMARKABLY—OR PERHAPS *NOT*, considering—Rod arrives at 6:29 p.m. And a nice surprise awaits: Except for a small sheaf of torn-out book pages crammed between the passenger seat and the center console, Rod's cab has clearly been spruced up. Rod, too. He must have ducked into a McDonald's men's room on the way over.

"You look nice," I say.

"Thanks. You, too. But you always look professional, Agent Navarro."

"Thanks yourself."

"No Moody?" he asks, pouting.

"She needs a break."

"Where to, then?" he asks as I break taxi tradition and settle into the front seat beside him. The smells from his Perrera's feast are already filling the car.

"SeaWorld," I say, "and start the meter."

"You sure?"

"Start it." Rod puts the cab in gear and the meter is running.

"We're going to watch Shamu while we eat?"

"No, we're going to sit in the goddamn parking lot."

Which is, in fact, what we do, since taxis are allowed in for free. I have Rod park away from the hard clot of cars close to the entrance gate, but not back in some distant corner. We might be having nothing more than dinner and a chat, but I want clean lines of sight in all directions. (This is why I don't pick Disney World. Except on Christmas Day, the lots there are *always* too full for this.)

"This is sort of like a date," Rod says as I unbag the containers and hand him his dinner. "Are we going to neck after we eat?"

"Yes, some serious necking," I say. "In fact, as soon as you finish eating, I'm going to place my hands around your neck and throttle you for making me come to Orlando almost every day."

We both laugh, even though Rod knows that I've felt like doing just that on more than one occasion.

Dinner doesn't take long. Rod is devouring the food, all but shoveling it in, while I snack on a bag of *chicharrones*—basically, fried pork skins, empty eating but comfort food for me as I try to put on some weight. When he's through, I bag everything and place it down by me feet.

Rod has NPR on, listening to a recap of the day's news.

"Rod," I say, "we know each other pretty well now. We talk more than most people do at work."

"We do. I mean, no one else knows about my situation," Rod says, looking down at his genitals.

"That's true, we talk about things few others do. And don't worry, Moody doesn't know." Another lie I'll live with.

"But you know, as much as we've talked, I have to tell you, I feel, I sense, that you're holding back, that you have more to tell me, lots more."

Rod looks straight ahead but doesn't say anything. He tries a little smile but he can't manage it.

"I think I know why, but I want to hear why from you." This is what I call a presumptive: I already know you did it; I just need to know why. It makes an admission much easier. "I can understand why answers," I tell him. "I have so far, haven't I?"

"You have and you do."

"Think about it. If I sense it, so does Koerner."

"Is Koerner giving you a bad time?" Now I don't answer, I just perform a deep exhale.

Rod is staring outside the window as tourists are making their way back to their cars after a long day—children in a zombie state, parents worn to the bone. Theme parks have one theme in common: They wear you out.

"You mind if we step outside?" Rod asks. "I need a smoke."

"Nope." I watch his hand carefully as he reaches into the glove compartment for his smokes and a beat-up plastic lighter that I'm sure someone else tossed away. I've been around Rod now for months, but I never let my guard down. I'm always checking for weapons, in case he decides to permanently end his misery—or mine.

Rod is looking up at a small airplane circling high above in the night sky, probably one of those sightseeing airplanes you can hire out of Kissimmee Airport. The plane's anticollision light flickers on and off every other second, as we both lean against the hood of Rod's taxi. I can sense his reticence, but there's no tension, maybe because we're enjoying this little outside venture and a breeze has come up.

"You know I play chess?" Rod begins.

"Of course, you told Agent Eways that the first day."

"My favorite game, though, is *Dungeons and Dragons*. I gave you that book . . ."

"I still have it," I say. "You want it back?"

He shakes his head no.

"Clyde was never into *D and D*. He preferred chess. But games teach you what Clyde was always saying: You have to have a strategy always—for whatever you're doing. You need to have a plan, a reason, options."

"It's the same for me, Rod," I say. "And for you. Lack of planning is courting failure."

"Conrad and I made so many plans. I was to be promoted and go to Heidelberg. I was going to have greater access and responsibility—Heidelberg is HQ for all of Central Europe—but I literally pissed it away."

I'm trying to dope out where Rod is going with this when he shifts direction on a dime.

"Joe, be honest with me. Now that the Wall is down, does all of this matter? My helping you, my reports, do they even amount to a hill of shit?"

"Rod, do you think for one minute that the Russians are going to be our friends? Other than North Korea, this is the most paranoid military power on Earth. They'll never trust the West. Do you think the KGB is suddenly going to become a stalwart advocate for democracy? They won't change, and let me tell you, it's not over yet. The KGB and the military have a financial stake in distrusting the West. They may just put an end to this perestroika experiment. They thrive on acrimony and fear—not 'Kumbaya' hand-holding. When the novelty wears off, the knives will come out."

"I suppose you're right," he says, taking long drags on his cigarette.

"Don't overanalyze it, okay? Snakes don't become less reptilian because they're treated nicely." More silence from Rod, which starts to bother me. I always use silence as a tool.

"You like flying, Joe?" Rod asks, looking at a plane high above SeaWorld.

"I do, but I've been kind of busy."

"You don't mention your daughter anymore."

"I know, it's tough when I'm on the road all the time."

Rod keeps staring at the sky, admiring his own smoke trail as it meanders with the breeze from the west. He's setting the pace, orchestrating something. I've never seen him so pensive in an interview before.

Suddenly, his head hangs forward as if he's no longer able to hold it up. He pulls out another cigarette, lifts his head back up almost as if it were a burden, and says, "I hope you brought a pen. You're going to need it.

"Charming Gorilla, Lion Heart, Atomic Demolitions Munitions List, Flicker, Peacetime Rules of Engagement, Cold Fire, Wintex-Cimex, Able Archer, USEEUCOM Emergency Action Procedures, Champagne Gourmet, Seventh Infantry Division (M) CONPLAN 4200, Candid Honor, Op plan for Twelfth Panzer." He machine-guns them at me. "Oops, sorry, let me repeat them for you."

I'm already writing in the margins of Rod's torn book pages when he repeats the list, as near as I can say exactly the same as before.

"Clyde and I clipped all of them, copied the plans, sold them to the Hungarians. Which one do you want to know about?"

"Able Archer is the one that sticks most immediately in my mind."

"Oh, yes," Rod says, "Able Archer. A good choice," and with that the cadence and tone of his voice changes, reminding me of Walter Cronkite narrating a documentary:

"1983: a perilous year in Cold War history. April: The US Navy sends forty ships, three hundred aircraft, and twenty-three thousand crew members, maybe the largest and most powerful fleet ever, into the North Pacific to test Soviet readiness in the region. Five months later, on September 1, Korean Air Lines Flight 007 is blown out of the sky near Sakhalin Island, over prohibited Soviet airspace. Among the 269 passengers and crew killed: Representative Larry McDonald, Democrat of Georgia. On September 26, with tensions already extremely high, the Soviet orbiting missile warning system incorrectly detects a single ICBM launch from the United States. This is followed by four more ICBM launches, also falsely logged. All that appears to keep the Soviets from responding in assumed kind is the very fortunate, cautionary restraint of a lone Soviet lieutenant colonel on duty at the time.

"Do you need his name?" Rod asks, retreating to more or less his own voice. I shake my head no, and he goes back to Cronkite.

"Seven weeks later, in early November 1983, NATO lays at the Soviets' doorstep the largest simulated nuclear attack ever put together. Known as Able Archer, the exercise is widely believed to have brought Moscow closer to launching a preemptive nuclear strike than it came at any other point during the Cold War—and that *includes* the Cuban Missile Crisis. But the story is more complicated than that because—ta-da!—the Soviets already have the *entire schematic for the NATO exercise* at their fingertips."

Ramsay actually chortles in his boyish, narcissistic way as he tells me this. He's transitioned from a more reserved and considerate personality at the beginning of this interview to his true character.

"Courtesy of?" I ask, sure of the answer, which Rod immediately gives me by making a modest bow.

"C'mon," I tell him, "this is bullshit. If the Russians had the Able Archer plan, they wouldn't have gotten in such a lather. They would have had proof in hand that it was an exercise, nothing more."

"Joe, Joe, Joe," Rod answers, a benevolent smile now spreading across his face, "that's the beauty of it."

"The beauty of what?"

"The Russians bought the plans from us through the Hungarians, then became convinced that we'd sold them misinformation meant to provide cover for a real NATO-led attack. You know that paranoia you just talked about? We got the money. They got the ulcers. And of course, once they realized Able Archer was exactly what we'd told them it was, they knew they could trust us even more. It was beautiful!"

Yeah, I'm thinking, *and millions of people might have died while you and Clyde were polishing your bona fides and burying more Krugerrands in the wintry German countryside, you bastard.* But there'll be time for saying that later. For now, I'm pressing Rod to give me a gloss on some of the other plans he's just named. The more detail work we have on these documents, the easier it's going to be to make our case in court.

"Start with the first one you remember clipping," I suggest.

Rod, still on his high, is only too happy to comply.

"I can tell you exactly which one it was. I was still being tested. Clyde told me he wanted the latest update of CONPLAN 4200. These were updated all the time, and it's what the Hungarians were interested in. So I copied it along with all the changes. I forgot what Conrad got paid, but it was a lot—at least twenty thousand dollars."

"Wait, what the hell is a CONPLAN?" I ask, not because I don't know but because I want him to tell me that he knows.

"These are the *contingency* plans, Joe," Rod explains in his most patient voice. "I told you about this before, way back with Al Eways. If something unexpected happens, it details for all the troops from the generals in theater on down what everyone will do. CONPLANs are crucial for forward-deployed troops."

"I'm sorry," I break in again, "but what was the classification of this document, just so I understand?"

"Oh, secret," Rod says, as casually as if were giving me the time of day, "although some of the CONPLANs did have top-secret annexes."

Me, with a third follow-up for courtroom purposes: "So how important was the information in the document, this CONPLAN 4200?"

"Extremely. Everything is laid out precisely as to what we would do. Let's say the space shuttle goes down in a foreign country, or a military jet veers off course and is forced to land behind the Iron Curtain, there are contingencies for that. It's the bible of what to do when things get all snarled up. Weren't you listening when I talked about this?"

I ignore that—let him think I don't remember. Instead, I try to drive another nail into Rod's legal coffin: "And you copied it? Did you read it?"

Rod, getting short with me now: "Of course I read it, I had to add the most recent additions. How could I know what was new and what old if I didn't read it?"

Then, and this is when it becomes truly scary, Ramsay closes his eyes as if blocking me out and begins to quote verbatim from one of the more interesting parts of the document, telling me the page number and even noting that the information can be found on the bottom third of the page on the left side.

I'm blown away by this, but I'm not going to let the moment go untested.

"I bet you can't repeat that," I say, pulling out more of the book pages to write on. Unfazed, Rod sits there silently, almost as if he's expecting a kiss, then repeats every word down to the last syllable. Then, for good measure, he tells me what copier he used and how he had to struggle with the oversized staples that bound the document.

"Okay, genius," I say when he's through, "I'm going to check this out one of these days to see how accurate you are."

As I fold the pages and stuff them in my pocket, Rod calmly steeples his fingers as if he were chairman of the Federal Reserve—Annoying Habit #22, by the way—and says simply and decisively, "You'll find it's accurate in its entirety."

Rod drives me back to the Embassy Suites pretty much in silence. He's got the radio on, maybe because he doesn't want to hear me lecture him once again about hygiene, household finances, keeping a tidy cab, the usual stuff. Rod has told me several times in different ways that he wishes he'd met me earlier. "If someone like you had been my father," he once said, "things might have turned out differently for me." Maybe. But sometimes I feel more like the henpecker in a worn-out marriage. Still, something powerful happened in that SeaWorld parking lot, something deep. A barrier came down. In a way the quiet between us as we creep along International Drive is honoring that.

At the hotel, Rod spots my Bu-Steed off to the left and pulls up behind it while I fish $146 out of my wallet and wonder how I'm going to expense this. "All this for a cab ride?"—I can already hear the Bu-Accountant moaning. Rod walks around to my side with arms outstretched, as if he's relieved, and gives me a hug. For once, I don't bother to check him for weapons as we embrace. He could have shot me hours ago if he wanted to.

"Thanks for your help, Rod," I say, relieved at how the evening has turned out.

"There's one more thing, Joe."

"Yes, of course, I'll tell She-Moody you miss her."

"No, it's not that. There's more. That apartment was knee-deep in paper."

"What apartment, Rod?"

"The secret one," he says. "The one Clyde rented so we could process all the stuff I was clipping."

16

JOSEF SCHNEIDER
PLAZA #4

Conrad and Ramsay's "secret apartment" hits the national security community like a Johnny Carson monologue: It's a riot!

"Rented an apartment?" one guy at the Washington Field Office says with a tone of absolute incredulity when he phones to talk about my FD-302 on the subject. "Maybe word hasn't gotten to Tampa yet, Joe. Spies Don't Rent Apartments."

"Knee-deep in stolen documents?" another guy at FBIHQ faxes me back. "C'mon, Navarro, you make it sound like these guys were running an Espionage Sam's Club—'Pile 'em high! Watch 'em fly!'"

When I relay the news that Rod had started videotaping "clipped" documents right in the middle of Disney movies, they tell me that he's probably watched one too many Disney specials himself, and maybe I have, too, if I'm going to accept such nonsense at face value. Word that Rod had perfected (though never actually built) a briefcase that could erase the same videotapes in a pinch by dropping them between two magnets—"degaussing" is the proper term—only earns further heaps of derision: "Oh, the guy's a regular Edison."

One might think the army would be upset in the extreme when I let them know that Rod once saw a Black Book on the floor in the apartment. The Black Book, after all, is the army's equivalent of the President's Daily Intel Brief—the latest satellite imagery, intercepts,

237

and other vital information for theater commanders around the world, top-top-top-secret stuff. Instead, no one seems to be perturbed in the least. Black Books, I'm told, don't disappear, and they don't end up on the floor of an apartment rented by spies.

When I inform Langley that Ramsay and Conrad used their rich harvest of stolen documents to scam other intelligence services, they laugh at the possibility of a spy working with multiple services. When I further tell Langley about the DAVID Scam in which, according to Rod, Conrad posed as a Czech intelligence officer and sold some of that excess harvest to the CIA for $120,000, they explode in righteous indignation.

For a while, it's almost amusing, but before long, the "secret apartment" is being hung like a millstone around my neck, proof that Rod has been gaming me, dropping these bread crumbs so that I'll keep coming back, keep buying him dinners, keep being his best little buddy in the world.

It doesn't help either that Rod's otherwise no-fault memory isn't doing us a hell of a lot of good when it comes to locating his and Clyde's little hideaway. Part of the problem is lack of resources. When we asked WFO to supply us with a street map of Bad Kreuznach, they responded with a tattered, twenty-five-year-old tourist flyer put out by whatever the German equivalent is of a chamber of commerce: a teeny map surrounded by large banner ads for what I'm sure were overpriced tourist traps. I just can't believe this is the best the Bureau can do. Actually, it is the best WFO can do.

Then there's the human resource issue on our end. There's no missing Rod's devotion to Terry Moody, but as Terry's delivery date nears, she's traveling out of town less and less and eventually won't be leaving the office at all on her ob-gyn's orders. Susan Langford has been filling in for Terry and doing a damn good job of it. For one thing, Susan can be gut-roaringly funny, comic relief when the tension gets too thick between Rod and me. She's also first-office-agent young and full of energy, but every time Susan lets loose her heavy

Southern twang, Rod and I both, I think, grow a little sentimental for Terry's flat midwestern accent and the common sense that seems to go along with it. Bottom line: Susan is no Mrs. Moody in Rod Ramsay's eyes, and that's a big deal. For the first time, I think I'm seeing some target fixation when it comes to preferences from Rod.

All things being equal, Rich Licht would probably be a better fit than Susan for the interviewing. Rich is so new to our office that he's still commuting from Orlando, where he broke into the FBI. That could be a real advantage the next time Rod calls with, say, the clap and needs instant, on-site attention. What's more, in addition to being a really sharp young guy, Rich has a law degree, and you don't get through law school without learning how to ask questions, and especially follow-ups.

But Lynn Tremaine and especially Terry Moody have offered more than enough proof that Rod prefers to have at least one woman present when we meet. Besides, I need Rich in the office, following up leads. In practical terms, too, I'd be risking insurrection if I started dragging Rich up and down the highway to Orlando with me. The head of the steno pool tells me that the ladies in the office have declared Rich the "most dreamy agent going." Even out-of-it Navarro has noticed how heads turn when he walks by. If I robbed the stenos of their eye candy, my FD-302s would start getting typed up at a snail's pace or worse.

There's also the possibility that Rod is doing just what the chorus in DC says he's doing: playing with me, screwing me over, dragging this whole thing out to what sometimes seems to be the end of time.

Whatever the reasons, or combinations of them, time and again Susan and I have asked Rod to envision himself walking from the front gate of the Eighth ID base to the apartment, and time and again, Rod has missed a turn or gone up a wrong alley and taken us instead to the ruins of the castle of the Counts of Sponheim, or to the medieval Saint Nicholas's Catholic Church, or some obscure spot along the ancient town wall—where, of course, he has to deliver a half-hour lecture on the old Roman Road or the Frankish Empire or the famed Rabbi Ephraim bar Elieser ha-Levi, who was broken on the wheel in this very spot seven centuries ago, etc. Worst of all is when Rod leads us out of town on these meandering virtual tours to one of his favorite Riesling or Silvaner wineries and we have to suffer through yet another dissertation on grape varieties, soil types, and God knows what else. Susan is enough of an oenophile to find these diversions amusing, but she's not the one getting beat over the head to solve this little puzzle or, alternatively, to prove that the puzzle is a Rod Ramsay red herring.

The few "remembered" addresses we've teased out of Rod so far have managed nothing more than to piss off several respectable property owners once we convinced the German authorities to check them out. Now the Germans are starting to join the WFO and FBIHQ chorus, claiming that virtually everything Rod has "admitted to" has been invented. One recent communiqué from Bonn said that "according to the Germans, 'it is incontrovertible that this apartment does not exist.'"

"Incontrovertible?" Susan says when I show her the teletype. "Who uses words like that?"

"It's German," I tell her, "for fuck you, stop wasting our time, stronger message to follow."

A FEW DAYS LATER, I am in Orlando on other business, so I ask Rod if we can have a quick meeting at the Embassy Suites, just to talk all this over.

"Sure," he says, but when he gets there, nothing has changed. He's knocking himself out, he says, trying to remember the address, the network of streets and alleys that got him there, landmarks, anything, but it's all blank. He's never had anything like this happen to him before.

"Just keep trying," I tell him, knowing that I'm asking in effect that he hand me the rope that will hang him. "Up in Washington, they're all over me about this. They think maybe the apartment doesn't really exist."

I have to excuse myself for a few minutes after that. For a guy who eats so little, I've been dealing of late with a lot of gastric discomfort. When I come out of the bathroom, Rod has slid back the glass door and is standing on a tiny balcony, not even large enough for a folding chair.

"Joe," he says, "I'm willing to jump if that will make them believe I'm telling the truth about the apartment. I don't want anyone to think you're lying to them."

I'm touched—how could I not be?—but for multiple career and personal reasons, the last thing I want on my record (and replaying hour after hour in my head) is a suicide.

"Rod," I tell him, "please come back in and sit down. Please. We'll find a way to make good on this." And, thank God, he listens.

Later, after he's gone, the surveillance agent in the parking lot tells me that he all but pissed his pants when he saw Rod leaning out over the balcony railing. He says that he momentarily wondered if I'd had enough of Rod and was going to make him jump—a comment that horrified me.

WHEN I GET BACK to Tampa that day, I head straight to Rich's office.

"Get on the horn and talk to our assistant legal attaché in Germany," I tell him. "We're not waiting to go through HQ channels anymore. Tell him this is personal for me. Tell him how frustrated we are with both the army and WFO and have him find an aerial photograph of Bad Kreuznach."

"Where is he going to find one of those?"

"Don't know, don't care. Get him on it."

Three days later, the legal attaché, Ed Beatty, calls me late in the morning our time.

"It's on its way to you," he says.

"What is?"

"I thought about your predicament, and I remembered that after high school I worked on a road crew. We always had aerial photos. I went to the Office of Public Works and bought a photo of Bad Kreuznach, for thirty-seven deutsche marks. You'll have it in a day or so."

"God bless you, Ed."

"Forget God," he says. "Just subpoena me to testify. That should be good for at least a week in sunny Tampa. It's colder than a witch's tit in Bonn this time of year."

"I'll keep you here for a month," I assure him.

"Take care, Joe. Glad I could help."

"A million thanks."

One phone call to one guy who cares and is willing to get off his ass. Why is it often so hard to find people who want to help?

AS SOON AS THE aerial shot arrives in Tampa, we have the photo unit in the office blow it up to poster size. Then Susan and I roll it up and dash to the Embassy Suites and another Rod meeting that I promise will be short in the extreme.

Short, in fact, it is. Rod stands for maybe two minutes, hands on hips, studying the map, then puts his finger at the front gate of the base and begins tracing his walk, calling out street names and familiar points of interest as he goes. Finally, he takes the grease pencil I'm holding, stares, circles what looks like a residence in a quiet neighborhood of houses and apartments, and says, "This is it—Josef Schneider Plaza number four," and with that we all exhale.

I give him a hug and so does Susan. "Are you sure?" I ask.

"Sure as can be," he says. "Now can we get something to eat?"

TWO DAYS LATER, THE Germans grudgingly send an under-cover car to drive by Josef Schneider Plaza #4. As they roll slowly past, certain they're on the trail of yet another bogus lead, an elderly man, puttering in his garden, steps forward to greet them, identifies himself as Carl Gabriel Schmidt, and then knocks them completely off their feet.

"I knew you'd be by to see me eventually," he says. "Come inside."

Conrad, he confirms, rented the apartment and changed the locks, and afterward he and a "young friend" (whose description fits Rod Ramsay to a tee) spent a lot of time up there, always with the lights on, very bright lights.

And with that singular confirmation of something no one knew before—not the Germans, not the army, certainly not WFO, not even the Swedes—this investigation takes on a whole new, more serious perspective. Rod Ramsay can no longer be ignored. Neither, I hope, can I.

17

HOLY SHIT!

Two things:

Number One, Rod wasn't bullshitting about the document he recited for me from memory. I fired his version off to the army, which has the original in inventory, the very night I wrote it down. When the army finally gets back to me, the teletype begins: "This is beyond incredible . . ." Every word, the page number, the page placement—Rod got it all dead on. When I show Koerner the long paragraph Rod apparently memorized while he stood over the copier at the Eighth ID and the army's confirming reply, he damn near falls out of his chair. He knows: This kind of capacity doesn't come along more than once or twice in a lifetime.

Number Two, I and whoever is going to be able to help me (Langford, Moody, or perhaps someone else) have been green-lighted to go all-out over the next week to see what else Rod has to tell us. The Able Archer stuff clearly alarmed any number of Washington desk jockeys. Rod's astounding feat of memory has begun circulating through high circles, too. And although we don't yet know for sure all the documents that were littering its floor (and probably never will), Josef Schneider Plaza #4 has proved to be exactly the place Rod described.

"If this, then what?" seems to be the question of the day at Fort Meade, Langley, and even in that dead-between-the-ears zone on Pennsylvania Avenue known as FBIHQ. Oh, that and "Why are we learning about this only now, four freaking years after the Conrad investigation began?"

First, though, some practical business: Back in November when he blew through the Tampa office, Director Sessions tasked me with providing round-the-clock surveillance on Rod, one more load on my plate but a reasonable request. Here's the downside, though: 24/7 surveillance is a hugely expensive operation, not just for the raw numbers of people involved—more than a dozen in this case—but also for the infrastructure they need, such as motel rooms, meals, gas, etc.

In the real world of commerce, businesses get around such problems by issuing credit cards to their employees. Not the FBI, though. Our agents are expected to use their own credit cards and then put in at the end of the month for expenses. Normally, that's not a huge problem, but when you add to the tab an operation of this size, systems tend to break down and invoices lag. That's what has happened here. All of us involved have pretty much maxed out our personal credit cards when HQ finally pulls its act together long enough to send the Tampa office a wire transfer of exactly a quarter of a million dollars.

To facilitate distribution, Koerner hands me the wire-in paperwork and orders me to get the funds from the bank in small bills, but I'm not alone. She-Moody has been ordered to follow me, with instructions from Koerner to "bring him down if he looks like he's going to bolt with the dough."

All the way back from the bank, Terry walks a few steps behind me and off to the side.

"Why don't you walk beside me?" I finally ask. "This feels weird."

Her answer: "It's easier to shoot you in the back this way."

Honestly, you really can't make this shit up.

It's not until we're in the car late that afternoon, heading to Orlando once again, that Terry drops her own bomb on me. Her ob-gyn has moved up the no-travel date. A week from now, she has to go on desk duty full-time.

DINNER IS A SORRY affair. Rod claims that he filled up at lunch, but when Terry excuses herself early on for the bathroom, I let him know that she's in her stretch run—that, in fact, this might be her last trip with me to Orlando—and as I anticipated, this puts him in the dumps. The question is how to use that to our advantage, and I'm hoping I have an answer.

Upstairs, I've reversed the usual seating order. Moody and I are at either end of the sofa. Rod is in Terry's place, the easy chair, facing both of us. I want him back in the role he likes best: Professor Ramsay, Mr. Smart Guy.

"Rod," I say when we're all settled in, "tell us about the Pershing missiles. What were they doing in Germany?"

"How far back do you want to go?"

"As far back as you think necessary. Right, Agent Moody?"

Terry nods in agreement as Rod shakes a cigarette out of his pack and pops open a Coke from the small cooler I've left by his side.

"Welllllll," he says, with a little dramatic flourish, "the story really begins with the Soviets. Beginning in the late 1970s, they started deploying SS-20 ballistic missiles along their western border, threats not only to Europe's major cities but also to key NATO air bases in Great Britain. Jimmy Carter believed that we should first negotiate with the Kremlin to get them to roll back the SS-20s, then, if that didn't work, respond in kind by deploying missiles along Western Europe's eastern border, aimed at the Soviets' major cities, air bases, etc. Are you with me so far?"

"Right there," I say, as Terry chimes in: "This is *very* useful."

"Good. Good. Ronald Reagan, of course, had a different plan. He was less interested in negotiating with the Soviets than in forcing them to their knees. In mid-1983, NATO, at Reagan's urging, announced it would begin deploying US cruise missiles to Italy and Britain, and Pershing II ballistic missiles to West Germany. Finally, on November 22—twenty years to the day after John Kennedy's assassination [Rod adds, as if he were dispensing dimes to indigents]—the West German parliament approved the deployment, and the next day the Pershing IIs began arriving on German soil."

"How did the West Germans feel about that?" Terry asks, honestly unaware, I think, of just how pissed off many of them were. Rod would have chided me for being naïve if I'd asked the same question, but this is Terry. She's a short-timer now, maybe a last-timer, and Rod is nothing but tolerant tonight.

"I'm sure, Terry, you won't be surprised," he responds magnanimously, "that many West Germans were less than thrilled to find themselves on the front edge of the Western World's nuclear shield. Even if the Soviets didn't launch a first strike, mistakes happen. Signals get tripped up, missiles launch that aren't intended to leave their silos, volatile materials get mishandled, and . . ."

"And?" More alarm in her voice, but alarm now that I recognize as intentionally feeding our guest lecturer's needs.

Rod: "There's no dialing history back then."

My turn to jump in, the voice of reason: "Of course. Of course. We've all seen *Dr. Strangelove*. The wingnuts take over. Slim Pickens rides a nuke right down the Kremlin chimney. But in the real world, Rodney [stretching it out], all these weapons are ass-deep in fail-safes, are they not?"

"True, Joe," he answers, stretching my name out just as long, "very true. You've done an *excellent* job with your homework." He pauses for a laugh, his own, before he goes on. "Nuclear missiles like the Pershing IIs have two key safeguards, to be exact: permissive action links—PALs to their pals [another ha-ha]—and SAS nuclear authenticators, also known as SNAs or 'cookies.' But not exactly Oreos [yet another ha-ha, looking primarily at Moody this time]. What's more, at military bases with operational command over nuclear-weapons materials, PALs and cookies are kept in the innermost sanctum: the Emergency Action Center, a small room—think of the movies, Terry, *cinéma noir*—where red-alert messages are received that deal with the utilization of nuclear material."

Me: "And that would include the Eighth Infantry HQ at Bad Kreuznach?"

Rod: "Yes, of course. The Eighth ID had responsibility for the deployment and use of nuclear satchels and artillery munitions along the Fulda Gap to stop Soviet tanks."

Terry: "Satchels?"

Rod, waving his hand grandly: "Nuclear mines, Terry, that have been parceled out through German villages along the frontier, not that the villagers have been told about them."

"My God!" Terry says with a slight gasp.

"Basically, it's a suicide defense concocted in Bonn," Rod explains, "just in case NATO lacks sufficient tanks to stop a Soviet advance. The Germans, you know, have vowed they'll never be occupied by Russians again. Never again," he says for emphasis.

In truth, I have no idea where this is going, and I can see that pregnant Moody desperately needs to pee again, but Rod is clearly so vested in the subject by now that I don't want to stop.

"Just to make sure I understand, Rod," I say, jumping in. "These nuclear satchels can't really be activated without these permissive action links and authenticators . . ."

Rod manages to nod approvingly while also furrowing his brow.

"Am I missing something?" I ask.

"A little something, yes."

"And that would be?"

"It's not just the satchels, Joe. All the nuclear weapons in Europe operate under the same command-and-control structure. The same code that activates the satchels also activates the Pershing missile and, of course, vice versa."

"I see. And these PALs and cookies are stored in the Emergency Action Center in what I assume is probably a vault of some kind?"

Another approving nod, this time without the censorious brow.

"And that's basically the nuclear firewall? Sounds a little porous."

"It does," Moody agrees.

"I'm afraid, Joe and Terry, that you're missing one final element."

"And that would be?"

"The PALs and cookies are kept inside a safe that can be opened only by two people operating two separate lock combinations that are themselves changed every time new EAC custodians rotate in."

"Ah," I say, "now that *does* sound fail-safe. There are a lot of mean dogs between those little puppies and anyone trying to get to them without authorization."

Rod agrees. "It's as fail-safe a system as humans can design."

This all sounds nice and compact as I tell it here, but when I look at my watch, four hours have gone by. The back of my shirt, I realize, is soaked clear through. (Another thing I should probably see a doctor about: I seem to be sweating far more profusely than usual.) Rod, I can see, has to pee so badly his eyeballs are all but floating in their sockets.

"Time for a bathroom break," I announce. "Terry, why don't you go first. I'll follow."

WHILE ROD'S IN THE bathroom, I drag the furniture back into its old configuration. Rod will be on the sofa once more, Terry in her usual easy chair off to his side. I move Rod's cigarettes and ashtray to the end table beside where he'll be sitting but keep the cooler on the table next to where he was. I'm just wheeling my swivel chair in from the bedroom when Rod reemerges with his face still damp.

"Terry needs the chair," I explain, waving him toward the sofa. I wait till he's settled in and shaking a fresh cigarette from the pack to begin.

"Why don't you tell Agent Moody, Rod?"

"Tell her what?"

"How you clipped the PALs and cookies."

It's a guess, a hunch, nothing more. If I've screwed it up, we'll be back to square one, or worse. But something about that last response—"as fail-safe a system as humans can design"—sounded to me as if Rod was walking up to the edge of his own vanity. And who better to bring his narcissism to full bloom than Terry Moody, on what might be his last chance to impress her?

Rod needs me—I'm his friend, his father, his confessor, his life coach, for crissake. But Terry validates his manhood. Her interest in him is proof that he's not a multifaceted loser who's been cuckolded for months in his own camper. That's why he got so blue when I told him she was being pulled off the case—I see that now—and I'm hoping that he won't be able to resist validating himself forever in Terry's eyes with this, his greatest coup (if, indeed, it was). And right on cue, he lays it at her feet, like the most precious present ever bestowed on anyone.

"They were stupid," he begins, speaking directly to Terry. "Lazy."

"They?" I ask.

"Maybe, Rod," Terry says in a softer voice, leaning his way, "this would be easier if you took it from the beginning."

Rod pauses again, nods in agreement, then restarts in earnest.

"The Hungarians and Czechs had both let us know that the Soviets were extremely interested in the nuclear capability and technology of the West, especially when it came to command, control, security, and release procedures," Rod says, with what I take to be relief in his voice, a burden of memory soon to be lifted. "Clyde had been grooming me to be promoted to Heidelberg, where I'd have access to even more sensitive material. I told you that the other day, Joe."

"I remember," I say. "The Central Europe HQ."

"Exactly, but I didn't want to go. I liked Bad Kreuznach. I liked being near Clyde. He was teaching me so much, and the Eighth ID had plenty of nuclear secrets of its own, so . . ."

"So?" I prod.

"So I did what Clyde kept urging me to do. I showed some initiative. I became entrepreneurial."

As custodian of top-secret documents at the Eighth ID, Rod goes on to tell us, he occasionally had legitimate reason to visit the EAC, but even without (in this instance) Clyde's guidance, Rod knew a good thing when he saw it, and he began ingratiating himself to the personnel in the EAC by doing favors for them—lots of favors, from running errands, to buying them cigarettes and helping fill other daily needs for guys who couldn't venture far from their message center.

This was all absolutely against the rule book, of course. Vault custodians are supposed to live like Trappist monks, but Rod, after all, had all the right clearances and was himself the custodian of classified material, so what risk was there?

Eventually, Rod tells us, he settled on two guys in particular.

"If they were working the overnight shift, I'd drop by on my way to work with sweet rolls. If they were doing 4 p.m. to midnight, I'd bring coffee. After all, we all had the same clearance, and I was the document custodian. Being vault custodian is one of those jobs you *want* to be excruciatingly boring. I wasn't supposed to be in there, but in the end, I was in and out of there—basically, anytime."

This of course was kindness with a purpose, and indeed, Rod's two marks quickly began satisfying Rod's insatiable curiosity by explaining how procedures worked in the EAC: the two-man safe, for instance, and the treasure trove inside it. Anything involving nuclear weaponry was obviously time-crucial. If you're told to activate the nuclear satchels, you definitely want to do it *now*, not in five minutes, or even one minute. To minimize any time gap between command and execution, both men kept their combination locks one digit, one tiny twist, away from completion.

"How did you find that out?" I ask.

"I bet 'em."

"Bet them what?"

"Nothing. All I had to say was 'Let's see who is faster.' Typical male bravado—they raced each other to see who could open it the fastest, right in front of me. Turns out, they both did the same trick—one digit off."

"Wow!"

"Yeah, right? Amazingly stupid of them to show me."

"No shit," I say, thinking about how dangerous this is.

"Two days later I came back and hung out until they needed a smoke break. So I said, 'I'll cover for you'—they never took longer than seven minutes."

In fact, I'm sure he had their daily routine timed out perfectly.

"I waited till they were out the door and, click, click, I had a PAL. It's just like a credit card, basically. I slipped it in my wallet. Clyde was elated. The Hungarians were ecstatic. They probably danced a *barynya* at the Kremlin."

Using the same methodology, he tells us, he was able to clip not one but two SAS nuclear authenticators—redundancy. More approval from Clyde. More medals handed out in Budapest. More dancing in Red Square.

I don't want to break into his recitation, but finally I can't help myself. "Rod," I say, "you were stationed right there. Weren't you concerned about your own safety, selling this stuff to the Soviets? Those missiles and satchels were defending you, too."

"You don't get it, Joe," he says. "It was never about the PALs and the cookies. For Clyde and me, it wasn't about going to war. It was about alchemy—about turning the PAL and the cookie into gold. The Soviets would pay a fortune for anything having to do with nuclear material. It was like Clyde said: selling the most valuable thing in the world—information. These things were commodities."

He pauses for a minute to let that message sink in, then turns to Moody and lays another present at her feet.

"What I didn't tell Clyde was that I had another cookie, one I kept for myself."

"Of course, you didn't," Terry says, sounding like a mother who knows her own son.

"I didn't tell Clyde about the second cookie because I wanted to keep it for a rainy day."

"And you still have it?" I ask.

"No," he says, "I broke it apart the best I could, then burned the pieces behind Mom's trailer, after the second interview with you and Lynn. I thought you were coming back with a search warrant."

As he's saying this, all I can think about is how the Washington Field Office ordered us off this case for a year. What else did Rod destroy or sell while egos were preening in Washington?

Then, as only a man with a steel-trap memory can do, Rod proceeds to describe his backyard bonfire to the nth detail—smells, smoke textures, and how the material degraded under heat. And all the while I'm saying to myself, *Remember all this, remember every word, Navarro.*

AT 1 A.M., I order Moody to bed, close the door behind her, and place a quick call to He-Moody, who must be wondering. (Not so many years ago, Luciana used to wait by the phone, too. Now she seems to know it won't ring.) Terry and I had come up in two cars, thinking she could get an early start back home. Instead, I tell He-Moody, she'll spend the night here and drive back in the morning. Besides, the room is already paid for. By the time Rod is through in the bathroom, I've got a cup of coffee for him, brewed in the suite's two-cup pot.

"Where's Terry?" Rod asks.

"Off to sleep," I say, nodding toward the closed door of the suite's bedroom. "She's tired, so let's hold it down."

"It was a game, Joe, a business. Clyde and I weren't planning to fry the lederhosen off of all those German villagers."

"Games have consequences, Rod."

He contemplates that quietly for maybe five minutes, sipping at his coffee, a cigarette burning beside him, eyes again on his knees. Then he looks up and says one word, and shakes me to the core.

"Crypto."

"Crypto?" I ask, although I already suspect where this is headed.

"These guys—they were the guardians of the PALs, right, the nuclear cookies. They had to know how to decode cosmic top-secret docs, and do it damn fast. That's how the army communicates about these things. I got them to teach me all these different elements of cryptography. It was fascinating. And then . . ."

"Then?"

"I carted off as much information as I could about cryptography, and eventually I was trusted enough to be handed the keying material they stored for destruction because they didn't want to go out in the cold and do it themselves at the fire pit we used for document destruction."

"And you and Clyde sold the cryptography materials to . . ."

"Of course, the Russians were thrilled."

Thrilled? *Thrilled*, for fuck's sake. Here, I'm thinking, is when and where I finally lose it. This is where Moody wakes up to a loud noise and a bloody mess on the carpet. Only one other time have I wanted this badly to do serious physical harm to Rod. It was one of our fatten-Rod-and-Joe steak dinners. I'd had Rich Licht and Marc Reeser follow us to Orlando and take a table nearby so they could see the subject of our investigation in the flesh. Rod was at his worst—paternalistic to Moody, all but patting her on the head as he droned on; dismissive of me every time I tried to break into his soliloquy. I'm not sure what almost put me over the top, but at one point I glanced over at Rich and Marc and saw them both half rising from their seats, looking our way, and that's when I realized I was gripping a steak knife in my right hand, almost ready to lunge at Rod.

But I held it in that time, and I hold it in this time, too, and thank goodness I do because Rod isn't quite through yet.

"I have to tell you—at the secret apartment, there was crypto material that wasn't coming from me. Clyde must have had another source because I definitely saw crypto stuff there that didn't come from our EAC."

Jesus, I'm wondering, *what else?* But now I really have hit a wall, and Rod suddenly looks talked out.

"It's past two, Rod," I say, "time for your beauty sleep."

I can't stop myself, though, when he puts his hand on the doorknob—old habits die hardest.

"Anything else?" I ask.

"Like I say, Joe, it was just clipping. It was about money, nothing else. I want you to know that."

Tired as I am right now, I'm still not over the urge to go after Rod. I don't want to be in this room with him. I don't want to touch him. When he turns my way for our departing *abrazo*, I have to choke down the disgust I feel raging inside me. I can't allow myself the pleasure of being disgusted. I let the stomach acids do that for me.

It's almost three in the morning when I finish up my notes and sit back for a moment to contemplate what all this means. Unless I'm wrong, Ramsay and Conrad have rendered useless the very systems designed to keep communications safe and nuclear command and control inviolate. The whole underpinning of Cold War détente, mutually assured destruction, was anchored in surprise and secrecy—now there's none. But that's an assumption, and FBI agents learn early on that assuming makes an "ass" out of "u" and "me."

I write a note for Moody, letting her know that I've called home for her, and am about to start for Tampa myself when the enormity of the night finally gets to me and all I can think of is another blackout at the wheel and what I'd be carrying to the grave with me if the worst were to happen. With that thought in mind, I stretch out on the sofa, cover myself with a couple of bath towels for a blanket, and turn the light out behind me.

*   *   *

IT'S 10:59 A.M. THE next morning when I walk into Koerner's office, say, "Holy shit!" and drop my FD-302 on his desk.

"Holy shit?" he says, reaching instinctively for his Rolaids bottle.

"I'm just saving you the trouble of reacting on your own," I say, and I'm out his door.

Thirty minutes later, I'm sitting in my office with the door wide open and can hear Koerner's distinctive walk from his six-three frame. I steady myself as he pokes his head in. "Holy shit, Navarro. Son . . . of . . . a . . . bitch!"

ALL THIS NEW INFORMATION is driving everyone crazy, not because people necessarily believe what Rod has told us—resistance in certain quarters is still epic—but because anything involving nuclear command and control has to go to the Joint Chiefs of Staff, and now they, too, want to know what the hell is going on.

Terry and I have gone back to Rod several times, trying to corroborate his "clipping" and whether EAC personnel at Eighth ID actually helped him intentionally as he said—and if so, were there others who also might have been compromised? Meanwhile, Rich Licht has been putting on his attorney hat, trying to see how we might compel Rod to reveal who else is involved by using a grand jury or granting "limited-use immunity" or something else legalese.

He's describing various schemes to us one morning when I say no.

"Why?" he asks, a little put out.

"Because, even if this does work, it will take too long and has too many moving parts."

Terry Moody, still helping out on the case but no longer traveling, throws in her two cents next.

"Rod is simply not going to mention names," she says. "I'm sure he realizes at some level that he's going to jail, but he doesn't want anyone else to go with him, at least on his testimony. Every time Joe and I ask about other people he worked with, he talks about their lifestyle—

they're drug abusers, they were Clyde's poker-poker pals, they're this, they're that—but he almost never names someone unless it's a long-ago minor infraction like selling fuel coupons. He might have a distorted sense of right and wrong, but he seems to be loyal to his friends."

Reeser is next up at the plate. "Moody's right. If Rod was going to name names, he already would have."

"So?" I ask impatiently. "We're not getting anywhere."

"So," Marc says, "if he won't tell us, why don't you use that voodoo body-language shit to get it out of him?"

Rich, I can see, is suppressing a smile at the very thought of this, and Marc for all I know has come up with this body-language suggestion just so he can end the meeting and get to his four-thirty hockey game. But I've been validating these techniques ever since I graduated from the Utah Police Academy in 1975, and if there was ever a time to use them, it's now.

"Marc," I say, "get hold of the army. Now. Stat. I want a list of everyone who worked in the EAC during Rod's time at Eighth Infantry in BK, and I want a list of anyone known to have closely associated with Ramsay."

"What are you going to do, Joe?" Moody asks. "He's not going to hand anyone up."

"I agree," I say. "Conscious Rod won't."

"So?"

"But Subconscious Rod will."

BETWEEN THE ARMY AND the encyclopedic Marc Reeser, we come up with thirty-two names in all. I write each on a separate three-by-five index card, in big letters so it is easy to read, and then I ask Rod to join me for a quick game before dinner. The "before" part throws Rod for a bit of a loop—we *eat*, then we *talk*—but I want him a little unmoored, and I'm counting on his intellectual competitiveness to make my job easy.

"A game?" he asks on the phone, already warming to the idea.

"Trust me. You'll like it."

By the time Rod arrives, I have the coffee table pulled up in front of his place on the sofa and my own swivel chair pulled up closer to him than usual.

"Here's the way it works," I tell him. "I'm going to flash these cards in front of you very fast. As I do, all I want you to do is come up with a word or two that describes the personality of the person named on the card. I know a little bit about each of them, and basically I want to test your recall. And remember, keep it short and quick, the first thing that comes to mind: nice guy, asshole, uptight, snob, white trash, or whatever you want to say, but just a word or two. Just personality traits or quirks, not involvement. Got it?"

"Got it," he says. "Let's do it," as if this is a schoolyard race between two eager boys.

I'm eager, all right, but for a different reason. I've chosen my words carefully, knowing Rod always uses "involvement" as a euphemism for espionage. I've told him not to think about *involvement*, but in fact by doing that I've primed him to think about that very thing. The mind focuses more easily on what it's told not to do than on what it's told to do.

"Okay," I tell him, "here we go."

I flash each card just long enough for him to read the name—perhaps no more than a second. I'm no more than two feet away, so I can see his face clearly, and in particular his eyes. For Rod it's just another game: how well can he remember, how accurate is his recall—his focus is on speed. Not mine.

My focus goes way back to 3.5 million years ago and early hominids on the plains of Africa. When our ancestors saw a threat in the distance—a lion or a pack of hyenas, any threat—their pupils would constrict. Today, we still share this involuntary reaction with all mammals for one good reason: the smaller the pupil or aperture, the clearer and more defined things become. That's why people who need reading glasses can, if in need, punch a pinhole in a piece of paper and look through it. Do that, and you'll see as clearly as if you're wearing glasses. Photographers use the same technique to increase the depth of field on their cameras.

What most people don't know is that the threat can also be written. The brain uses shortcuts—heuristics—and doesn't differentiate between the thing itself and the representation of the thing, i.e., the word that describes it. A threat is a threat, and the faster you deal with a threat, even if it turns out to be false, the greater the chance of survival and passing on your genes. If any of these names represent a threat to Rod—because they conspired with him, because they could testify against him, because they saw something, or because they somehow participated with him—his pupils will show it.

For thirty of the names I present to Rod, in a very short period of time, there is absolutely no eyeball response. He seems to know all of the individuals, and his comments range from "cool dude" to "real pecker-head" to "dumber than dirt." For two, though—Jeffery Gregory and Jeffrey Rondeau—Rod's eyes squint when I hold up the card, and his dilated pupils constrict just enough for me to register the change. I don't even listen to what he says about them—the pupil constriction is enough for me.

BACK IN TAMPA, I ask the army to pull the files on Rondeau and Gregory and send me their ID photos. A few days later, in suite 316, where this all began, I take the fight to Rod.

"Do you think you're the only one helping us?" I say as I lay down photos of both Gregory and Rondeau. Rod looks at those photos for a moment, his eyes squinting with disdain, and then it's like someone has turned on a fire hose to maximum pressure.

"Those sons of bitches!" he shouts, and proceeds to tell me everything: how he'd used them to help gather secrets, sign for things so his signature wasn't always on the checkout list for documents, serve as lookouts, and help carry documents out or conceal them for him.

"These," he says, "are the guys who helped me carry out a ton of documents because they were too heavy in a duffel bag."

THE NEXT DAY, AS Marc Reeser comes into the office, I drop the news on him—Gregory and Rondeau signed, sealed, and delivered.

"Thanks, by the way," I add.

"For what?"

"For suggesting I use that 'voodoo shit.' I guess you won't be calling it that anymore."

"Only behind your back, Navarro, only behind your back."

18

FRENCH CUFFS
AND SUSPENDERS

For a moment as the four of us sweep into the J. Edgar Hoover Building, the FBI headquarters on Pennsylvania Avenue, I find myself thinking of old westerns—the good guys (us, naturally, in white hats) at one end of a dusty street, ready to take on the whole corrupt town. Why not? We're all packing heat, as FBI agents are expected to do when they travel. But the fact is, we've come in peace.

Jay Koerner, who led us here, is headed upstairs to work his contacts at HQ so we can move the Ramsay case along. I'm expecting good results, and I'm particularly glad Jay is willing to expend some capital on this effort. He's in a unique position: well respected at HQ but with no desire ever to occupy an office within its imposing walls. In Washington, you can get a lot done once people know you don't want their jobs.

Susan Langford and Rich Licht are here at my insistence. This is Susan's first big case and she's working hard on it, but her trepidation at not knowing everything she should is pretty obvious. I'm hoping this visit to the Royal Maze will calm her down some and make her feel ready for the challenges still ahead. Rich is a newbie, too, but he's rock solid and not easily fazed. I've off-loaded plenty of horror stories on him about dealing with HQ. Time for him to see the place in the flesh, especially the Division 5 floor where so many of our overlords hold court.

And me? I'm mostly looking forward to our midday trip out to Fort Meade, in Maryland, to meet with some people at the National Security Agency. Until then, I'm hoping to keep a low profile, stay out of trouble, and dope out what the hell at HQ is holding this case back, and I'm counting on Jane Hein to help me do all those things.

First, though, we need to get our temporary badges at the security office. That's easy. We're expected. Finding the right elevator bank is a lot harder. Even though I've been in the Hoover Building many times, I still take the wrong hallway, and we end up at a set of elevators I've never seen before, going places I can't imagine.

We puzzle it out eventually. I've taken a left when I should have gone right, or maybe two rights when I should have kept straight ahead. The exterior of the Hoover Building is what's known in architectural circles as Brutalist Modern, sort of intentionally ugly. Inside, though, the Hoover is closer to a Skinner Box, designed to see how well rats negotiate the endless hallways in search of rewards.

Jane's office is small, barely big enough for the four of us, but she's quick to make Rich and Susan feel welcome, and she's aware that all FBI agents travel on their stomachs.

"Let's go get some coffee and pastries," Jane suggests and leads us off to the cafeteria on the eleventh floor. Along the way, she gives Rich and Susan, both increasingly wide-eyed, a hallway-by-hallway tour, including areas so sensitive that no agents ever see their insides. The cafeteria is its own revelation, swarming at this morning-break hour with well-groomed guys in impeccable suits with colorful suspenders and French cuffs shooting out just so from under their coat sleeves.

"What's with the fashion show?" Rich asks.

"Teachable moment," I say, grabbing both Rich and Susan by their elbows. "What are all these Fancy Dans *not* wearing?"

Rich puzzles over it for a second, then gloms on to where this is heading. "Belts. Holsters. No one packs in here . . . or anyplace else he goes."

"No one's changing his own tires either," Susan adds, studying the beautiful French-cuffed shirts.

"Welcome to the world of no fieldwork, and no manual labor," I'm saying when Marc Reeser descends on the three of us like a hockey defenseman in overtime. That's the other purpose of this visit: a reunion. Marc has been recalled to HQ, at least temporarily, to help with the budget strains of our investigation. We all miss the hell out of him.

Once I've said hello, I leave the three of them to catch up in the cafeteria line and join Jane over by the twenty-foot-high windows overlooking Ninth Street. We sit with our backs to the view so we can watch the human zoo in front of us while we talk shop.

"IT'S ALL SET FOR one p.m. at the Antenna Farm," Jane says, using the shorthand for NSA HQ, a place that literally bristles with telecommunication equipment.

"Great. You coming?"

"No, you're on your own. I've got to mind the store. Besides, Jay is going to be tied up most of the morning, and he's asked for some time with me."

Over in the cafeteria line, Marc looks to be demonstrating slap shots. Whatever it is, he's got Rich and Susan in stitches. The people in front and back of them are looking on like the three of them have just farted very, very loudly. A fun house this building is not.

"Joe," Jane says, turning my way, "I can't tell you everything, but there are a lot of people above me and over at WFO who just have it in for you. They don't like that you took over this investigation, and not to sugarcoat things, they despise that you showed them up. This was supposed to be their golden apple, and you've taken it away from them. Up here, careers are made on cases like this—you know that."

"Are you fucking serious? This is what they're so upset about?"

A nod from Jane is all the answer I need.

"Thanks," I say, "at least, I think so. At any rate, I want you to know that we really appreciate what you're having to put up with. I tell our SAC you're the only real friend we have up here, you and Reeser, and you're the one stuck in the middle. You don't deserve to go through all this shit."

"Don't worry about me. I'm a survivor. Speaking of which, you look like you've lost more weight. You okay?"

"Yeah, you know, big cases, big problems, little sleep. I've lost my appetite, the stress of dealing with WFO . . ."

"Yeah, well, watch yourself. You've got quite a crew here to mind. How's Mrs. Moody? Just weeks away now, right?"

I nod, although Terry is closer.

"Do you miss her?" Jane asks, leaning toward my ear.

"Terribly. She's probably one of the few friends I have left, and she's so great to work with." My eyes actually start to water up as I say it, so I look away.

"She's a gem," Jane says with her hand on my arm. "Let's gather the troops."

Back in Jane's office, I have Rich, Susan, and Marc go through all the information we've gathered from Ramsay and what we've been able to corroborate thus far.

Rich begins by reviewing the thousands of leads that have gone out all over the US and to at least seven European countries, retracing everywhere Ramsay has lived, from Boston to Japan to Hawaii to Germany and elsewhere, including confirming the bank robbery that took place shortly before he left for Hawaii. We've also scoured by hand customs and immigration forms to identify entry into the US both by Ramsay and Conrad, something HQ and WFO never bothered to do.

Susan follows up with the documents that Ramsay has mentioned thus far as well as other material that didn't come directly from him but was seen at the—now well-corroborated—secret apartment in Germany. The list of documents, Marc confirms, is larger than anyone anticipated, and Ramsay has described each one accurately. We now have duplicate copies from the army, and Ramsay's recall of each is, as Rich puts it, "scary accurate, in the most minute of details."

Both Rich and Marc further confirm that the espionage tradecraft Ramsay has described is entirely consistent with what has been garnered from the army, the Germans, and the Swedes. Conrad, we've established to our satisfaction, did rely on Ramsay after he retired, and the two definitely traveled to Austria and elsewhere for meets. What's more, Conrad used video recording equipment, just as Ramsay told us, as well as photographic equipment that he also described.

For their part, the Hungarians—the new, post-Communist version—have been able to determine that Conrad and Ramsay made deliveries directly to the Hungarian Intelligence Service. Conrad also used dollar bills torn in half and those tiny souvenir cowbells as agent recognition signals, all useful at trial, especially since Rod kindly gave me one of those cowbells as a present. And of course, there was also the famous hello number that Rod thought we'd never make much use of and will now definitely be government exhibit number one at trial.

Even I am a little overwhelmed by the weight of all this evidence when Marc, Susan, and Rich finish up.

"You've seen all of my FD-302s," I say to Jane. "There's no question that Ramsay understood what he was doing and that despite the threat it posed to the United States, he was willing to assist in espionage. We need this guy arrested, and we need to start thinking about a trial and getting the US Attorney's Office in Tampa involved."

"Whoa, cowboy," Jane says, holding up a warning hand. "Believe me, Joe, I'm trying to get people to move on this, but they're resistant. The biggest hurdle is WFO and Internal Security. You have no idea how hard they're fighting this. They're doing everything they can to intercede."

"But why?" is all I can ask. "This is what I still don't get. We have more information to prosecute Ramsay than any other spy we've ever tried. Meantime Rondeau and Gregory are up to no good and we're waiting for what? Nothing will ever be perfect. This is as good as it gets. No . . . more . . . waiting."

"Joe, for crissake, you're preaching to the choir!"

"Okay," I say. "Sorry. I know that. But what about the leaks? The *New York Times*, ABC News, Bamford—they're all over this even before we in Tampa get the information."

"That pipeline has been going on here at HQ a hell of a lot longer than I've been here," Jane says. "I'm amazed at how much leaks out of this place, always to favorites, always with a purpose, and no one so far as I can tell does a damn thing about it."

"Well, somebody better start doing something about these leaks," I say, knowing I'm getting too excited again, "because we're damn lucky that Rod Ramsay hasn't already disappeared somewhere in Moscow. The Russians would pay a fortune for what he has in his head. Christ almighty, he knows the same go-to-war and contingency information that the generals in Europe know. And every time there's a new leak we have to scramble to make sure he doesn't run, and I have to talk to his mother, and Rod . . . Jesus, Jane, we have to arrest this guy."

"Joe, I try to sell this at every meeting."

"But this isn't vacuum cleaners. It's not Avon Lady shit, for God's sake. We shouldn't have to *sell* this to anyone. It's crazy that Jay has to spend the morning at Internal Security, trying to convince John Dion—the number two person in the ISS, for crissake!—of the need to at least brief Greg Kehoe on the details of the case. This is a huge case. Why would ISS even think about blindsiding the first assistant in the Middle District of Florida and not tell him what's going on in his own jurisdiction? Talk about nuts!"

All Jane can do is shrug her shoulders at this outburst, but Rich and Susan wear looks that tell me they're starting to realize how deep this tar pit is.

"One last thing," I go on. "Our leads in Austria. Tracking down the restaurants where Ramsay says he met with the Hungarians is going to be key. He's described those restaurants with particularity, but the names are blurry to him, and we need to confirm those places exist for trial."

"Speaking of Austria," Jane jumps in, "letters rogatory have come in from Germany, and the Director as well as Internal Security agree . . ."

"On what?"

"You'll be going to Germany to testify next month."

"Goddamn it, Jane, no! N-O! If I go, the news services are going to be all over that. My army source tells me it will be in open court. As soon as I walk into that courtroom, Ramsay will find out about it, and so will his mother. You think defense isn't going to ask where I interviewed Ramsay, and is he under arrest or will he be arrested? What am I to say to that? I'm not going to do it. You'll have to order me to go."

"That's easy. Agent Navarro, you are being ordered to go testify in Germany during the week of May 6. How is that?"

"Jesus, Jane."

"Joe, when the Director says jump, it's our job to say how high, not to question it."

"I just want it on the record that I'm opposed to this and that it will be a real security and containment problem for us."

"Noted. It's not your decision, Joe." And then, with a growing smile: "After you testify, I'll join you over there, and we'll travel together to Austria to see if we can find those meeting places."

ON THE WAY DOWN in the elevator, we drop Marc off at his floor, then stop at the FBI Recreation Association store next to the

Federal Credit Union so Rich and Susan can pick out some souve-
nirs: T-shirts, mugs, golf balls, towels, just about anything that will
hold an FBI logo. I'm thinking about a T-shirt for Stephanie when
it dawns on me that Luciana might take it as a slap in the face. They
get the T-shirt; the FBI gets me. Instead, I buy a "JR FBI Agent"
onesie, size 0–2 months. She-Moody is due a week from Friday.

19

INSIDE THE ANTENNA FARM

Marc rejoins us a little while later, and the four of us head out in a borrowed HQ car to NSA headquarters, with a quick lunch break along the way. Just getting into the Antenna Farm parking lot is a hassle, but the security desk is a whole other story, mostly because of me. My security clearances are sky-high, but the NSA computer system has me down as "Joseph" while all my credentials use my legal name: "Joe."

Eventually—as in after half an hour of valuable time—the problem is cleared up, and we get waved through to the inner sanctum, where we're greeted by a woman and two men, told to leave everything but paper and pencils behind (no pens), and led immediately into the most well-manicured secure room I've ever seen. Not until the door has been shut and all our ears have popped in the newly pressurized environment are introductions forthcoming.

The NSA people use first names only: Emily, the woman, clearly in charge although no titles are given or name tags worn; Leonard, the older of the men; and Henry, younger, with three pencils stuffed in his shirt pocket. On our side, I introduce everyone by first name, last name, and title: special agent or, in Marc's case, senior research specialist.

Emily gets us immediately down to business once I'm through, sounding every bit the senior manager. "Thank you for coming. We appreciate it. Obviously, we're very concerned with all of the NSA equities that are at issue."

"Of course."

"Leonard and Henry are two of our top technical people in this field and can assist with the validation, investigation, and corroboration process. If what your resource has told you is true, we've never had so many systems compromised seemingly at once, but while we're concerned, we're also highly skeptical."

"I would be, too," I say, "if it were anyone but Roderick James Ramsay."

"Do you believe everything he says, Mr. Navarro?" Henry asks. He's clearly a worrier and under considerable stress. The hairs on his left eyebrow have been picked almost clean, and the skin beneath is red with worry.

"No," I answer, "I don't believe everything he says. That's not my job. My job is to get Ramsay to open up, to memorialize [pure Bureau-speak] what he says, and then to validate it."

"I see," says Leonard, perhaps nearing seventy years of age from the way he walks, speaks, and dresses. He looks like a Harvard mathematician working out of a basement office with no windows—a place where chalkboards, not whiteboards, are ubiquitous and well worn, just like his elbow patches.

Emily is the one not from central casting. She seems to be wound very tight; even the hair in her bun has been done to an extreme. From her inflection I'm thinking multiple PhDs but not a mathematician. More likely, she's an engineer. If I had to bet money right now, I'd put it on MIT. Her clenched-teeth manner of speaking says she's lived mostly within the northeast corridor, but the way she stands with hands behind her back and her chin ever so high also tells me she probably has done a stint or two in England, maybe liaising with GCHQ, the NSA equivalent.

"We've seen your reports, the FD-302s as you call them," Henry begins. "Obviously, you have been capturing Rod's words, but words can be misleading. We do have some questions for you."

"Ask away."

"Prior to this matter, had you been exposed to any NSA equities? In other words, did you know about permissive action links, did—"

I stop Henry in his tracks.

"I gather what you want to know is whether my previously existing knowledge of your 'equities' could have, through osmosis, entered Rod's mind? Did I poison the well? It's a reasonable question, but the answer is no—I had no prior exposure to any of these systems. Everything I've written about came directly from Rod and was introduced by him into the conversation."

Emily goes next, in a tone bordering on arrogance, or at least academic superiority. I suspect from her manner that she looks down on just about everyone, Henry and Leonard included.

"Why would he tell you these things? If he's as smart as you suggest and the army IQ exam seems to confirm—although that's hardly a definitional test when it comes to intelligence—he must have known that he was feeding you evidence of his own crime."

I'm about to answer when Rich, who's promised not to say anything, jumps to my defense: "Because Joe treats him with respect."

I look at Rich with the same look my dad would use to put me in my place when enthusiasm got the best of me, and take it from there.

"I do think Rod does respect me, as Rich says, but he also trusts me, and at this point I'm probably the only friend he has left."

"And that's it?" Emily asks, looking perplexed, as if trust weren't a basic human motivation.

"I wish there were more to it," I allow, "but yes, it is just that. He likes me, and we get along." I can see from Emily's face that this goes against everything she's seen on television about interviewing, and quite possibly everything she understands about human nature as well. NSA hires engineers and mathematicians. They're all experts at quantification and the abstract—social engineering, not so much. If I were to tell Emily right now that one of the reasons Rod confided in me even at his own peril was that I'd helped him deal with the clap, the top of her head might just blow off in dismay.

Leonard the Elder, as I now think of him, looks up from his notes just then and picks up the questioning. These people are as scripted as I am, I'm thinking, but I'm dealing with the suspected and accused when I ask these questions.

"Rod claims that the permissive action links were compromised. But did he ever describe them—a physical description, that is?"

"He did, and you have that, of course, but whether he described them accurately, we have no idea. I'm sure you realize that we've requested a copy, for evidentiary purposes, but we have nothing so far that would allow us to corroborate what he said."

Henry looks to Emily for guidance before speaking next, and we all endure an uncomfortable three-second silence until she slowly nods her head.

"Well," Henry resumes, "we have looked at what you wrote, of course, and Ramsay must have seen these materials and manuals—of that we're convinced. But did they go to the other side?"

"Thus far, everything Rod stole, Conrad stole, or unidentified others stole at Conrad and Ramsay's request was sold to the other side, sometimes multiple times. Does that answer your question?"

It must have, because at that moment all three NSA reps look at each other with repressed fear. If their jaws tighten any further, I swear molars are going to break.

"What about the SAS nuclear authenticators?" Henry continues. "Do you really think he stole those also?"

"I do, Henry. I think that was his ultimate challenge, the ultimate moneymaker. That's why he kept one for himself—it was going to be his last bargaining chip. But then he panicked and destroyed it when I showed up. The way he described destroying it, with such specificity and without hesitation, mind you—I have no choice but to believe him even if it's the kind of thing that puts a nail in your coffin."

It's Leonard's turn again now. His voice is softer but in an odd way more chilling.

"I have to say, we didn't believe any of it at first—you or Ramsay. That is, until we replicated the burning sequence. These materials are always shredded or destroyed chemically, but we burned it exactly as Ramsay described to you, even going outside and using a disposable cigarette lighter. We broke it apart as he said, we went exactly point by point, and all the materials—and there are multiple ones, some exotic—burned exactly as he said: each differently, each consistent with the special chemicals that go into each component. As far as we're concerned, he couldn't have made that up."

"I'm actually glad to hear that," I admit, "because we had no way to validate it on our own."

"Another thing," Leonard goes on. "Ramsay's description of how he got around the two-custodians safe system. Frankly, it seems a little, I don't know, Hollywoodish to us. The simple fact is that no one other than custodians is allowed in the EAC."

"No one is allowed to rob banks," I say. "No one is supposed to murder or embezzle from their employers or bring million-dollar bricks of cocaine over the border, but you know, Leonard, it happens all the time. You want to know what I think?"

He nods, without checking with Emily, the luxury of an employee nearing retirement, I'm guessing.

"I think these guys are so bored over there that rules go by the wayside, which is why you see drugs, alcohol, spouse cheating, prostitution, and whatever else. Rod either saw the combinations to each safe over time, or as he said, these guys really do leave it so that the next turn is the one that opens the safe just in case of war. Either way, from what I know and from what you've told me, Rod had access to these materials, and to him all material is measurable not by the danger it poses for America or the West or even the world, but by how much someone is willing to pay to possess it—in this case, the Soviets."

"Russians," Emily corrects.

"Russians now, Soviets forever. We're their number one enemy and always will be whatever the hell they end up calling themselves."

"What about the cryptographic keying material?" Henry asks, jumping into the fray.

"Color it gone," I say. "That would have been the easiest to take because on cold days those guys in the EAC weren't going to go to the burn facility as they were supposed to, and neither were the communications folks, especially when ever-helpful Rod Ramsay was headed there."

By now, I can't help noticing that our three new NSA friends are looking even more troubled than when we entered the secure room. A joke jumps to mind: *Was it something I said?* But thankfully before I can repeat it, Emily takes up the narrative:

"This is the worst compromise we've ever endured," she says, "worse than the John Walker case. Walker compromised the navy, a major breach, to be sure, but trivial in comparison. Now the other side has *everything*. They can reverse engineer our nuclear command-and-control system if what Ramsay claims is right." The lipstick is gone from Emily's lips, rubbed raw through her constant pursing and touching.

"Actually, Emily, it's worse than that," Leonard says, pushing up to a standing position. "It's bad enough that they can reverse engineer it and that they are reading our messages in real time, but it will be worse by far if we ever get to nuclear stand down."

Now he really has my attention, and Marc's, Susan's, and Rich's, too.

"We never envisioned this situation when we designed the system," Leonard continues, with the authority of someone who might well have been in on that design. "We were trying to build speed and suppleness into the system, for obvious reasons. But if someone were to replace a nuclear authenticator with one that looks real but with numbers that are wrong, launch would be impossible, and there would be nothing we could do about it, even if incoming were headed our way. You don't even need a spy to take anything, the way Ramsay did. All you need is a spy to replace something—the real authenticator with a phony one, easier by many magnitudes."

My stomach, already in bad shape, just sinks at this. All my worst fears are being validated, and to make things worse, we still don't have authority to arrest Rod.

"'This man needs to be arrested immediately," Henry says with the nodding concurrence of Leonard and Emily.

"I agree," I say, "but it is not up to me."

"Understood," Emily says. "We aren't entirely out of the prosecutorial loop here in the capital. But we're willing to come to Tampa and help out with validating all this, if you'll have us."

"The more the merrier," I say, never even thinking if Jane Hein or the Washington Field Office is going to object. "But you must know that I'll be testifying at Conrad's trial in Germany, and some of this is going to come out."

"Why?"

"Because it's the truth and because I may be required to testify to everything Ramsay has said."

"Oh, this is bad," Leonard says, sitting down.

"You *think*? You're worried about your equities, and I can understand that, but I'm worried about Ramsay's fleeing and all the knowledge he has in his head."

Emily, back to the sure-footed senior manager she was at the start of our session, delivers the afternoon's verdict: "We'll fly down to Tampa next week with some things that have been sterilized to show Ramsay to see if he's making any of this up. We must be scientifically sure."

"That's fine, by all means. Rich will give you a call with the contact information. But I can save you the time—everything that can be checked will check out."

"We shall see," Emily says, with an even larger dose of upper-crust incredulity. And with that we're thanked and ushered out.

I'M BACK ON THE old Baltimore-Washington Parkway, heading to DC to turn in the Bureau loaner, when the enormity of what we've learned hits me again.

"How are they going to explain this one to the president?" I say aloud. "And when?"

Marc's answer is cynicism itself. "That's easy. Once they've figured out how to blame the whole damn thing on you, Joey boy. That's the way Washington works."

20

MULTIPLE CHOICE

Emily doesn't make the promised trip to Florida, but Henry and Leonard do, not one week but two after our NSA meeting and still using first names only. They insist on being met at the plane, and I do. Handcuffed to Henry's wrist, just like in the movies, is a fireproof suitcase made of material I've never seen before, containing the essence of our national security in a photo array.

We jump in the Bu-Steed with no time to spare, head to Orlando, and check in at the Embassy Suites. On the way up in the elevator, Henry expresses surprise that the front desk folks know me by name.

"They should," I tell him. "I've been here more than twenty times in the past half year."

Our first job is to settle Leonard and Henry into their room next door to—and connecting with—our usual suite 316. We've come to this arrangement for three reasons. First, they're not supposed to be seen by Rod. Second, more important, the material they've brought with them "technically" shouldn't leave their sight. However, they've been allowed to bend the rules so long as they're in the connecting room. Third, most important, they've been told not to watch, hear, or in any other way witness Rod interacting with the materials they've brought. Otherwise, they could be compelled to testify in court—about the last thing anyone at the National Security Agency wants to do.

As Henry is unlocking the briefcase chained to his wrist, both men admit that this is the first time they've been out operationally "on an investigation," and both seem nervous enough about what they're doing that I give them my two-way radio with earphones so they can monitor the surveillance frequency. I tell them to sit on the floor the entire time Rod is next door.

"Floor?" Leonard asks, clearly worried about how his seventy-year-old bones are going to take to this.

"For quiet," I explain. "Furniture creaks. Your bones won't creak until you try to get up again."

This at least gets a smile. As I close the connecting door behind me, they look like young kids getting to play with their first set of walkie-talkies.

I'm studying the photo array booklet twenty minutes later when Rod knocks on the door. Once again, I've gotten him here by promising a test—it's like waving meat in front of a lion.

"Rod, I really appreciate your coming in." I give him an *abrazo* as usual and wave him to his customary corner of the sofa. "I have something very important and urgent." The words aren't casually chosen. I want him to focus right now on the "importance and urgency" of what I just said, not on what he might potentially see.

"Here's the way it's going to go. I would like you to look at the objects in this photo array and identify for me any items that you saw, took, stole, and/or gave to the Hungarians. Only items you can positively identify from your own experience, please."

Rod looks over at me as if to say "Is this legit?" I nod yes, and then without a moment's hesitation, he begins to scan the photos. NSA has managed to build in essence a booklet full of interesting stuff, but I have no idea what might be real or fake. I suspect Ramsay is curious, but he's like a radar that hits on real targets.

"Page two A4, page three B6, page four C7," he says in a single breath, and with that he closes the booklet and heads to the door.

"I gotta run," he says. "Working tonight." To Leonard and Henry, this would sound alarmingly casual, I'm sure, but I know this is Rod strutting his stuff, like a chess grandmaster who jumps from table to table, checkmating everyone in sight.

"Are you sure? Don't you want to consider your answers any further?" I say as he grabs one of the bottled waters before reaching the door.

"No. We're good, right?"

"Of course," I say, and he's gone, the very shortest Rod interview ever. I knock on the door and Leonard and Henry jump up from the floor surprised. (Well, in Leonard's case, not quite "jump.")

"What happened?"

"He looked at the book, and he had to go."

"What? Is he coming back?"

"Not for this. He's working tonight."

As I say this, my beeper indicates surveillance is on him in the parking lot. Henry, still listening to the walkie-talkie, confirms.

"So what did he say?"

"Page two A4, page three B6, page four C7."

"Oh my God," Henry says as I hand him the booklet. "He got all three."

Leonard echoes him: "All three." If his chin were tucked in any closer to his neck at this moment, he would probably pass out. "All of them."

"Gentlemen," I say, as Henry starts to stow the booklet back in his fireproof briefcase, "I know you need to take that back, but this is now a government exhibit. So I will note that it is in your custody. You'll have to save it for trial, and I'm going to write a receipt for you to sign. Please don't alter or change the booklet in any way—it must be preserved as is. This is evidence and subject to the federal rules of criminal procedures."

"What?" both of them say almost simultaneously.

"Welcome to my world, guys."

As for me, I can't help thinking beyond government exhibits to the larger implications of this little test we just ran. Not only has Rod validated what he told us a few weeks earlier; he's turned our world upside down, yet again, because now there can be no doubt. Things are worse than anyone imagined—the worst security breach in US history.

21

UP CLOSE AND PERSONAL

Things to do before leaving for Germany:

Check in with Henry and Leonard [No Last Names] at NSA to make sure they know Rich Licht will be coordinating with them while I'm gone. Since that first visit in early March, the two have been back almost weekly to Orlando, each time with some new test for Rod, hoping (or so I read between the lines) to disprove that he actually did clip NSA equities and sell them to the other side. And each time they leave for home with even longer faces, ever more convinced that Rod did exactly as he's said.

Make up for my now three-month deficit in firearms and related training before Shirley and Brian, the instructor, have a cow on the office floor. Unfortunately, this doesn't go well. The shooting range I can handle in my sleep, but when Brian begins lecturing me on the need to maintain proficiency in hand-to-hand combat, I tell him, "Go fuck yourself and get out of my way." I'm just too tired, too beat down to handle this crap. "I'll have to report this, you know," Brian bleats. "Good," I say. "Then maybe they'll pull me off this case, and I'll get some rest."

Prepare for Clyde Conrad's trial. My army sources tell me there are gaping holes in the prosecution's case against Conrad, holes that only Rod Ramsay's story can fill. Since I'm going to be, in effect, Ramsay's surrogate at the trial, that means me. For a solid week I sift through what are now thirty-six volumes of material and hundreds of pages from Ramsay, getting names and dates right, refreshing my memory for trial as though it is a performance, which is exactly what court is: a theater where you have to be believed.

Maybe most important, tell Rod what I'm doing. I think long and hard about this. Is he more likely to bolt if he hears secondhand, through the press or maybe some buried contact, that I'm testifying at Clyde's trial or if I tell him myself? Either way the risks are huge. Rod is fluent in German, Japanese, and Spanish; he could lose himself in any one of dozens of places, not excluding Russia itself. And of course, he's inherently volatile with a proven track record of reckless behavior and rash decision-making. In the end, I opt for the direct approach. "Rod," I tell him over a quick lunch on International Drive, "my masters have ordered me to Germany to testify at Clyde's trial. It's not at all something I want to do." I'm studying him for any sign of distress—arched eyebrows, pursed lips, that bobbing Adam's apple—as I tell him this, but all Rod does is swallow, lean back slightly in his chair, and say, "Bring back some good Riesling, okay?" Like I told Emily at that NSA meeting, it's all about trust. Just to be safe, though, I task Susan Langford with calling Rod every day while I'm gone, hoping her syrupy diet of "sweetheart," "hon," and "doll" will keep him coming back for more.

DEPARTURE MORNING DOESN'T GO quite as planned. The overnight traffic from HQ brings word that I'm one of only six agents (out of twelve thousand nationwide) selected to the single most elite unit in all of the FBI, the new National Security Division's Behavioral Analysis Program. It's an honor, to be sure—I didn't even know I was under consideration—and proof that at least one person near the top of the Royal Maze still loves me, or at least respects my abilities. But this also means more work, more travel, and less time for everything else, family included, and I can tell no one about it, not even Koerner. We're to report directly to the assistant director for national security or, in his absence, the Director himself.

By the time I finish digesting all this and letting the assistant director know I'm on board, I've got to dash for the airport. My plan had been to stop by home on the way—a goodbye kiss for Luciana, instead of the wave I gave her this morning as I raced through the kitchen—but now I'll have to call from Tampa International, time allowing. Not until I'm retrieving my suitcase from the trunk do I remember the two presents stowed there for young Caitlyn Moody, born into this world on April 18: the onesie I bought a month back from the FBI souvenir shop, still in its plastic store bag, and a beautifully wrapped box from Luciana with I'm-not-sure-what inside.

MY TRAVELING COMPANION TO Germany, Ihor O. E. Kotlarchuk from the Internal Security Section, probably has orders to keep me from stepping all over my dick before, during, and after the trial. That would bother the hell out of me with any other ISS attorney—and I do mean *any* other—but Ihor is the one person I like at ISS and the only one who'll even return my calls. He's also very funny—a connoisseur of food, wine, and women—and (God bless him) honest about what really goes on in his section. By the time we land in Frankfurt, I've got a pretty good fill on just how much the front-office people at Internal Security dislike me and on how they absolutely hated being forced to brief Greg Kehoe just a few days back on the case. The latter is no surprise. Greg has a hell of a track record as a prosecutor, but reading him into the case is tantamount to admitting that Internal Security has lost control.

From Frankfurt, we're whisked to a compound outside Koblenz, forty-five miles away, where the trial has been under way for several weeks. One of the first people I meet there is Gary Pepper, the army investigator without whom Clyde Conrad would never be facing these espionage charges. Gary looks like he's still in his late twenties, but he's already an investigative tour de force. As he describes for me his own multiple days of testimony, now finally completed, I can tell we're going to mesh just right. He's been using detail after detail to build a narrative that places Conrad at the center of his spy ring, just what I intend to do.

That's the good news. The bad news, Gary says, is that the media is all over this case. The *New York Times*, the *Stars and Stripes*, *Der Spiegel*, the *Guardian*, *Le Monde*—they'll all be in the courtroom. Even the newly liberated Russians have sent several credentialed "journalists" who still somehow manage to look like thugs from the KGB.

"The 'Espionage Trial of the Century,'" Gary says. "That's how they're playing it. That's why they've got us out here at this compound, but you can forget about privacy and anonymity once you walk into that courtroom tomorrow."

Truer words, in fact, have been rarely spoken.

Koblenz, in the morning light, turns out to be a beautiful place, even pristine. The State Superior Court Building is one of its highlights—a lovely old pile overlooking the Rhine and Mosul rivers. One of my minders tells me Koblenz is usually a quiet enclave, a place where everyone's privacy is respected, but when I try walking into the courthouse without being noticed, one reporter immediately calls out my name in unmistakable American English—"Yo, Joe, over here!"—which I ignore.

The wood-lined courtroom itself must date back at least a century or more. It smacks of age and gravitas. So does the arrangement. This isn't like an American courtroom: a judge in the front, jury of peers to the side, plenty of open space between all parties. In Germany, cases like Conrad's are heard by a panel of six judges, chaired by a senior judge. This panel weighs everything you say, can question anything stated, and often does.

I no sooner take all this in than I'm led past a gaggle of courtroom visitors to the witness chair. The last man I pass on my left is so thin and gaunt that I barely recognize him. From the many photographs that Rod had shown me, I assumed Clyde Conrad was still blond-haired and full-faced. Those candids always put me in mind of the confident CEO of a shady enterprise. But the Clyde Conrad I'm walking by now is white-haired and at least thirty pounds lighter than his booking photo. His chin is perched uneasily on his two thumbs with his index fingers spread to just underneath his nose.

Rod has been talking about this demon for over a year, building him up in my imagination into some sort of evil titan. Instead, Conrad looks like one of those ex–Nazi prison guards from World War II who get arrested every decade or so—so underwhelming.

It's only when I sit in the witness chair that I realize I'm going to have more than enough opportunity to study Clyde further, and incredibly close up. Back in the States, witnesses and the accused are put at a reasonable distance, not close enough to claw at each other. In Koblenz Superior Court, though, the witness and accused are no more than a yard and a half apart. If Clyde were to lean slightly to his right and I leaned an equal amount to my left, we could hold hands.

Next to Conrad, his defense attorney sits slightly slumped in his chair. At their own table farther away, the two prosecutors sit ramrod straight.

"Herr Navarro," one asks, "could you please tell the court precisely how you got involved in this case?"

And with that, the show begins. For the next day and a half, nine hours of testimony in all, I take the court from Al Eways and my first meeting with Rod Ramsay, on the very day Clyde Conrad was arrested; through the early interviews with Lynn Tremaine; my year of no contact; how Rod then began to talk to me and Terry Moody, reluctantly at first, but each time with a little more information, until the confessions and revelations started spilling one on top of the other; and finally up to just a few days ago when I last saw Ramsay and told him I was going to Germany.

"And what was his response to that, Herr Navarro?" Conrad's attorney wants to know.

"He asked me to bring him back some good Riesling."

At least two of the judges find that amusing, but Conrad sits stony-faced. Every once in a while as I testify, though, I catch him with the hint of a smile, on the left side of his face, the more honest side, especially when I say something he knows is accurate. One such moment comes when I describe how Conrad had sent Rod into the document vault to steal a file, then started banging on the door to scare him. It's obvious to me that Conrad wants to laugh—he's reliving the moment and deeply proud of how he tested Rod—but he catches himself at the last moment.

This is far from a nine-hour monologue. The defense counsel, the panel of judges, even the prosecutors pelt me with questions. Conrad's attorney seems especially upset that I do all this without a single note in front of me. Time and again, he'll scribble furiously as I answer some question, then ask me the same question an hour or two later to see if I change a fact, a time, even the wording. I don't, at least not by enough to be meaningful in the least.

"How is it possible to deliver this testimony without notes?" he exclaims on the second day, throwing his hands dramatically into the air. "It's not. It's simply not."

I could tell him how it's possible: not because I'm clever, but because this is what I've lived for two years. Rod's words, his voice, his story—it's all so etched in my brain that Luciana used to complain that I was repeating Ramsay's interviews aloud in my sleep. That's the reason she gave for moving her bedroom into the den: One of us had to have a chance to rest. Or maybe because there were three of us in the bed every night, Rod included.

When I get to the most sensitive area of my testimony—the material from the Emergency Action Center, NSA's "equities"— the judges ask a lot of questions on all sides of the matter, but I get the impression that this is just one leap too many for them.

Fundamentally, they don't think Rod could have done it, could have taken what he confessed to taking. If I were allowed to testify that NSA has already verified that Ramsay is telling the truth, we could end the matter right here and now, but then we'd have to get into how Leonard, Henry, and others corroborated Rod's account, which would quickly lead us down a slippery path at the end of which top-secret matters would get divulged in open court. Score one for the Conrad team—and Clyde's smirk tells me he knows he's holding a winning hand on this issue—but the way his head keeps dropping lower between his shoulders also tells me that he knows the EAC material doesn't really mean that much, at least to his immediate future. I've already corroborated all the other documents that have been introduced, including the OPLANs and CONPLANs Conrad and Ramsay were so eager to sell. Throwing PALs and cookies on that pile would just be adding more fuel to an inferno.

As I expected, the court is openly surprised about the secret apartment. That seems to beggar everyone's imagination. But what concerns them the most, as it turns out, is why Ramsay is talking to me at all. And it's not just the judges. Defense counsel also wants to know if the government has made promises to Ramsay, if he's received Miranda warnings, if Ramsay is being paid, if he's worked out a deal with the prosecutors, and most unnerving—and this is when all the reporters, even the Russian ones, break out their pens and start writing furiously—why is Ramsay not under arrest?

One of the jurists is particularly appalled: "Herr Navarro, surely he is in some form of custody, no? With all the evidence you've presented, how could he not be?" The question, I should add, isn't directed solely to me. It resonates with everyone in the audience because everyone in Germany seems to get it—Ramsay should be in the clink by now.

What can I say? That spineless bureaucrats fretting over their careers have refused to act? That Ramsay's arrest is hung up in a pissing match between Tampa, the Washington Field Office, and FBIHQ? In the end, I opt, as I too rarely do, for tact:

"In espionage matters, Your Honor, only the US attorney general can make that decision, and he has yet to do so."

THE JUDGES HAVE JUST finished thanking me for my time at the end of my second day on the witness stand when Clyde Conrad clears his throat in what I take to be a meaningful way, and I look over at him. His face during my nine hours of testimony has run a gamut of emotions common to psychopaths: from narcissistic glee at hearing his "genius" confirmed, to the ice-cold stare he levels at me during short breaks or when I say something particularly damning, to a look best described as reptilian indifference, the outward and visible manifestation of a mindset that allows psychopaths to commit horrible crimes and do terrible things without feeling the least bit of remorse. There's something of all that in the way he stares at me now: animosity, disdain, the tacit assumption that everything about him has value and nothing about me does.

I'm literally inches from Conrad as I leave the witness stand. Maybe now is the time to let loose with a little anger and disdain and even triumph of my own. I've finished what Gary Pepper started, and between us, I'm sure Clyde Conrad will not be digging up his hidden jars of gold coins anytime soon. Take that, you son of a bitch! But the truth is I feel neither joy nor sorrow. In fact, at that moment as I walk past Clyde Conrad, I feel absolutely nothing for him, as though he's already dead.

THAT NIGHT WE HAVE a nice private dinner with the army folks, including Gary Pepper, and some of the investigators from the Bundeskriminalamt, the German equivalent of the FBI. Ihor, of course, has grabbed a couple bottles of Riesling for us, and one more for me to carry back to Orlando for Rod. We're into maybe our fourth liter when Ihor leans over to me and says, "Joe, the sum total of these two days has been jaw-dropping—nicely done."

Of the many nice pats on the back that night, Ihor's is the best, and also the last. In the morning, I'll be leaving for Austria to hook up with Jane and begin searching for the meeting spots Rod has told me about. The last thing I need is to wake up with a splitting headache, and Ihor and the Germans seem to be settling in for a long, long night.

I'm passing by the front desk at the compound when the night clerk asks me if I am "Herr Navarro," then hands me a fax that he says has arrived from "Tampa, in Florida America."

I wait until I'm upstairs to read it just in case I can't control my reaction—a wise move since, in fact, I cannot. The message is only seven words long:

"RR cannot be located. Call office stat."

Not until I land in Vienna just before noon the next day do I find out what happened: Surveillance followed the wrong Yellow Cab out of Orlando International. For twenty hours before he's found again, and just as news of my testimony in Koblenz starts circulating around the world, Rod Ramsay is on the loose and below the radar. For three of those hours, I lay in a bed in Koblenz, West Germany, convinced I was having a heart attack. So rattled was I that in the morning I forgot to pack Rod's Riesling. It was still on the dresser as I left for the airport in Frankfurt.

22

PLACES, EVERYONE!

Imagine the setting: an old building with poor lighting and anemic air-conditioning somewhere I can't identify in the Greater Washington, DC, metropolitan area—a secure, off-site location furnished with Department of Defense hand-me-downs from World War II and before. We're in a large conference room, gathered around a slightly scarred table big enough to sit twenty and, today, filled to the brim. And just like in junior high, everyone is sitting in packs.

The delegation from the Department of Justice? Together, and tight as ticks. Ditto the representatives from the army, from NSA, from FBIHQ, and from our office. Terry Moody, back to work at last and beaming from her new motherhood, Rich Licht, Marc Reeser, and I all sit to Jane Hein's left, with me on the wing, next to Dale Watson and the espionage squad he supervises at the Washington Field Office. Greg Kehoe is to Jane's right, elbow to elbow with the folks from Internal Security.

Watson begins the meeting by talking about information received from the Swedes. Why? This is probably the last thing that should be on the agenda. We can't use anything the Swedes are saying at a trial—it's all hearsay. Far better to spend our time on that small thing called "the trial of the century" in Germany or thank the army for having identified Conrad. But Watson's thinking is as slow as his Southern drawl.

When others in the room interrupt to talk about more pressing matters, such as the investigation of Rondeau and Gregory, Watson shuts them down just as he's tried to shut me down throughout this investigation. In fact, I know exactly what's going to happen next because I've lived this for over a year. I know who'll rant, who'll sit back complacently, who'll cower like sheep, what everyone will say and object to and harp on, and who, of course, in the end will get kicked in the nuts: me.

So why have I come? Because we somehow have to coordinate the largest espionage case in FBI history and make an arrest before everything falls apart, me included. And I've brought my core group with me (Susan Langford excluded, so someone can be by the phone in case Rod goes missing again or calls in from the ledge of a tall building) because through all this bureaucratic shitstorm, I'm determined that someone, goddamn it, will say thank you to them.

That contingent—the Tampa group, the very people I want to experience some gratitude, to feel some love—is predictably the first to come under withering assault.

Watson's superior from WFO decides he has something nasty to say and barges into the monologue, acknowledging the presence of "the young, but I'm sure hardworking, First Office Agents Moody and Licht" and then lamenting "how this large and delicate case requires the expertise and nuanced handling of a much more experienced office"—WFO, for example. And in that short presentation I realize why the word "patronizing" was invented.

Another senior manager from WFO jumps in, asking, "Why do we have a line attorney here?" with the same tone of voice she might use to object to, say, a dead mouse in her Diet Coke. "This is a counterintelligence working meeting."

Jane informs the group that Greg is actually the first assistant in the Middle District of Florida, and as if scripted, someone grumbles from the Washington Field Office side that the only attorney present should be the first assistant in the District of Columbia.

Greg himself ignores this salvo—he's been a trial attorney too long to let this insult raise even a single eyebrow. But other gloves come off immediately. Everyone starts taking shots at us, even though we've done all the work, including the crime scene work WFO never saw fit to do. In a burst of hyper-enthusiasm, one of the senior managers from WFO even questions why *any* attorneys are being brought into the case at this stage.

"Premature, I would say," he concludes, tugging on his pastel French cuff for effect.

Does he even know about the Koblenz trial? The nine hours of testimony, all directly related to Ramsay? Can he even imagine the flight risk we're now under with our only prosecutable suspect? Maybe not. Maybe it's true what they say—once you're inside the Washington Beltway, common sense is sucked right out of you.

Next, right on schedule, come the more personal attacks on me. Moody, Licht, even Marc Reeser (generally well liked at FBIHQ) are miscalculations enough—rookies on a case that needs seasoned hands—but why, Agent Navarro, would you insist on taking control of this case when (a) the WFO is ground zero of FBI field offices, (b) all the relevant big players (NSA, CIA, NSC, more initials) are in the Washington area, and (c) Tampa has so little experience in these *major* espionage matters?

Once again, playing my part, I just sit there and listen, even though I've worked more spy cases than anyone on Watson's WFO squad.

Then it gets worse: I'm being uppity, running an investigation it's not my place to run, asking other offices to do our work, placing demands on our legal attaché in Bonn and the other offices in Europe, etc.

It's when I'm accused of being "imperious" that I decide I've heard enough. I stand up to speak, but before I begin, I take the desktop podium that has been sitting idle by Watson and move it so that both the podium and I now tower over him. Then I start in.

"Guilty as charged," I say, raising my hands in surrender. "I have pursued this investigation because that is what I get paid to do and that is what Agent Moody and Agent Licht also get paid to do. We did so with the support of my special agent in charge. If you have issues with how we've proceeded, I suggest you take those up with him, not me. As has been suggested more than once, those supervisory issues are well above my humble FBI pay scale.

"Now, with that out of the way, let me tell you why I brought Agents Licht and Moody with me today, and asked Marc Reeser to join us as well. The fact is, I thought you might want to take this opportunity to thank them for a job damn well done. For hustling to make up for what was not done in this investigation."

Here, I admit, my voice begins to rise.

"Thank Agent Moody, for example, for the untold hours she's put in helping to interview Rod Ramsay, the countless trips back and forth between Tampa and Orlando, her deft skill in getting Rod to relax and open up, and for doing all this not only while handling all the other duties expected of a special agent but also while being pregnant with her second child."

I pause for a second, just in case someone wants to mumble his or her gratitude, but that would be off script, and no one is going there.

"Thank Agent Licht for the hundreds of leads he's sent out and tracked, leads I regret to say that no other investigative agency involved in this case thought to pursue."

Silence.

"Thank Marc Reeser for what I hope we all acknowledge is his remarkable talent for assimilating vast amounts of data and finding the links. For helping us find information and generating leads no one else has pursued since 1986."

This, at least, gets a small nod from the FBIHQ contingent.

"Thank, for that matter, the surveillance team that has sacrificed so much, has spent their own money while awaiting reimbursement, has worked so hard, has been away from home for months at a time, and has never lost Rod Ramsay—"

"Correction," says one of the minions from WFO. "I believe

your crack surveillance team lost Ramsay just the other day. It's a wonder—"

"You're right, one time, we did lose him for about twenty hours. Have any of you here ever tried to do surveillance on a Yellow Cab in an airport taxi queue? Any of you?" I say, looking down the WFO line. "We're lucky we lost him only that once. With all the leaks out of Washington, I'm frankly surprised we haven't seen him being received in Moscow with a bouquet of flowers."

Have I just gone off script? Maybe. But I recover gracefully—and I hope teach gratitude by example—by thanking the other offices and legal attachés present, the army folks for cooperating with us, the Swedes in absentia, even WFO for hosting this meeting even though we clearly should be holding the powwow in Tampa. And then I move on to the real points of my presentation: (a) the need to continue this investigation in Tampa, where we have the main suspect, the evidence, the thousands of pages of investigative materials, and the best testimony for a trial (as opposed to the WFO, where they have mostly petty jealousy and cheap vitriol to add to the mix); (b) the details of my testimony in Germany, so everyone in the room will know what I was required to let out of the bag; (c) the fact that, post-testimony, Jane Hein [nodding her way as she nods back to me] and I were able to corroborate Rod's descriptions of multiple meeting sites in Austria, thus significantly bolstering the case against him; and (d) the final and inescapable fact that Rod Ramsay now represents a significant flight risk who needs to be arrested "before he runs, disappears, defects, and/or destroys evidence."

"We have," I conclude, "only a few days, maybe just hours, to act. We need to make a decision. Today. Here. Now."

One of the Internal Security attorneys, no surprise, jumps on this: No decision, he says, will be made "today, here, now," putting me in my place. Yet another representative from WFO says that as far as they're concerned, the lead investigative office is still WFO and not Tampa. This, of course, is where the script has been headed all along, but instead of feeling that I've been kicked in the crotch, I'm feeling more like someone strong is pressing the palm of his hand with increasing pressure against my chest.

I drink water from the table, but that doesn't seem to help. I'm actually beginning to feel dizzy, not just anxious, when Greg Kehoe stands up beside me, quietly suggests I take my seat, and clears his throat before turning to the crowded conference table. Greg is a perfect gentleman, good-looking, full of life, but he does not tolerate bullshit, and this meeting has become so thick with it they should be issuing waders. Time for him to break his silence.

"Gentlemen, ladies, this case isn't about CI matters, secret meetings, or 'equities.' It's about a criminal enterprise." He says this with a smile, hoping to bring people down from their high horses, but in a voice that absolutely commands attention, even from the cuff shooters, maybe especially from them.

"It's a very simple case—a case about criminals who violated the law, stole documents, sold them to a foreign power, put this nation and others at risk, and frankly we're lucky to have at least one person and possibly more to put away here in the United States. *Capisce?*" I've heard Greg use that word hundreds of times, but something about the way he says it now, with a heavy Queens accent, seems to jolt everyone to attention. I can almost see their ears lifting, the way dogs pick up threatening sounds.

"Folks, you talk like this demitasse of secrets isn't going to spill, that if we just sit on this long enough everything is going to be okay, and we'll all get back to where we used to be. Well, I got news for you: That train has already left the station. The shit hit the fan way back when Zoltan Szabo got recruited and turned things over to Conrad. And if that isn't bad enough, it gets turned over to Ramsay, who flips the whole damn thing into Secrets'R'Us."

As he speaks, I can tell that most people in the room are frankly surprised by how much Greg knows about the case.

"Color me crazy," Greg says, stepping out in front of the room with his arms palms-up, "but someone needs to go to jail. It's that simple.

"People are going to look at this and ask: What did you do? What did you who are paid to protect us do? What are you going to say then, huh? Tell them you gave the case to the Germans out of the goodness of your hearts? Judicial hands across the sea—that kind of thing? Are you effing kidding me? That doesn't pass the stink test, not even at the Fulton Fish Market, and lemme tell you, it's pretty smelly there."

Greg smiles as he says this, but trust me, no one he's talking directly to is smiling back with him.

"Boys and girls, it's up to us to put criminals in jail. Since when do we outsource justice, especially when it comes to spies? You tell me. Do we outsource that to the Germans? Do we outsource it to a Swedish detention facility with conjugal privileges?

"I don't want to be a pimple on the butt of progress here, but all you're trying to do is shine shit—excuse my language, Mrs. Moody and Jane—and you can't shine shit no matter how much effort you put into it. A crime has been committed, for God's sake, a serious one last time I checked. If we were at war, I'd be asking for the death penalty."

Greg looks now directly at the DOJ-ISS representatives and speaks almost in a growl.

"And what are you going to tell the American public? That you in this room decided to keep this disjointed investigation going the way it is? That you couldn't make a decision about an arrest that should have been made months ago? No, we have a duty to the American public, something you in the cloak-and-dagger arena seem to have forgotten."

Greg walks over to his briefcase.

"Folks," he says, lowering his voice, a technique he has mastered in court, "I'm leaving here shortly. But I can tell you this. We're going to prosecute Rod and anyone else we can get our hands on. We're going to run a grand jury in Tampa, in the little old Middle District of

Florida, and we're going to start papering the world with subpoenas," he says, looking at me and Rich Licht, who'll help prepare them, "and we're going to lock in testimony because so far as Joe Navarro and I can tell, no one has bothered to think about that."

As he says that, more than a few people in the room begin to squirm in their chairs—literally, not just figuratively.

"Yeah, somehow, you guys have forgotten about locking in testimony. What, you think that if someone said it, it will be there at the time of trial? Who the hell taught you about trial work? Perry Mason? You ever put a case together for court? It's not testimony until we lock it in through a proper federal grand jury. All we have is what people have said, but that doesn't mean crap at trial if we don't lock them into their testimony, if we don't subpoena records and make those available and ready for the court."

Greg has begun gathering his things now, but he's not quite through, and unlike earlier in the day, no one dares to interrupt— not even the senior managers from WFO, because Greg has few equals and certainly none in this room.

"Let me be perfectly clear," he says. "Neither I nor the US attorney for the Middle District of Florida are going to shirk our responsibilities. I can tell you unequivocally that enough is enough. I will personally trample on anyone who obstructs justice or interferes. You seem to have forgotten the trust the American public places on us to exact justice, no matter how it comes to us, no matter how imperfect, and to put people in jail. We have a duty to the American people, and frankly we have no legitimate explanation for what we've done so far."

By now, the DOJ guys are frozen in place, looking straight ahead. I can see the veins on their foreheads throbbing.

"Enough," Greg concludes. "Get off your asses and make a decision. We're impaneling a grand jury in Tampa, and we *will* indict. And you have my word on that. Good day, ladies, gentlemen."

With that, Greg smiles at Moody, Licht, and Reeser, shakes my hand, and whispers in my ear just loud enough for those nearby to hear: "Don't take any more shit from these lemmings. Got another meeting. See ya at the airport." He's walking out and sucking the air from the room with him when Jane rises from her seat, runs Greg down from the back, then shakes his hand and thanks him for coming all this way. The stares she gets for that tell me that Jane Hein has just become a traitor to her class.

GREG NEARLY MISSES OUR flight back. Not until we're strapped in and lifting off does he tell me that he went straight from our off-site meeting to the Justice Department itself to meet with Bob Mueller, who definitely has the attorney general's ear.

"It's over," he says.

"Over?"

"The fighting. The delays. All the shit. The AG apparently called the Internal Security Section and told them to get the hell out of our way."

"Son of a bitch" is all I can say. The case that will never end is finally going to trial.

"You know what happens next?" Greg asks.

"Sure, of course, the arresting document, arraignment . . ."

"No, Joey, Joey," sounding suddenly a lot like an extra in *The Godfather*, "dat's next-next, ya know. I'm talking *next*."

"Okay, I give up. What happens *next*?"

"Next," Greg explains, "watch your back. The knives will come out when you least expect it."

23

"DOES JOE NAVARRO KNOW ABOUT THIS?"

By the time we land in Tampa late on the night of June 5, I'm having trouble swallowing, maybe because of a lump that has appeared under my chin. It's so sensitive I hold a cup of ice to it most of the flight, while Greg Kehoe snores lustily beside me. Just hauling my briefcase through the terminal and out to the car park leaves me short of breath.

The next day, June 6, 1990, the State Superior Court in Koblenz sentences Conrad to life plus six years, the longest sentence ever handed down in West Germany in an espionage case—proof that, in that country, at least, this really was the spy trial of the century. By noon on the sixth, the switchboard at our Tampa office is dangerously close to being overloaded. Newspapers and media outlets from all over the world are calling with questions about Rod Ramsay. Did he get immunity for his testimony? What are his trial dates? Where is he in custody? I want to shout back: "What immunity? What testimony? What trial and custody?" But what good would that do?

Instead, I labor down the two flights of stairs to Greg's office and find him locked in an animated conversation.

"We have to pull the trigger now, this moment," I say, leaning heavily against his doorjamb.

"Soon," he tells me, covering the mouthpiece. "The pricks at ISS are dragging their heels."

"Soon," I say, "is too late," and trudge back up the stairs, again feeling like I'm summiting Mount Everest, struggling for every breath.

My next move is to call Ihor. He doesn't have the clout to make anything happen at the Internal Security Section, but as always, he has a close ear to the ground.

"Kehoe's philippic the other day was like a Pennsylvania Avenue earthquake," he tells me. "He rattled the shit out of the front office here, and the AG came down on them a few hours later like a ton of bricks. Something's about to happen. Paper is heading your way. You didn't hear it from me."

Sure enough, Ihor's "paper" arrives three hours later, with a cover communication from FBIHQ: "Attorney General has authorized arrest of Roderick James Ramsay by COB [close of business] June 7. Coordinate at once with First Assistant Gregory Kehoe, US Attorney's Office, Middle District of Florida."

MY FIRST CALL IS to Rod, who has phoned yet again, worried about his future, while I've been ranting away. He wants me to assure him, face-to-face, that the walls aren't closing around him.

"Maybe you could come over tomorrow?" he suggests. "I could pick you up at the hotel. We could just ride and talk, or maybe get some lunch and eat it in the car like before."

"No can do, Rod," I tell him, "but I'll tell you what. Why don't you come over here tomorrow and let me put your mind at rest. I'll cover the cost of gas. I've got a big surprise for you."

"What?" he asks, clearly nervous about where this might be heading.

"She-Moody!"

"Terry?"

"Yup, she's back from maternity leave. I know she'd like to see you. Say noon?"

Duplicitous? Hell yes, and even worse that I've used Terry for bait. I know these lies are eating away at me somewhere deep inside—it's my Catholic background. But Rod seems happy to comply, and he now has Agent Moody's company to look forward to, always a treat.

Next, I place another call to Ihor.

"Got it?" he asks.

"Yeah. And . . ."

"And what?"

"Ihor, it's four in the afternoon and we have until close of business tomorrow to arrest Ramsay. When are we going to get the charging complaint?"

"What charging complaint?"

"Wait a minute. That's what your office does!"

"Not this time. You're on your own."

"What the fuck?"

"Joe," he says, before hanging up, "the front office is dumping it on you guys."

Instead of cursing at a mute hunk of black Bakelite, I hustle down as best I can to Greg's office once again and tell him that ISS has put us on life support and we'll have to draft the charging complaint ourselves. I then sit quietly while Greg questions out loud the paternity of everyone in the Internal Security Section and the relative chastity of their mothers. It takes him a couple minutes to calm down, but then he commands two legal pads from his secretary, and the two of us head off to his conference room and begin drafting the document that will officially charge Rod with violation of a federal law—and thus give us standing to arrest him. The document will also allow us to conduct a search at multiple locations—including Rod's vehicle, his mother's vehicle, where he currently lives, and his mother's house—for evidence of espionage activity.

"When is Rod coming over?" Greg asks after we've been working maybe an hour.

"Tomorrow," I tell him, "around noon."

"You know, Joe," he adds another ninety minutes later, as we're putting the finishing touches on a first draft, "you gotta have a plan in place."

"Oh, gee, Greg, you think?" I say. "I hadn't considered that." But as Greg well knows—since I've been stepping out of the conference room every twenty minutes or so to use his desk phone—I've been working on the plan almost as hard as we're working on the affidavit. For starters, we'll need added surveillance to watch the campground closely all night and follow Rod out when he leaves in the morning, a hotel room for the meeting (Moody's job), and a command post somewhere else in the same hotel. Then there's the arrest—where are we going to do it so it's safe? and when?—and also the problem of other law-enforcement agencies that might just trip over us if we don't give them advance warning. The US Marshals Service, for instance. We can't let them be surprised that a major arrest is coming down. Nor can we just brush off the local police. US marshals are cowboys—piss them off and revenge is almost certain—but if a squad car of local cops happens upon a bunch of plainclothes FBI agents with drawn guns, lead might start flying in all the wrong directions. We also have to set out over 160 initial interviews to be done worldwide within eight hours or sooner of Rod's arrest. Thank God for Rich Licht and Susan Langford, who put the finishing touches on that project. There's no FBI office that won't be affected by what's about to go down, and the ripples will be felt as well by many of our attachés in Sweden, Germany, Austria, and Japan—even Italy and the UK.

By now, it's past eleven o'clock at night, and I'm rousting more agents from their beds to get everything set up for tomorrow. Midnight has come and gone when Greg finally finishes faxing our affidavit to the night-duty lawyer at ISS; it's past one when the night lawyer faxes it back with dozens of nitpick edits that only a government attorney would ever think of inserting.

"Why didn't he write the damn thing himself?" I ask Greg.

"Because that requires effort," Greg says, his pencil busy checking through changes. " 'These are the timid souls who neither know victory nor defeat.' "

"Where did that come from?"

"Teddy Roosevelt. Speech at the Sorbonne. 1910."

"I would have thought they weren't helping because now no one is going to pat them on the back when this is through."

"That, too," Greg says, diving back into the draft.

Months, even years, of work have now been reduced to writing the legal instrument that will initiate the judicial process, a critical document that will have to stand the test of time and the scrutiny of the courts. And there's nobody I'd rather have at the other end of that editor's pencil than Greg. Half an hour later, his head pops up again. "By the way, have you prepared something to send to the NSC so they can brief the president?"

"For crissake, let HQ worry about that, Greg."

"You don't want the president to be asked about a spy arrest in Tampa and have to say, 'We'll get back to you on that.' Trust me, the White House wants to know—yesterday—and the National Security Council will be extremely pissed if they haven't been alerted in advance. I've run into this with the Noriega case. Leave them out of the loop, and there'll be hell to pay. You've got to brief State, too."

"The State Department?"

"Yeah, State. You know, Germany, NATO, missiles, all those little issues. Our friends abroad might like a teensy heads-up on tomorrow's events."

"I'm ahead of you on that one. Jane, your new best friend at FBIHQ, is handling that. As soon as the affidavit is signed, the message will fly."

"Speaking of affidavits, tomorrow," he continues, waving the draft over his head, "you'll need to go before Judge Elizabeth Jenkins and swear to this. Good thing your boy isn't showing up until noon, eh?"

*   *   *

I LEAVE FOR HOME at 4:30 a.m., kiss Stephanie a tardy good night—or good morning?—without waking her, spend half an hour under the hottest shower I can stand, shave, dress in something comfortable (a standard dress shirt and tie would scare Rod to death even if I had the tie at half-mast), and look longingly at my bed, wondering when I'll ever share it again. In the kitchen, I stare inside the refrigerator for a few minutes, hoping I'll be inspired to eat something but knowing that, even if I do, I won't be able to hold it down.

Luciana is on her side, facing the door, breathing gently and evenly, when I check on her in the den.

"Soon," I whisper into the dark. "It's almost over. We can be real people again."

I have a feeling her eyes are open, but there's no way to tell.

I'm back in my office by 6 a.m., reviewing Rod's case and firing off the few briefings I didn't get off late last night before my vision went almost double. By eight o'clock, I've sent off the last of those—to our FBI legal attachés in all major European cities, who'll shortly have to brief their law-enforcement and counterintelligence counterparts as well as deal with local press queries, all of which will henceforth be directed to the US Attorney's Office in Tampa. I've also left a message for Jane, who's probably still out on her morning run, assuring her that she'll have a copy of the affidavit as soon as possible after it's signed. Once that happens, the FBI loses all authority over the case. DOJ runs the show and the ball is squarely in Greg's office.

I spend part of the next hour taking a physical inventory, and the results aren't promising. My chest is pounding, I have trouble breathing, the room seems to spin around me at times, and now both sides of my mouth on the underside are sore. When I try to calm things down with some yogurt, the cold hurts my mouth too much to go on.

A little before nine o'clock an anonymous caller from the 202 area code thanks me for an unidentified heads-up about an unmentioned subject and then proceeds to tell me in a very clipped shorthand how the early-morning meeting with President Bush had gone:

"When POTUS was told about the PALs and SNAs, he looked like a ghost had walked across the Oval Office." There's a surprise. Apparently, the national security people didn't have him fully in the loop. Ouch.

" 'What are we going to tell the Germans?' he asked Scowcroft. 'As little as possible.' "

Click.

Poor Germans. "As little as possible" is exactly what I gave up at Conrad's trial, so much so that the judges doubted anyone could have stolen the keys to the nuclear castle. Will Bonn ever know how naked we left them? In any event, it pays to have friends at HQ even if they have to remain secret.

Half an hour later, I've just set up radio contact with our campground surveillance unit when Terry Moody pokes her head in my office, waves a tentative good morning, says, "Joe, I think you'll want to see this," and leads me to a south-facing window that conveniently looks out on the US District Court for the Middle District of Florida. We're in steamy June, but outside the sun is coming up on a beautiful day, one of those picture-perfect advertisements for the Sunshine State Gulf Coast.

"Nice," I say to Terry, longing to be out in my kayak and knowing I don't have the strength to paddle more than a few minutes. "Thanks."

And that's when I follow her eyes down to street level and see *three* TV news trucks parked at the curb in front of the courthouse, with "ABC" blazed boldly on their sides.

"Not local," Moody tells me. "I checked them out on my way into the office. License plates are all from Washington, DC."

"Bamford," I say. "Shit!" But it comes out so tamely that Terry immediately turns her focus to me.

"You holding it together, Joe?"

"No," I want to say, "I'm really not," but at least I'm beyond shock that someone at HQ would have tipped ABC to this, the final scene in the Ramsay story. I'm asking myself how different this kind of institutional sellout is from espionage itself when the hand radio I've carried over to the window crackles alive and I hear a disembodied voice saying, "Iris 9 to Gunga Din. Iris 9 to Gunga Din," words designed to get your attention in the middle of a tornado.

"Over," I answer.

"Eyeball on the package, and he's moving."

"Shit! Moody, we gotta get going!" I say, running for the stairs with Moody right behind me.

We planned on noon. Even if Rod dawdles all the way down I-4 and misses the Tampa turnoff, he'll be here no later than eleven o'clock.

"Go!" I shout to Moody, pointing in the general direction of the downtown Hyatt, her choice for the best place to rendezvous with Rod. Simultaneously, I break for Greg's office. A clean affidavit, approved by ISS, is just rolling off the fax when I bust through his door.

"No time to explain," I tell his secretary as I grab the still-warm stack of papers and do what I can to bust a move to the street below. *We have time*, I tell myself. *We have time. We have time.* And short of disaster, we absolutely do.

"YOU CAN'T GO IN there," the courthouse guard says to me.

"Sure I can," I say. "You know me. I'm FBI." I flash my credentials just to put him at ease.

"You're carrying a gun," he explains. "No guns, you understand? Them's the rules."

"But this is an emergency." It's a sweaty June day, despite the pristine view from the window ten minutes ago. The affidavit in my hand is going limp with the heat and humidity.

"What part of 'can't' don't you understand?" the guard asks.

"Look, I only have minutes. How about I leave the gun with you?"

"Can't do that."

I get it, actually. The senior judge has forbidden FBI agents to enter the courthouse with guns. Sensible, surely. This guard is powerless. Yet, if there's an assault on a federal judge, the FBI has to investigate, and we're not going to walk in the courthouse door stripped of any protection. You have to be schizophrenic to understand these rules, but I don't have time to argue.

"Can I lock my service pistol up somewhere?" I ask, cajole, beg.

With that, the guard casts me a fishy look and walks us over to a bank of new lockers at a pace that tells me he's never been in the trenches or anywhere close to them, but we still haven't gotten to "enter." After I secure the weapon, he tells me I have to walk through the magnetometer before I can go upstairs. Here is another humanoid I will always remember as a speed bump on the road to success.

"She's in her chambers," the guard says with a sour smile as I enter the elevator. I just hope there isn't a line of other federal agents waiting to have their criminal complaints authorized. For once, things go well—sort of. Judge Jenkins welcomes me in, her morning courtiers are nonexistent, but then she launches into an examination of the document that I can describe only as pedantically thorough.

By the time she asks me to raise my right hand and swear that the details herein are accurate and the full circumstances made known to me so help me God, we're down to twenty-seven minutes, less if Rod has the pedal to the metal. As I race to the Hyatt, I can barely read my own watch I'm breathing so hard. What's more, there's no time to rest once I do get to the room. Within seconds, it seems, I have three radios going: the command post, the surveillance unit following Ramsay, and the arrest team—each feeding me updates and each update ratcheting up the tension I'm already feeling.

Just to add to the fun, Dorothy Ramsay's worried calls to my office switchboard are being helpfully patched through to the Hyatt front desk and up to me. Each time one comes in (every four minutes, by my count), I have to rush around and mute all three radio connections so

Dorothy doesn't glom on to the full extent of my treachery. Apparently, there's a news reporter at her house. No wonder she's questioning my attempts to assuage her fear.

"Dorothy," I tell her, "that's what reporters do when they have nothing real to report on. They go on expeditions. They fish. They try to manufacture a story. Don't—"

"I don't want to know anything more, Mr. Navarro," she interrupts. "Rod is burden enough." And she, too, hangs up on me. A morning for rejection, all richly earned.

Moody, meanwhile, is trying to calm me down, but even she acknowledges what I've been through and all the commotion going on.

"I don't know how you do it, Navarro," she allows. "I really don't—this is turning into a carnival."

For my part, I sit on the couch trying to steal whatever rest I can, but there's no time for that either. My chest is heaving just from the exertion of getting here. This is ridiculous. I can run two miles with all my SWAT gear on, for crissake, or—correct that—once could. I don't know what the room temperature is set at—meat-locker cold, maybe—because I'm soaked clear through from my running and shivering like a leaf in a gale when surveillance makes one last call upstairs to say that Rod is on his way. The Eagle has landed, I'm thinking, when he knocks on the door for the very last time and Moody lets him in.

"Mother Moody," he says with a big grin. She does her best to grin back, but you don't have to be a body-language expert to see how hard she's trying.

"And Joe," he says, now turning toward me and giving me a good once-over. "Man, you look like dog poop."

"Thanks, Rod. Nice to see you, too." And that's when I notice: We're wearing almost exactly the same thing: khakis, penny loafers, and salmon-colored polo shirts. In a way, I'm not surprised. Rod is a master of mimicry, but as this showdown nears, Rod and I have also been drawing nearer to one another in a multitude of ways. More and more, he's been echoing the terms I use, my syntax, the general tone of my voice. He's even held me up as a role model to his mother. Clothes, I suppose, are just a natural extension of that, even if at the moment we happen to look like a textbook example of evil twins.

In the professional literature, this is known as "transference and countertransference"—whenever you spend this much time with another person, you begin to take on each other's characteristics and even bond subconsciously. This is the main reason FBI deep-cover agents have to be pulled out before they succumb to the antisocial behaviors they've been sent undercover to root out. I think I'm well short of that with Rod—I have no urge toward espionage—but I also can't ignore the fact that he's infinitely interesting, highly intelligent, incredibly fragile, overwhelmingly pathetic, and soon to start a second life behind bars. How could I call myself human if I simply hated such a man? What's more, hate takes energy. I have no energy left and certainly not for that.

The three of us have spent about fifteen minutes on the usual introductory chitchat—how he's eating, cab fares, what books he's been reading (and tearing apart as he goes through), today's traffic report on I-4, Moody's infant girl (a robust eight pounds fourteen ounces at birth), my incompetence in forgetting the promised bottle of Riesling from Germany—when even Rod has had enough.

"Well," he says, a serious look spreading across his face, "I've heard the rumors about an arrest." His lips and chin are quivering.

Just as seriously, I reply, "Rod, I have no intention of arresting you. Mrs. Moody certainly isn't going to either."

Maybe the "I" should have been a little more emphasized, but what I've just said is the absolute truth. Making the arrest is a big, big deal in the FBI. You lead the perp walk with your FBI jacket on; you're the one in front of the cameras when the media gather for the follow-up press conference. Get credited with a collar as big as Rod, and your career is pretty much golden. But this morning I informed our Tampa bureau, HQ, and everyone else that I wouldn't do the arrest, and I meant it.

My rhetoric was lofty and heartfelt: "A lot of people worked on this case, and they need credit," I told Koerner, who disagreed but in the end acquiesced to letting Rich Licht lead the arrest team along with Susan Langford, an honor richly earned by both. What I didn't tell Jay was that I didn't want to be anywhere near the Hyatt parking lot when the arrest happened. And Moody agreed. The joy of finally putting this guy in cuffs was taken from us piece by piece months ago. This is no sporting event to celebrate, no trophy to hold up. This is a tragedy.

Our little white lie behind us, Terry, Rod, and I try to get back to the conversation, but I think all of us know this just isn't right. Moody is trying to be cheerful, but she looks closer to tears. I'm worse than exhausted. Transference expert that he is, Rod is slipping into our own miserable moods. We're just on the short end of testy and grumpy when I decide to end it. None of us is in a mood to talk.

"I'm sorry to have brought you all the way over here, Rod," I say. "I just don't feel well. Correction: I feel shitty, and your mom has been calling me and she's concerned. Would you mind if we got together another day?"

"Please go see your mom as long as you're here," Terry adds. "Let her know you're okay. She's been so worried."

With that, Terry and I both get up and give Rod a hug, covering between us as much of his body as we can to make sure he isn't carrying a weapon—a last Judas moment to end our forty-two interviews.

"Well, see you later," Rod says at the door, with a small wave. He lingers with his hand on the knob, almost as if he's trying to will me to ask "Anything else?" one more time.

Almost before he's gone, I collapse on the sofa while Moody radios the arrest team waiting in the parking lot: "Target leaving hotel." Around us the three radio frequencies, now back to life, are blaring away, but I'm not listening. The chatter on all three frequencies has turned to an almost unbearable cacophony.

"Come on, Joe," Terry finally says, "we have to go." But I don't move. I can't. Moody is just lifting me to my feet when I hear cheering in the background from the command post and Rich Licht radios in his report: "Rod is in custody without incident." And with those words communications start flying to FBIHQ, Justice, everyone involved. Within seconds, the Germans and Swedes know, too, and no doubt the Russians as well.

I'm still frozen in place when Rich calls back and tells me to "squawk Delta 3," a code phrase for switching to an alternate, little-used SWAT frequency no one else in the Bureau is monitoring. Terry has to help me, but we finally get the frequency up and working.

"You know what Ramsay's first words were, Joe, when we cuffed him?" Rich asks.

All I can do is stare at Moody. I can't even imagine what the answer might be.

" 'Does Joe Navarro know about this?' "

24

STAYING ALIVE

Moody and I sit in that room at the Hyatt Hotel for what seems like an hour after Rod has walked out the door one last time. It might be only twenty minutes really, but when you're too exhausted to move, when you're sweating profusely in an air-conditioned room, when you feel a fever burning up through your head, when you're shaking uncontrollably, minutes seem like hours.

Terry offers to have an agent pick us up for the trip back to the office, but once she gets me on my feet, I want to walk, to feel my body moving. Maybe whatever is wrong with me will just go away now that Rod is in custody. It doesn't. What is usually a ten-minute walk turns into a forty-minute trudge with She-Moody supporting me every step of the way.

Spirits are high when the elevator finally opens onto the fifth floor of the Tampa office. Most of my colleagues have been in the dark about the Ramsay case. Now word is out, and the mood is celebratory—an arrest! a perp walk!—but I feel just the opposite. I sit in my office for as long as I can stand it. The room is swirling around me. People talk but it isn't registering. I make sure I thank everyone involved, then go into the bathroom and lock myself in a stall, just to decompress.

By then, I've discovered a swollen lymph node in each underarm to go along with the odd, bilateral swelling beneath my chin. That is part of it—I don't know what the hell is wrong with me, but the signs are scaring the hell out of me. Worse, though, is a sense of disconnect with everything going on around me. Moody, of course, knows what I've been through over the last year and a half. Koerner, too. Kehoe, Licht, Susan Langford, and a few others have seen some of the worst of it, too. But somehow, happy talk and high fives seem the wrong way to end it, and not only because my mind is fogged in.

What I need is rest, bottomless amounts of it, but there's more work to be done on Rod's case. I have to testify the next day at his detention hearing, and it's going to be a zoo—the first opportunity for the public to hear what's been going on, defense counsel's first crack at me and our case as well. At this moment, I'm not sure I can hold up to an attack. Sleep is almost out of the question—I'll be rehearsing my courtroom answers all night long—and I'm far from in top form in any event, mentally or physically. After hiding in the bathroom for almost an hour, shivering from the fever, I talk myself back into the game.

"Where have you been?" Moody asks.

"Resting my head."

"The boss is looking for you. They want you to attend the press conference."

"You go."

"Not me," says Moody. "If I want to go to a circus, I'll wait until Ringling Brothers comes back to town."

"I've got to get ready for tomorrow," I tell her, "and I feel terrible."

"Honest truth, Joe, you look awful. Go home. I've never seen you like this."

"I know you mean that well," I say, gathering my things and giving her a hug. "Thanks for everything, Terry. I owe you a lot."

"Joe—"

But whatever she's going to say, I don't let her finish the thought.

"I gotta go. Cover for me, okay? I don't want to be here. I need to rest."

I slip out the back door, avoid the media, and somehow make it all the way home without once again falling asleep at the wheel and careening through a strip mall.

THE NEXT DAY, JUNE 8, I testify at Rod's detention hearing while the accused sits across from me and his mother glares at me from the audience like I'm a whore in church. Mark Pizzo, Rod's defense attorney, tries valiantly to tear into my methods and me. Mark looks like the actor Andy Garcia (my fellow Cuban-American) and possesses impressive street smarts. And I've got to say, he rises beautifully to the occasion with maybe four dozen reporters on hand, hanging on his every word. Meanwhile, Rod at the table beside him is doing everything he can to unnerve me. His eyes burrow into me the entire time I'm on the stand.

One line of questioning clearly gets to both of us, even though I'm uncertain where Mark is heading with it other than to show that I'm a conflicted emotional mess—which, of course, is not far off the mark.

"Isn't it a fact, Agent Navarro," he says, "that you hugged my client just about every time you met, before and at the end of your interview session?"

"It is," I agree. "I gave him an *abrazo*, a friendly hug."

"Would it be safe to say, then, that you cared deeply about my client?"

There it is in a nutshell—love, hate, the whole endlessly contradictory nature of Rod's and my relationship; a petri dish of transference and conflicted emotions—but I'm not going to go there.

"I hugged your client, Mr. Pizzo, because I wanted to see if he was armed. He had, after all, told me that he once robbed a bank."

If I read Rod's eyes right, he looks a little crushed by that, and in truth, I feel like a shit for saying it. But I'm sure the moment makes no difference in the outcome of the hearing. In the end, Rod is remanded to the custody of the US Marshals, pending trial. There's no question of his being out on bond. If ever there was one, Rod is a threat to the security of the United States.

WHEN I LEFT THE house that morning, my fever was hovering around 102. It isn't any better on the way home so I stop at the office of yet another Cuban-American connection, Dr. Juan Ling. Juan, it turns out, is away at a medical conference, but his nurse can see I'm teetering on the edge and draws enough blood to get the testing started. Even that, though, makes me queasy. Add in the heavy sweating that has been going on for days and the cement legs I was feeling even before my madcap dash to the Hyatt on arrest day, and I can barely get out of the car when I finally pull into my driveway late that afternoon.

"Daddy!" Stephanie yells happily when I walk through the front door. To her, this is something almost new in history—a father home in daylight. But all I can do is smile at her, pat her on the head, and make straight for my bed. For her part, Luciana just stares at me as I move awkwardly through the house, seemingly in slow motion, unable to say a single word. I want to cry but I'm too tired even for that.

For the next three weeks, I do try to go to the office regularly. There's plenty more work to be done. I have to prepare for a trial, continue the investigation of Rondeau and Gregory, identify who else might be involved, corroborate everything Rod has said, plus the endless paperwork—this *is* the FBI, after all—but I can't complete more than two hours' work at a time.

Somewhere in there, too, Jim Bamford calls to say that he thought we'd mounted a "magnificent investigation." The only other time we talked, months earlier when he called with yet another leaked tidbit about the Ramsay case, I told him what I'd say to any journalist under similar circumstances: "I can't talk to you, and I can't confirm what you're saying. If you're going to publish, publish. There's nothing I can do about it, or you." This time, I think, he means the compliment sincerely, with no ulterior motive, and I take it that way. I have no beef with Bamford. Whoever has been telling him secrets hasn't derailed the investigation. What has gone off the tracks is my health and my natural defenses.

Everything in my life, it seems, has turned upside down. For months I got by on at best three hours of sleep a night. Now I fall into bed almost as soon as I get home and have to struggle out in the morning twelve hours later. The fact that more sleep isn't helping suggests a more serious problem, and my stubborn refusal to accept the reality of what's happening to me physically isn't helping things.

Finally, I'm able to get in to see Juan Ling, who pores over me for an hour, reviews the blood tests, gives me four prescriptions to have filled right away, and orders me to go home with bed rest and no work until further notice.

"I suppose I could go in every other day for a while," I concede.

"No work," he demands. "None! Joe, here's my clinical assessment: You're a mess." And then he kindly details just how big a mess I've become: exhaustion, a high white-blood-cell count, Epstein-Barr virus, anxiety and panic attacks, and an enlarged spleen. Every lymph node in my body is swollen from my neck down to the insides of my legs.

"You have too much stress in your life, and I suspect you're clinically depressed. In fact, you have many of the features of post-traumatic stress," Juan cautions.

"You think so, Doc?" I try to make it sound like a joke, but by now, Juan is in no joking mood and I suppose neither am I.

"Listen to me, Joe. You have to take your life and your health back, or you're going to die. You hear me? You either get in bed and rest now, or you *will* die. Your immune system is compromised, your lymph nodes are trying to clean up your blood, you have a fever that would knock out a horse, and you're suffering from these anxiety and panic attacks because your body is screaming at you to stop. 'Stop or die'—that's what the attacks are telling you.

"Cuidate coño!" he blurts out in Spanish, trying to get through to me. It's an admonition we Cubans give to each other: "Take care of yourself, dammit!"

JUAN TURNS IT AROUND for me. I start listening to what the attacks and all the other symptoms are saying, but that's only the beginning. Illnesses I never imagined or thought only happened to others become my constant companions.

For nearly nine months I lie in bed completely drained of energy, incapable of getting up on my own even to pee, living in a kind of hibernation. I can see my daughter through the window playing in the backyard, but I can't raise my head or even smile as I try to enjoy those moments. Depression, I can tell you, is a terrible thing—you cry over the smallest happening—it attacks your mind and it doesn't want to let go. People don't understand that you're in mental anguish, pain so bad it makes you think about killing yourself just to end it. That's how bad it gets for me.

The physical part of all this—at least I can see and feel it coming on. The depression catches me by surprise. I don't realize I'm in the maze until I'm so deep inside I can't imagine a way out. Thanks to a terribly structured insurance system, I see multiple therapists—some good, some terrible. Insurance rarely pays for the best mental health care, if at all, but I'm caught in a further Catch-22 because I can't talk about the work that has led me into this box canyon until the FBI finds a clinician cleared at the top-secret level.

Some of the therapists suggest, like Juan, that I've gone through post-traumatic stress. Others tell me viruses can bring on depression, while still others say that I've spent too much time with Ramsay. One literary-minded therapist and I spend an entire fifty-five-minute session talking about what he calls my "white whale" problem, as if I were Captain Ahab and Rod my Moby Dick. "Ahab could have turned the boat around," the therapist keeps insisting. "Why didn't he? Why didn't you?" I have no idea. Even in my tired, sick state, I know this white whale theory is a flimsy intellectual construct from someone who's never been through anything like what I'm trying to crawl out from under. That whale was whatever Ahab turned him into in his own mind—his tormentor, his obsession, evil incarnate. Rod Ramsay, goddamn it, is *real*, and it was my sworn duty to pursue and bring him to justice no matter how many roadblocks my superiors placed in front of me.

Then there's the FBI explanation: Many agents suffer depression from the weight of their work but keep it secret so their record will stay clean and the longed-for twenty-five-years-and-out won't be jeopardized. Instead, they turn to alcohol or other addictions. That much, at least, I've avoided, so far.

My own diagnosis is that I'm mentally and spiritually drained. I've lost faith in so many things, and I've had to deal with so much that I never saw coming: plans derailed by other offices; the intransigence—and, later, skepticism—of WFO and HQ; endless hours of preparation to ensure we didn't fail; the constant fear that Ramsay would disappear; the frightening suspicion that Rod had other secrets, that others were involved, that the Soviets had everything they needed to wage *and win* a war; the endless lying to Ramsay and his mother to keep them from securing an attorney; and the constant need to be creative, to find the right key to get Rod to tell us yet one more secret he was holding back.

The toll of all this feels like a millstone around my brain.

Perhaps, too, there's an existential dread associated with what I've been through. Since 1947 the eggheads at the *Bulletin of Atomic Scientists* have been maintaining a so-called Doomsday Clock, with the minute hand moving ever closer to midnight, the point at which global disaster occurs. For almost two years now I have been one of the very few people aware of how close "midnight" actually is. Everything I've done—all that stomach-churning prep work, the ceaseless sprinting, the refusal to take no for an answer—has been at least partly spurred by my fear that America—and maybe the world—might not have much time left. Rod Ramsay has handed desperate people the means to lash out in an apocalyptic way. He has left the choice up to them, not us.

I've known plenty of agents who've never felt the need to look back once a case is done. I've been that type of agent myself. But this hasn't been the usual case, and Rod isn't your everyday felon. In one way or another, he's with me every day of the nine months I lie in my bed, wondering and questioning if I'll ever heal, ever be myself again. And to be honest, there are times I think I *will* never be the same again. How could I be?

IN THAT WEIRD TWILIGHT state I find myself slogging through, for so many months after depression sets in and illness saps all my strength, the question of why Rod finally told me his secrets keeps surfacing—in my own head, of course, but also in queries from prosecutors and conversations with the few visitors who dare enter my dark world. Speculation is all over the place: transference (at some level, he longed to be me), narcissism (the Smartest Guy in the Room Syndrome), a guilty conscience, and on and on. With the exception of the guilty conscience—Rod is incapable of guilt; he has no moral compass—there's something to all of them, but I think the best answer I ever get is from the one person who comes to know Rod and his motives almost as well as I do: Mark Pizzo, his defense attorney.

"In the end, Joe, you seduced him," Mark tells me, sitting in his office a year or so after Rod's sentencing as part of a plea agreement. "Everything you did was so contrary to what he expected from having watched hundreds of hours of police dramas. He thought he could beat you. He never realized how slowly and insidiously you were luring him into cooperation."

"Really?" I ask.

"One hundred and thirty-seven pages of admissions he made. You know what a nightmare that is for a defense attorney?"

"I didn't think about that."

"I wanted to know, too," Mark answers. "As part of our deal to cooperate with the government before sentencing, I asked Rod directly why he gave up so much, made all these admissions, put the rope around his own neck. You know what he said? 'Because of Joe. Anyone else I would have told to fuck off, but Joe never seemed to be aggressive. He respected me. He never wrote anything down. After a while, I felt I could trust him, even if I knew my trust would never be rewarded. I couldn't help myself.'"

At some remote level of awareness, I know that large changes are taking place in the shadow worlds of intelligence, security, and nuclear weaponry as a result of what Rod has revealed. The army's "fail-safe" communication system has to be reconstituted to make it secure again. Unknown to the Germans demonstrating against them, the Pershing II missiles stationed on their soil have been compromised by the efforts of Conrad and Ramsay.

Vetting systems for classified personnel have obviously failed miserably—they, too, must be reworked from the ground up. In the wings, all the spies Ramsay and Conrad drew into their scheme have to be rounded up and emptied of whatever secrets they hold. Critical procedures have to be changed as well. Who will henceforth be chosen to be document custodians? And using what criteria? How will documents be stored or destroyed going forward? The list, I'm sure, is endless, but in my bed, with the curtains drawn against the relentless South Florida sun, this all feels as if it's happening in a galaxy far away. It's no longer my fight, but in my mind I keep kicking and punching as though it were, and that, too, grinds me down. The leads that haven't yet been run down, the many holes still to be found in the investigations—I place those squarely on my shoulders.

*   *   *

EVENTUALLY, I DO MANAGE to let go and get better, healthy enough to return to work—although I don't go back to the SWAT team or to flying surveillance immediately. The CI caseload hasn't diminished while I was away. Jay Koerner is glad to have me back in the fold. The Behavioral Analysis Program, it turns out, is a good diversion for my interview and nonverbal skills—a chance to work with bright, highly motivated agents I can learn from.

And Rod Ramsay's arrest doesn't end that matter for me either. For the next seven years, I serve as case agent for multiple trials in federal court in Tampa: Jeffrey Rondeau and Jeffery Gregory are sentenced to eighteen years each. Kelley Therese Church, née Warren, an army typist who became the fourth generation of the Conrad/Ramsay spy ring, recruited by Conrad after Ramsay left, gets twenty-five years. Rod is finally sentenced to thirty-six years—all deserved, but oddly, for years after, I get annual Christmas cards from Rod and his mother. Motives are always hard to read, but I like to think that they both realize I had a job to do and did it as best I could. More than once in these messages from prison, Rod thanks me for being a good role model—he holds no animosity toward me, or Mrs. Moody. After a time, though, I ask the Tampa office to intercept any further communications from Rod. I don't want to read them anymore. I can't.

Clyde Lee Conrad dies in Diez Prison, in Koblenz, in 1998 at age fifty, of a heart attack. Zoltan Szabo, the godfather of the spy ring, is luckier. He remains in Austria, a so-called neutral country, and is never brought to trial in the US. In fact, Szabo still receives his US Army retirement check every month—no, you really *cannot* make this up. It's directly deposited into his account. I talked with him once for several days at a location I'm not allowed to reveal. For some reason, he's been reluctant to come to Tampa to repay the visit.

Even today, I can still raise the hairs on my arm by thinking of how terribly, almost fatally, compromised the security of the West was at the height of Rod Ramsay and Clyde Conrad's espionage.

At Conrad's trial in Germany, after I and dozens of others had testified, Chief Judge Ferdinand Schuth concluded that had the Soviets chosen to attack with the knowledge they possessed via Conrad and Ramsay, NATO would have been left with two options: "capitulation or the use of nuclear weapons on German soil." These measured words shook the intelligence community as well as the military. No one suspected it was this bad.

Ironically, others calculated the consequences as being even graver. At Ramsay's sentencing—in federal court in Tampa, in August 1992— General Glenn K. Otis, Commander in Chief, European Command (CINCEUR) from 1983 to 1988, testified through a signed affidavit that Ramsay and Conrad's acts of espionage had left the West so vulnerable and so stripped of its own defensive capabilities that its defeat "would have been assured" had the Soviets acted on their intelligence and launched an all-out war. That statement alone appears in no other espionage case in the history of the United States. To repeat: The defeat of the West, including the United States, *would have been assured.*

That's where Ramsay and Conrad left America and the West— without a plausible chance to defend itself. Not the Berlin Crisis, not even the Cuban Missile Crisis, had bequeathed the West the *certainty of defeat.* Both the German and the American courts were in agreement on this. Nothing in the annals of Cold War or American history comes anywhere near it.

DURING THE NINE MONTHS I spend lying in bed, all too often I ponder what this case has really been about. Each day yields a different answer. Sometimes it has been about being lucky enough to see a cigarette shake when it shouldn't have. Other days it's been about acknowledging that no security system is ever truly safe—that predators in whatever form can undermine any system. Espionage is always a threat, and it can have existential ramifications. As investigators, we need to dig deep and not assume we know everything that's out there—we never do. We also need to keep in mind that not everyone in the Bureau or in Washington, DC, has our back. As one old-timer told me, "We FBI agents make our own luck."

At a deeper level, the Ramsay case has also been about human frailty—avarice, hubris, jealousy, contempt—a facile criminal mind, and what happens when these go unchecked; about a moment in time when we were minutes away from assured destruction had the dice of history rolled just slightly differently; and about a scrawny, sad, fucked-up genius whose life could have been so much more. All that potential, all that evil—that's what I can't let go of.

"You're now in charge of the family," my father told me when he left us that tearful night in Cienfuegos when I was only seven years old. That's what I've always tried to do, exercise proper stewardship over my duties—not the least of which was to defend this nation that I love so much from "enemies both foreign and domestic." Not until I was an adult, though, did I read Nietzsche's warning about the abyss that so many of us in law enforcement look into daily— the abyss that holds monsters known and unknown and is always staring back. I ignored that warning to my terrible detriment and to the detriment of my family.

ON THE DAY I began my sick leave, I drove to the office in the morning to turn in my Bureau car. Before I could depart—Luciana was waiting outside to drive me back to bed—the special agent in charge of Tampa called me into his office to say that as a result of the Ramsay arrest FBIHQ was recognizing me for my hard work. He handed me an envelope that I placed in my coat pocket next to my FBI credentials—I was too tired to open it.

Weeks into my recovery, as I slowly made my way to the bathroom with the help of my wife, I noticed a bank receipt on the dresser.

"What's that?" I asked Luciana.

"I deposited that check," she said, "the one you got from head-quarters your last day at the office."

"How much was it for?" I asked, barely remembering the moment.

"Five hundred dollars, but after deducting for taxes, Social Security, and insurance, it came to $327.36."

"Five hundred dollars doesn't go far these days, I guess," I said, but I couldn't even muster a smile.

"No, it won't go far," Luciana agreed, "but you'll be home for Stephanie's birthday this year, and one more thing—you're alive, Joe."

Just then I started to cry, bawl like a baby—for the first time in my life I felt so helpless. Settling me back in bed, with Stephanie helping as best she could at my side, Luciana repeated words in Portuguese that we often said to Stephanie whenever she fell and hurt herself:

"Chore nao. A vida e boa."

Don't cry. Life is good.

Indeed it is.

ACKNOWLEDGMENTS

Early in my writing career, fellow author, friend, and mentor Toni Sciarra Poynter warned me that often the most difficult task in writing a book is the acknowledgments. She wasn't kidding—there are so many people to thank. In all of our endeavors, we're assisted by others who provide guidance, assurance, encouragement, or insight. This is true in writing a book, and it was no less true in conducting an espionage investigation that spanned a decade.

Ten years is a long time for any investigation, and the number of people who along the way helped or assisted me can't be accurately measured—but what *can* be measured is my profound gratitude for their efforts.

First and foremost, I want to say that this country owes an immense debt to the US Army Intelligence Security Command (INSCOM) and in particular the Foreign Counterintelligence Activity (FCA). It is they who, acting on a tip from the CIA, looked at over 250,000 service members stationed in Germany and narrowed their focus to one individual passing highly classified documents to the Soviet Bloc. To me, the sheer enormity of this task is still breathtaking and yet they, alone, did it. It was their hard work that identified two American traitors: Clyde Lee Conrad and Zoltan Szabo.

With superb guidance from Lieutenant General Ed Soyster and Colonel Stuart A. Herrington, this team of dedicated individuals accomplished the near impossible—without equal in US history.

Along the way I got to meet or work with Norman Runk, Al Eways, Al Puromaki, Bob Gaiter, and Mike McAdoo. But of all of these highly professional INSCOM-FCA special agents, I want to single out Gary Pepper, with whom I got to work closely for years. He is the finest investigator I've ever teamed with; I certainly learned much from him and I was inspired by his unparalleled tenacity.

I want to thank all of the dedicated men and women of the FBI, past and present, who work so hard to "protect and defend the Constitution of the United States from enemies both foreign and domestic," as they swear to do the day they take their oath. I know what they sacrifice every day, and I'm eternally grateful.

In particular, I want to thank the Tampa Division of the FBI for the work that they do and for the assistance they provided us in this massively complex investigation. While there are fifty-nine major field Offices in the FBI, the Tampa Division is one of only a handful that has prosecuted an espionage subject. They've done it five times.

Julian "Jay" Koerner, Lynn Tremaine, Marc Reeser, Rich Licht, Susan Langford, Jane Hein, and especially Terry H. Moody deserve special thanks for their sacrifice, guidance, hard work, and dedication—this is also their story.

I must also acknowledge Ihor O. E. Kotlarchuk, who assisted me on so many cases over the years and helped me navigate the national security labyrinth at the Department of Justice. For his help and friendship I'm very grateful.

Likewise, I must also thank former First Assistant US Attorney Greg Kehoe, who brought this matter before the courts, for his dynamic leadership, unwavering resolve, and intellect. To say that Kehoe is a giant when it comes to jurisprudence only begins to recognize his gifts.

To Donna Bucella, who served as the US attorney for the Middle District of Florida, a hearty thanks for clearing away so many obstacles on so many cases. And many thanks also to my friend Assistant

US Attorney Walter "Terry" Furr, who for five years aggressively pursued this case with me.

For twenty-five years I didn't want to talk about this case; I preferred to keep it squarely behind me. Over a period of years, though, Steve Ross, my friend and literary agent at Abrams Artists Agency in New York, was able to coax out of me, with great delicacy, some details regarding it. Ultimately, he convinced me to go forward with a book, saying, "This is a story the American public must know."

Steve is not just a peerless literary agent, he is a fantastic human being. Through his trust and gentle guidance, this project came alive. It is he and his wonderful group at Abrams Artists Agency Book Division that I must thank for getting this story told.

Thanks, too, to David Doerrer at Abrams, for helping advocate for this story with publishers around the world, and to Paul Weitzman for getting the proposal into the hands of George Clooney and his partners at Smokehouse Pictures.

Deserving of special thanks is Howard Means, a great writer in his own right, who, to assist me, took time from his busy writing schedule (he was then working on his latest book, *67 Shots: Kent State and the End of American Innocence*). I'm very grateful that he agreed to help me mold my thoughts into a coherent narrative. I've learned much from him about the art of writing.

Creating a proposal is one thing; telling the tale from start to finish and getting it published another. Here is where Rick Horgan, vice president and executive editor at Scribner, and his staff came in. It is he who looked at the proposal and saw its potential. He asked all the right questions, and once the manuscript was completed he tackled it personally. In his capacity to bring out the best in authors Rick has few equals. I couldn't have asked for a better publisher than Scribner or a more talented editor to guide me through the process. My thanks also go out to Scribner team members Colin Harrison, Sally Howe, Jaya Miceli, Pete Garceau, Laura Wise, Mia Crowley-Hald, Chris Milea, and Richard Willett, whose contributions were crucial.

I could not write this book without giving thanks to my family. Through their sacrifices and loving example, my parents instilled in me a love of family, hard work, and a profound appreciation for this nation that took us in as refugees. Whatever success I've achieved in life is due to their influence; I'm indebted to them for so much. To my family near and far, thank you.

Lastly, but most especially, I must also heartily thank my dear wife, Thryth, for her love, dedication, and patience, as writing all too often distracts me. She is my anchor for the things that matter. With her help, I was able to draw out of myself some of the experiences I was reluctant to talk about for so long. Her kindness and love are never far from me.

INDEX

ABOUT THE AUTHOR

For twenty-five years Joe Navarro was a Special Agent with the FBI in the area of counter-intelligence. He was also a founding member of the FBI's elite National Security Division Behavioral Analysis Program, which focused on the behavior of spies, terrorists and criminals. He has since left the Bureau and now lectures widely on non-verbal communication. He is the author of the international bestseller *What Every BODY Is Saying*. You can find him at JNForensics.com.